HERITAGE
OF INDUSTRY

February 2002

Tony

... from one Kiwi to another Kiwi, we must always enjoy our common heritage and roots.

with warmest regards

.... and also from a Bulgarian

love Deyana

HERITAGE
OF INDUSTRY

DISCOVERING NEW ZEALAND'S INDUSTRIAL HISTORY

NIGEL SMITH

REED

To the memory of Maurice Buttimore

FRONT COVER (CLOCKWISE FROM TOP LEFT): Pumphouse, Kawau Island (Nigel Smith); Gum digging at Sweetwater, Northland (Northwood Collection, Alexander Turnbull Library, National Library of New Zealand/Te Puna Mātauranga o Aotearoa, 051975 ^{1}/2); Invercargill Water Tower (Nigel Smith); Bush locomotive on a tramway near Raurimu (Alexander Turnbull Library, National Library of New Zealand/Te Puna Mātauranga o Aotearoa, 71728 ^{1}/2).

BACK COVER: Brunner Mine (Alexander Turnbull Library, National Library of New Zealand/Te Puna Mātauranga o Aotearoa, PA1-0-498-36).

Established in 1907, Reed Publishing (NZ) Ltd is New Zealand's largest book publisher, with over 300 titles in print.

For details on all these books visit our website:
www.reed.co.nz

Published by Reed Books, a division of Reed Publishing (NZ) Ltd,
39 Rawene Rd, Birkenhead, Auckland 10.
Associated companies, branches and representatives throughout the world.

ISBN 0 7900 0804 1

© 2001 Nigel Smith
The author asserts his moral rights in the work.

Edited by Peter Dowling and Brian O'Flaherty
Designed by Graeme Leather

First published 2001

Printed in New Zealand

Contents

NOTE ON WEIGHTS AND MEASURES

In some instances imperial measures have been used in this book.
Conversions are as follows:

Measures: 12 inches = 1 foot

                             3 feet = 1 yard = 0.9144 metre

                             1 acre = 0.405 hectare

                             1 pint = 0.568 litre

                         1 gallon = 4.546 litres

Weight: 16 ounces = 1 pound = 0.4536 kilogram

                          1 ton = 20 hundredweight = 1.016 tonnes

Money: 12 pence = 1 shilling

                 20 shillings = 1 pound = $2 (at 1967 value)

PREFACE

Heritage of Industry records a search for the remains of New Zealand industry, some of which date back over a century and a half. To contain such a theme within a single volume demands selectivity. It follows that the industrial heritage sites included here are just a few from thousands, selected for their historical significance or their ability to illuminate the toil, ingenuity and perseverance that went into making this country.

Brief details of the location of the industrial sites mentioned in this book are given at the start of each chapter, listed in alphabetical order and accompanied by maps. For more detailed information readers are encouraged to visit the local museum, information office or Department of Conservation office. Where appropriate, DOC should also be consulted prior to extensive bush walking, and care should be taken to avoid disused mine shafts and other industrial hazards. Please respect private property.

Nigel Smith
Auckland, August 2001

ACKNOWLEDGEMENTS

In producing this book, I have become indebted to many writers and researchers. Primarily, Geoffrey Thornton's *New Zealand's Industrial Heritage* (1982) is, and is likely to remain, the most comprehensive and authoritative work on this subject and a substantial debt is owed to him by all subsequent writers. A number of industries have comprehensive histories. Gold mining, with J.H.M. Salmon's *A History of Gold Mining in New Zealand*, dairying with Eric Warr's *From Bush-burn to Butter*, and timber with Thomas Simpson's *Kauri to Radiata*, for example, are fortunate in this regard. Other industries — frozen meat, coal mining are just two — have many excellent studies of individual companies, locations and themes that are too numerous to mention here. These are detailed in the bibliography. Sincere thanks are extended to the authors of all these essential works. The brochures and on-site noticeboards provided by the Department of Conservation have also been of great assistance in interpreting the history so often hidden deep within New Zealand's bush.

Thanks are also due to the staff of numerous regional museums and historical societies around New Zealand. Whether professional or amateur, they show unbounded enthusiasm and an abundance of local knowledge that is passed on unstintingly. The following have been particularly helpful: Mary Brockbank, Waikouaiti; Katie Clements and Linda Wigley, Huntly; Kirsty Davies, Wanganui; Terry Harpe, Mystery Creek; Lindsay Hazley, Southland; Paul Hewson and Livingston Baker, Patea; the late Alistair Isdale, Thames; Peter Lawn, Blacks Point; Heather Lindauer, Russell; Janet Maunsell, Whakatane; Alastair McLachlan, Riverton; Greg McManus, Rotorua; Nona Morris, Pukekohe; Peter O'Neill, Wellington; David Phillip, Coromandel; Joe Pihema, Gisborne; Pauline Pulford, Timaru; Janet Riddle, Mercury Bay; John Robertson, Edwin Fox Society, Picton; Esme Stevenson, Tokomaru; Poppy Short, Waiuku; Kathleen Stringer, Oamaru; David Verran, Auckland City Library; and Rita Wright, Ashburton.

New Zealand is also fortunate in having a scattering of enthusiasts who freely give much of their leisure time to maintaining, recording or generally keeping a watchful eye on our industrial heritage. Thanks are extended to the following for sharing their knowledge and enthusiasm: Bob Bradshaw, Dunedin; Ossie Collinson, Bluff; Jim Dangerfield, Dunedin; Jim Lundy, Ashhurst; Bill Lundy, Benhar; Fiona McNaughton, Highcliff; Haki McRoberts and David Wairua, Maungaroa; Lois Mills, Ongarue; Kate O'Malley, Benhar; George Ottaway, Waimiha; and William H. Pitt, Wellington.

Corporate New Zealand has also made a contribution to the creation of this book, extending the privilege of viewing heritage that is now part of a busy working environment or passing on information. Thanks to: Kim Hannah, Anchor Products; Greg Jackson, Trust Power Limited; Tanya Lindsay, Glaxo New Zealand; Neville Martin, New Zealand Dairy Board; D.G. McEwan, Milburn New Zealand; Barbara Pendrey, Watercare Services; John Welch and Bruce Neagle, RNZAF; and the administrative staff at Chelsea Refinery.

Photo credits are due to: Alexander Turnbull Library, National Library of New Zealand/Te Puna Mātauranga o Aotearoa; Blacks Point Museum; The Bush Tramway Club, Pukemiro; Clyde Historical Museum; Yvonne Coles and Brian McClintock for access to their comprehensive collection of old New Zealand postcards; the Edwin Fox Society; Gisborne Museum; Rotorua Museum; Southland Museum; the Tokomaru Steam Engine Museum; Watercare Services; and Whakatane Museum. Otherwise the photographs are the work of Nola Smith and myself, or from our collection.

Votes of thanks are also due to friends Val Baillie, for giving an initial spur to the project, John Webster for fielding numerous queries, Bill and Jill Williams for reading the manuscript, Tony Fayerman and Alastair Sorley for pointing me in the right direction in uncharted territory, Sandra Gillespie for ongoing support, and my wife Nola, constant, uncomplaining companion around the most distant nooks and crannies of industrial New Zealand and my essential guide along the uncertain paths of new technology.

INTRODUCTION

'A young country is a real heritage,
though it takes time to recognise it.'
KATHERINE MANSFIELD

When Britain recently submitted a list of nominations to UNESCO for recognition as World Heritage Sites it came as a surprise to many that it mainly consisted of heritage from the Industrial Revolution. It was a belated recognition of the importance of the common man and woman and their workplace in the history of the nation — and, commercially, of the interest of tourists in them. Move over cathedrals and palaces: there is still money to be made down at the mill — or at the redundant railway station, the decaying dockyard or the ancient ironworks.

New Zealand is usually thought of as an entirely different case. The words 'industry' and 'heritage' do not readily trip off the lips of Kiwis and certainly not in the same sentence. Ours has been a predominantly agricultural society, not the southern hemisphere's cradle of industrialisation. Ask about the heritage of our industry and the usual response is just a quizzical look and a few faded folk memories.

Certainly the earliest entrepreneurs to these shores — mostly whalers and alluvial gold diggers — left few permanent memorials behind them. They were not looking beyond the short-term horizon. For them days of back-breaking work were supported by dreams of the lush life. Usually all that is left are tales of exploration, danger and heart-rending privation.

Before long, however, many industries needed substantial capital equipment. From this point our search becomes much more productive. For instance, gold mining soon required stamper batteries and ancillary equipment to crush the quartz ore. This was often laboriously manhandled up our remotest mountain ranges. Much of it is still there. In the bush of Coromandel and the West Coast, and in Central Otago, there are waterwheels on mountain tops, stampers in distant gullies and boilers in stream beds. There are also ghost towns out there in the wilderness — Bendigo, Macetown, Waiuta — where the haunting aura of once vibrant communities still lingers among the ruined cottages. They are lost civilisations in miniature. The good news for the adventurous is that all this is tucked away among savagely beautiful scenery.

Sometimes old gold towns have staggered uncertainly into the twenty-first century. St Bathans, Otago, for instance, has been reduced to a single-figure population but its one-sided street frontage should be on anyone's UNESCO wish-list. Nearby Ophir is more substantial but no less alluring. Just occasionally serious gold money was invested in sustainable real estate on a larger scale. Clyde, in Central Otago, Reefton on the West Coast and Thames, capital of the Coromandel, have all nurtured their past with enthusiasm and have gems of colonial architecture to show for it.

Coal mining developed around the same time as gold but often lasted much longer. Brunner, an icon of early industrialisation, was established in the mid-1860s and for the next half century that part of Westland's Grey Valley became as heavily industrialised and polluted as many back in 'the old country'. Today it is a fascinating microcosm of the early coal, coke and brick-making industries. A little to the north the eighth wonder of the engineering world, the self-acting Denniston Incline, was an audacious piece of Victorian self-confidence. There, 600 m up the scarp face of the desolate plateau — where on a clear day you can see forever — the detritus of industry is scattered across the barren landscape. Yet Denniston is just one of many vibrant, often politicised mining communities that added a different dimension to the growth of the nation. To imbibe in the pub in Blackball or to visit the Miners' Hall in Runanga is to travel back to days when men risked death by explosion or miners' phthisis — and then had to fight for the meanest of lunch breaks and the decency of a pit-head bath.

New Zealand's timber industry dates back over two-and-a-quarter centuries if you count from the first recorded felling of a kauri tree by a European. Serious timber milling, however, started around 1840. A gung-ho harvesting of a vast natural resource followed. At first it can appear that little is left to bear testimony to this systematic devastation. When an area was logged out, the mill, tramlines and wooden viaducts were either shifted or left to rot. Yet not all has been lost. The regrowth bush of the Waitakere and Coromandel ranges still hides the skeletal remains of the driving dams that once flushed out kauri with elemental power. Many old tramways have been turned into walking tracks. Charming Creek in Westland and Port Craig, Southland — which also boasts the magnificent Percy Burn viaduct — are good examples. Abandoned structures and machinery linger unexpectedly in the undergrowth, often accompanied by an informative notice from the thoughtful folk at the Department of Conservation (DOC). Many old bush locomotives have been salvaged and are now smothered with love in a number of preservation societies.

Not all New Zealand was logged. Much was wantonly incinerated. Bush-burn established the farms of Taranaki, the central North Island and many other areas, but was both contentious and dangerous — though it certainly opened up the country for the great staples of New Zealand's export trade, frozen-meat and dairy products. Luckily a few of the earliest icons of the frozen-meat industry still receive the respect that is their due. Prize examples are Totara Estate, North Otago, where sheep were killed before the first successful shipment of frozen meat aboard the *Dunedin* in 1882, and at Picton the *Edwin Fox*, which was used as a floating freezing works for many years after her sailing days were over.

The development of railways also left icons dotted across the land, including a handful of handsome viaducts. Railway stations survive from as early as the 1870s. They are fairly simple, functional buildings but within a generation George 'Gingerbread' Troup was creating more elegant structures, including his masterpiece in Dunedin. By the 1930s the grandiose termini in Auckland and Wellington were built to celebrate the dominance of rail, which it was thought would never fade.

Further examples of our heritage abound in a variety of other industries but a common picture quickly emerges. Firstly, much of New Zealand society in the late nineteenth century was dependent on a dominant local industry — we were not merely the agricultural society that is ingrained in myth. Secondly, if we search around just a little, often among fantastic scenery, there is sufficient heritage to stir even the meanest imagination.

What's more, it can be a search that reveals not only metal, brick and stone but also traditional Kiwi ingenuity in all its glory. Our free-wheeling entrepreneurial forebears knew few intellectual bounds. There are examples of whales being caught in a net; of sulphur being mined in an active volcano; and of a timber-framed flour mill being saved from toppling over in a howling nor'-wester by tying it to its brick chimney stack and slowly hauling it upright. There is a railway spiral so tightly constructed that the front and rear of a train can be travelling in opposite directions at the same time. There was also the case — inevitably it now exists only in old photos and folk memories — of a 73-m single-span bridge on a logging tramway that became so rickety that the driver habitually dismounted, set the throttle to slow and let the engine chunter across unmanned.

It is also a story redolent with risk takers. Some became successful beyond their wildest dreams. Johnny Jones rose from a life skinning seals to become the proprietor of seven whaling stations, briefly owner of vast chunks of the South Island and died one of the wealthiest men in early Dunedin. His monument is Matanaka, a farm high on the headland above the site of his whaling station at Waikouaiti. Also in Dunedin, Arthur Burns, farmer and rumbustious politician, was middle aged and knew little about making woollen textiles but could recognise a window of opportunity when he saw one. He founded our first woollen textile factory at Mosgiel and made an excellent return on his investment. Diminutive Chinese, Chew Chong didn't know much about butter-making when, again middle aged, he peddled small goods around the bush-burn farms of Taranaki. Yet he was one of the prime movers in establishing early dairy factories and ended up a wealthy man. Little is left outside museums to commemorate Chew Chong but examples of the early dairy factory system he helped foster are everywhere — now often used by a multitude of minor industries from motor repairs to transport depots to local museums.

For others, risk was not rewarded. The Oxenbridge family spent three years digging a tunnel through a spur in the Shotover River in order to expose the river bed and extract the gold, only to discover a pile of old shovels, wheelbarrows and whisky bottles. Someone had beaten them to it decades earlier. The tunnel is still there, just above the Edith Cavell Bridge near Arrowtown. In remote Te Wae Wae Bay, English entrepreneurs poured vast sums into an early 'think-big' oil-from-shale plant around 1900. It closed within three years and they lost a fortune. Now the only remaining building is used for farm storage. In 1875 hundreds of hopeful diggers gathered in a field near Paeroa for what was literally a gold rush. Within a few days they were limping back to Thames and Auckland empty-handed, threatening to 'crop the ears' of the spreaders of false information. They symbolised the sad story of the world's miners — a good return demanded money as well as muscle. When well-heeled capitalists scoured the same ground a few years later they had the benefit of massive machinery and the latest technology. They made a substantial return on their investment. They also left behind some of our most abiding industrial heritage — the iconic pumphouse at Waihi and the Victoria, Talisman, Woodstock and Crown stamper batteries of the Karangahake Gorge.

All this may not add up to a list of UNESCO citations but it is not bad for a country deemed short on heritage and with supposedly little or no industry to speak of. It could be much better of course. In the dark ages of conservation after the Second World War a great deal of our industrial heritage was lost. The challenge now is to cling on to what remains — it is often our only link with the sweat and toil, the ingenuity and risk-taking, the lives of privation and misfortune that were the making of New Zealand.

1
WHALING

'... smelling like a thousand filthy lamps.'
DAVID MONRO, 1844

Look to starboard from the Interislander just after it enters the sanctuary of the Tory Channel from Cook Strait. In a sheltered cove in the lee of the bare hills lie the skeletal remains of New Zealand's last whaling station, established by Joe Perano in 1924.

Perano, who had previously worked at the family whaling station at Tipi Bay across the channel, ran an efficient and enduring business. From a shelter on Lookout Hill at the head of the Tory Channel whales were spotted through high-powered binoculars up to 15 km out to sea. Signals were sent by beacon, flags, or later radio-telephone to the small, fast whale-chasers already at sea. The ultimate was the *Miss Liberty*. Powered by a 450-hp converted aero-engine, she could reach a remarkable 45 knots. Dummy runs to fool the opposition, mid-channel collisions and mishaps with high-explosive harpoons were all part of the thrill of the chase. Whales were then often herded into the entrance to the Tory Channel like sheep pursued by automated aquatic sheep dogs.

The initial processing plant at Fishing Bay was quite small but by the time the annual catch peaked at 226 humpbacks it had grown to a sizeable operation. Winches and hydraulic rams hauled whales to the flensing deck at the top level of the factory. From there they were gravity fed for processing, primarily through a huge digester with a capacity of over 25 tons of blubber, guts and bones. After simmering for half a day in this over-sized pressure cooker, oil was drawn off and stored in 2000-ton-capacity tanks behind the factory. A semi-submersible tank could be towed into mid-channel to be picked up by ocean-going ships. By-products of whale-meat and whalebone were shipped out to pet-food manufacturers in Gisborne and to the market gardeners of Pukekohe.

WHALING

1. **Russell** The Museum is at 2 York Street. Phone 09 403 7701.
2. **Te Kaha** is 69 km north-east from Opotiki on SH 35. Kaiaio Marae, Maungaroa is 4 km further along. Private property. Can be viewed from the main road.
3. **Whangamumu** The steep, 4-km track to Whangamumu is signposted from the Rawhiti road, 28 km from Russell.

4. **Banks Peninsula** Most whaling stations — Oashore, Ikoraki, Peraki and Island Bay — were clustered along the south-western shore of the peninsula.
5. **Christchurch.** Canterbury Museum is in Rolleston Avenue. Phone 03 366 5000.
6. **Dunedin.** Otago Settlers Museum is in Queen's Gardens. Phone 03 477 5052.
7. **Fishing Bay and Te Awaiti** are on Arapawa Island. Access by boat from Picton.
8. **Kaikoura.** Fyffe House, 62 Avoca Street is south-east of the town centre along the Esplanade. Phone 03 319 5835.
9. **Kakapo Bay** is 54 km from Picton on the road that winds around the bays of Port Underwood.
10. **Riverton** is 38 km west of Invercargill on SH 99. Wallace Early Settlers Museum is at 172 Palmerston Street. Phone 03 234 8520.
11. **Stewart Island.** Prices Inlet is off Paterson Inlet near Halfmoon Bay.
12. **Waikouaiti/Matanaka.** From Waikouaiti (42 km north of Dunedin on SH 1) take Edinburgh Street and then a private road to the car park (about 5 km).

The Perano operation — faithfully recorded by Don Grady in his *Perano Whalers of the Cook Strait* (1982) — was as good as it got in the hazardous world of whaling and remained profitable until 1960. The following year the catch started to slump dramatically and the Peranos harpooned their last whale at 4 pm on 21 December 1964. With them the last of New Zealand's shore stations closed. Soon parts of the fabric of the factory were recycled to Picton — roof beams to build a hotel, the tanks to store tallow. In the early twenty-first century the iron skeletons, concrete foundations and a few other buildings are all that remain.

THE RISE AND FALL OF SHORE-BASED WHALING STATIONS

Appropriately New Zealand's shore-based whaling industry had ended where the saga began. Te Awaiti — known to whalers as Tar'white — was founded by Jacky Guard in an adjacent bay of the Tory Channel, probably about 1829. Whaling ships from foreign shores, equipped with on-board try-works, had hunted sperm whales in New Zealand's deep-sea waters from the 1790s onwards, of course. But they had only visited such places as the Bay of Islands for provisions, repairs and a little riotous R & R during voyages that sometimes lasted years. Hell-raising Kororareka, now Russell, developed as a service centre for the trade. It was Guard and Peter Williams, at Preservation Inlet, who established the first more-or-less permanent settlements dedicated to rendering down whales. Over the next decade many others sprang up around the coastlines of New Zealand, including those in Marlborough, Kapiti, Otago, Southland, on Banks Peninsula and in Northland.

Nothing quite like these early shore-based whaling stations had been seen before — or since. The process of rendering blubber to oil was uncomplicated. A winch hauled the whale onto the beach at high tide and a three-cornered scaffold was usually erected to aid stripping, or flensing, the blubber. Iron try-pots were kept constantly on the boil, the blubber dissolving in its own oil. As it could take up to two weeks to liquidate an average-sized whale, acrid smoke constantly polluted the air. Everywhere whale remnants littered the beach — vertebrae, ribs, putrefying offal. Dismembered whale carcasses floated just offshore. Birds, dogs and the occasional pig scavenged aggressively. Whalers' huts straggled along the shoreline. These Maori-built, one-roomed raupo cottages were standard issue to most pioneers of the time

19

but a whaler's furnishings had the distinction of items rough-hewn from whalebone. Inside, in stark contrast to the detritus that littered the beaches, a degree of domestic order was maintained by the whalers' Maori wives.

When the seas were generous men soaked in sweat, blood, oil and the mind-blowing local brew — rum-based arrack — toiled round the clock, for payment was strictly by results and the season short, usually from May to October. Such semi-permanent alcoholic anaesthetisation may well have been the only way to cope with the working conditions, and the whale-masters made sure arrack was plentiful and cheap. Most other necessities of life were supplied at inflated prices, however. This, together with deductions from pay for the inevitable lost gear, often resulted in little return for the workers after a season's toil. Indeed for many it heralded a descent into continuing debt.

Visitors recorded a variety of impressions. Many were missionaries who, intent on saving the souls of the ex-convicts, ship deserters and adventurers who manned the stations, were often shocked by their experiences. The Rev. J.H. Bumby went into virtuous overdrive after visiting the Tory Channel:

> … they practise every species of iniquity without restraint and without concealment. The very sense of decency and propriety seems to be extinct. The very soil is polluted. The very atmosphere is tainted.

Others were less censorious. E.J. Wakefield thought the whalers displayed the virtues of courage, frankness and hospitality and were astute judges of character. Even Bishop Selwyn was impressed by the numbers attending his services and by the whalers' love for their children — who were numerous.

Early shore-based whaling was the ultimate extractive industry. No one looked beyond the immediate horizon in this, the toughest of working environments. Much of the industry was based on the maternal instinct of tohora, the baleen or right whale. (They were 'right' because these slow-moving mammals were the whalers' favoured prey — they were easy to catch, buoyant when dead and provided a lot of oil and baleen.) When females gave birth in shallow inshore waters, the calves were slaughtered. The mothers refused to desert their offspring and they too were systematically butchered. It was a recipe guaranteed for species extinction and it almost happened — and very quickly.

For example, Dicky Barrett and Jacky Love, who had taken over Guard's station at Te Awaiti, had fruitful seasons in 1834 and 1835. Barrett even indulged himself with a fine fully lined timber house set on a small hill above the bustle and stench of the bay. By 1836, however, competition was intense. There were reported to be 70 or 80 whaling boats in Cook Strait alone and catches inevitably slumped. Towards the end of the decade, portly, happy-go-lucky Barrett had the good fortune to be bailed out of a failing venture in the most unlikely manner. William Wakefield sailed around the headland in the *Tory* intent on buying huge chunks of land for the New Zealand Company while the going was good. Much to his surprise Barrett, a man of modest education, was engaged by the company as pilot and interpreter. He was to play a pivotal, and ultimately unsatisfactory, role in the purchase of much of the Wellington and Taranaki areas. But that is another story.

By the early 1840s almost all the early whaling stations were in rapid decline. Not a moment's thought had been given to environmental considerations. It was not as though competition from the petroleum industry was even in sight. Kerosene did not oust whale oil as a lamp lubricant until after the sinking of the first oil well in Pennsylvania in 1859. Simply, stocks of right whales were aggressively fished out and it was uneconomic to continue in business.

SOME SOUTH ISLAND STATIONS

Many early whaling stations became New Zealand's first ghost towns. Very little had been invested in industrial or social infrastructure and most disappeared as rapidly as they had emerged. Flimsy buildings decayed in the salt air; whale vertebrae disappeared under shifting sands and try-pots were filched as garden ornaments. Just a few stations lingered sporadically.

Te Awaiti, Kakapo Bay and Riverton

The last whale-boat put to sea from Te Awaiti in 1916. The photograph from the 1890s on page 22 shows the settlement, the whale-boats and the whalers in fine detail, though perhaps they had all been spruced up for the occasion. One of the sleek whale-chasers is probably the *Swiftsure*, now in the Canterbury Museum, Christchurch. Built in Tasmania around 1863, the *Swiftsure* originally made a tidy

21

The backdrop is Te Awaiti, Tory Channel, complete with whale-rib fenceposts. One of the two sleek whale-chasers is the *Swiftsure*.

profit ferrying prospectors from Picton to the Wakamarina goldfield. She was then bought by James and Tom Jackson and fished out of Te Awaiti until around 1910.

Elsewhere, whaling stations occasionally merged into the wider community. For instance, tough, black-bearded Jacky Guard moved down the coast from Te Awaiti to do his whaling from Kakapo Bay, Port Underwood, in 1832. It must have been a happy move, for a century and three-quarters later members of the Guard family are still there. Jacky keeps a stern and watchful eye from the burial ground above the bay. It is a similar story at Riverton, on the south coast of the South Island. Captain John Howell established a shore station there in 1835, married a high-born Maori woman and started the European township with fellow seafarers. He is buried in the local cemetery and a memorial at the site of the old whaling station features two old try-pots.

Kaikoura

At Kaikoura, Fyffe House is a lasting reminder of the days when the town was heavily involved in whale hunting, rather than whale watching. Robert Fyffe established his whaling station just around the headland on Armers Beach in 1842. It was a propitious spot offering a sheltered anchorage, a freshwater spring and fertile land that supplied the whalers with potatoes. For a few years the station was very successful. At low tide, flat grooved rocks still mark the final path the whales took en route to the try-pots. The eastern wing of Fyffe House itself began life before 1852 as the cooper's cottage. Fittingly, it was distinctly up-market from the average whaler's hovel for the cooper was a prized and well-paid member of the community, his barrels being essential not only for whale oil but also for storing water and liquor. The original whalebone piles of this part of the house can still be seen. Robert Fyffe died tragically in 1854 while shipping whale oil to Wellington and it was to be his cousin George who greatly extended the building. A further claim to fame at Fyffe House is a rough wall on the property that is thought to be the earliest remaining example of the use of concrete as a building material in New Zealand.

Banks Peninsula

Further down the South Island, whaling and its memories have been part of life on Banks Peninsula for over two centuries. From oral tradition it seems possible that the pioneer whaler *William and Ann,* under Captain Eber Bunker, sheltered in the long harbour of Akaroa as early as 1792. Nearly two generations later five stations were established on the shores of the Peninsula, starting with Captain George Hempleman's settlement at Peraki in 1837. Hempleman's station was just as short-lived as many others but he stayed on to farm the area, again without much success. Hempleman did bequeath one item of rare value, however. His *Peraki Log* is one of our few detailed insights into the daily workings of an early whaling station. Elsewhere there is now only the odd reminder of the whaling days of the Akaroa area. Early cottages have been demolished but a handful of try-pots are scattered on the foreshore or have been preserved in local museums. Whalers' graves can be found in the local cemetery. Numerous placenames recall the early whalers, including several named after Joseph Price of Ikoraki. Tumbledown Bay is said to commemorate the sad fate of one Billy Simpson who succumbed to temptation when carrying a cargo of alcohol from one station to another and fell down the hillside, breaking his entire load.

Waikouaiti

Around the bottom half of the South Island shore-based whaling was dominated by one of the industry's few success stories. Johnny Jones allied a fiery temper and stone-hard fists to considerable business acumen and amassed an empire that other whale bosses could only dream about. From a penniless boy on a sealing ship, Jones somehow advanced so rapidly that by the time he was 30, in 1839, he employed 280 men in seven whaling stations. He ploughed the profits into spectacular land purchases that were said to total around two million acres. Most were soon nullified following the signing of the Treaty of Waitangi but Jones retained sufficient land to ensure a comfortable living following the inevitable decline of whaling.

Jones's premier station lay sheltered beneath the headland at Waikouaiti. Purchased by Jones in 1838 from the original owners, the Sydney firm of Wright and Long, it traded well for just a few years. Always keen to stay ahead of the crowd, Jones diversified from an early stage. Within two years he shipped a dozen or so farming families over from Sydney where they had lingered briefly and unhappily since emigrating from southern England. Life in a communal barracks and then in indigenous whare also proved less than idyllic and many soon tried their luck elsewhere. Yet sufficient folk remained to get Jones's feudalistic settlement off the ground and today the pioneers of the *Magnet* are remembered on a memorial cairn near the beach at Waikouaiti.

Jones moved to Waikouaiti a few years later, very briefly living down among the try-pots on the beach. It was hardly the ideal lifestyle for a man of substance. When David Monro visited he thought it was 'a picture of the most perfect neglect of anything like order or neatness', featuring a large shed 'in which the oil is tried out, greasy in the extreme, and smelling like a thousand filthy lamps'. But there was money in chaos and Jones soon built a splendid house on the headland and as whaling diminished he concentrated on farming. Monro was more impressed by Matanaka farm than with the degradation down on the beach. He reported: 'Mr Jones … is proceeding with great vigour. He has erected a most substantial large barn and other outhouses.' By this time, though cropping was initially erratic, there were 600 acres

Most early whalers left little behind except the occasional try-pot. At Matanaka, however, autocratic Johnny Jones established a farm on a headland above his whaling station at Waikouaiti that has stood the test of time. Many of the buildings date from 1842/43.

of fenced land, with around 100 under crops and 2000 sheep, 200 cattle and 100 horses. Soon horse-drawn threshing and winnowing machines had replaced the sickle and Jones's farms were in a position to supply foodstuffs to the emerging settlement of Dunedin and later to prospectors starting the long trek to the goldfields of Central Otago.

Many of the original buildings at Matanaka still survive high on that headland — stables, granary, schoolhouse, storehouse and a communal three-stall privy. They are the oldest surviving farm buildings in New Zealand. Decked out in red, set in a green pasture against the backdrop of a brooding sky, the Matanaka buildings have all the power and visual simplicity of an unfettered post-impressionist landscape. They are also amazingly well preserved — wind-resistant and waterproof despite nearly 160 years of howling southerlies.

From 1854 onwards Jones moved again to two imposing houses above the harbour in Dunedin (both of which are still standing) from where he could better manage his interests in shipping and finance. Johnny Jones lived on in Dunedin until 1869. Although always feared for his violent temper, which time did not allay, he was well regarded for an even-handed benevolence to most Christian denominations that was remarkable for the times. A firm believer in the civilising influence of Christianity, Jones endowed Anglican, Methodist, Presbyterian and Catholic churches. In its obituary the *Otago Daily Times* described him as:

… a large-hearted man with the simple instincts of a child, who fought with adversity and was improved by prosperity like few others of his kind before him.

TWO NORTH ISLAND WHALING STATIONS

Whangamumu

Although the glory days of shore-based whaling peaked well over a century and a half ago, fragments of the industry lingered on until the Peranos' business finally slipped into history in 1964. Few were more successful, and certainly none more newsworthy, than the station run by the Cook family at Whangamumu, Northland.

The simple statement that the Cook brothers caught whales in a net sounds like the ultimate fisherman's tale but it is true enough. South of Cape Brett whales habitually passed through a narrow channel between a high rock and the mainland. Sections of steel wire mesh, about 10 m square and held together by manila rope, were stretched across the channel. When a humpback whale hit the wire netting the ropes broke and the mammal was encased in the mesh, hampering its movements sufficiently to aid capture.

The Cook brothers, George Howe and Herbert Francis, who patented their

Whangamumu — remains of the old whaling station among the pohutukawas.

26

unique whale-snaring device in 1892 and used it successfully for nearly two decades, were the salty product of generations of whaling experience. Grandfather William Cook arrived in New Zealand on an English whaler in the 1820s. His son George commanded a schooner in the South Seas and whalers out of Sydney. In turn his sons George and Bert served for many years on a variety of whaling boats and by the early 1890s their seafaring experience was immense. Between them they had seen a sperm whale smash three whale-boats in an orgy of revenge, met the pirate Bully Hayes, witnessed a mutiny and almost been fatally ensnared by a harpoon rope. Even more pertinently, they had spent countless fearful and often fruitless hours in open rowing boats chasing the leviathans of the deep. By early middle age their minds turned to easier ways of pursuing their vocation.

George, writing under the by-line 'Lone-Hander' in the *New Zealand Herald* in the 1920s and 1930s, recorded many of the Cook family's experiences. There he wrote passionately of the day that finally persuaded the brothers to try something a little different. They gave chase after a spouting whale in an open boat around midday, rowing to a spot where the whale would logically resurface:

> But she did not — she came up a quarter mile nearer the shore. The boats put after her but again she fooled us … For hours she kept this up.

In the evening, when 'all hands were tired, hungry and thoroughly dispirited', they made one final attempt and were successful:

> At one o'clock next morning we grounded her on the beach. The boats were hauled up and the crew obtained food and rest, the first since noon of the day before. … This whale decided Cook Bros. future operations … It was recognised that a five-knot boat has not much chance of catching a six-knot whale, so a plan was thought of to handicap the brutes.

Early the following season netting began. Netting, amazingly obvious if topography allowed, proved an eminently successful way of pursuing their hazardous business. Telling of the first capture by net, George Cook was rapt by the simplicity and economy of it all:

> … the shore was only a few yards away. This was comforting to the crew … the whale was finished off a few yards from where he first took the net. Half an hour's tow put him on the beach.

In 1893 the Cook Brothers built a shore station in a sheltered bay at Whangamumu, just south of Cape Brett on a site that had previously been used for whaling as far back as the 1840s. A waterfall originally provided both fresh water and power. Within a couple of years of the first netting the operation was sufficiently buoyant for Cook's New Zealand Whaling Company to be formed with a capital of £10,000. Even so the business remained fairly small scale with about 20 whales a year, each valued at about £100, considered a good catch. Later, in 1910, the company enlarged its operations by purchasing the *Hananui II*, a modern steam whaler, complete with a bow-mounted harpoon gun. In 1915, 70 humpbacks were captured, while by 1927 the catch was up to 74, yielding 388 tons of oil and 70 tons of bone fertiliser. The Whangamumu station closed in 1931 after a dramatic downturn in prices. An attempted reopening during the Second World War foundered when an oil slick polluted local waters.

Today the remains of the Cook brothers' whaling station nestle almost innocently in one of Northland's more remote and beautiful bays. Much of it is still traceable among the pohutukawa of the shoreline and the gory business of dismembering and processing can be readily recreated in the mind's eye. The main, indestructible, concrete ramp was linked by a wooden bridge to the central flensing area. Leftwards up the hill were the mincer and digester from where oil was piped to holding tanks by the stream. The bulk of the meat and bones was then chopped in the factory and cooked in huge concrete vats. After 36 hours the fat that had risen to the surface was scraped off by hand while the meat, dissolved by cooking, floated out when the vats were emptied. The boiler that powered the process is still set in a brick housing behind the vats. Nothing remains of the few workers' houses that once occupied the terraces on the hillside.

The truly adventurous can also search the coastline of the peninsula beyond the bay for the large iron rings that were set into Net Rock and the adjacent mainland in order to secure that prized example of Kiwi industrial ingenuity, the Cook's patent whale net.

Te Kaha district

On Labour Weekend 1993, the century-old whaleboat *Hangutuwera* was welcomed home to Kaiaio Marae at Maungaroa, near Te Kaha, in the eastern Bay of Plenty. The

previous day she had been hauled with due ceremony around East Cape from Gisborne Museum, where she had been housed since 1958. Then, as the karanga rang out in front of the meeting house, *Hangutuwera* was carried on to the marae and placed in a specially constructed building, her natural resting place. Now the visitor can look on *Hangutuwera* and marvel at the courage and endurance necessary to chase a whale in a low-slung, 9-m rowboat, envy the strength needed to pull the six huge oars, and try to imagine the swirl of activity as a kilometre of rope unwound from the bilges when a stricken whale plunged for the depths.

Amid the feasting and singing that day, the oral history of whaling in the eastern Bay of Plenty was recounted in detail and with deep affection. This part of the life story of Te Whanau-a-Apanui was once in danger of being lost. Now *Hangutuwera*,

After catching whales in a net for many years, the Cook brothers turned to more conventional methods. The steam whaler *Hananui II* is seen here at Whangamumu wharf.

(Capt. G.P. Hall Collection, Alexander Turnbull Library, National Library of New Zealand/Te Puna Mātauranga o Aotearoa, 069217½)

together with the whaling murals in the marae's dining hall, ensures nothing is forgotten.

No one knows quite when whaling started in these parts. Certainly folklore, and the variety of local European surnames, suggests the traditional techniques were learned from offshore whalers in the earliest days. Later in the nineteenth century there were many reports of whales being landed at various spots along the Bay of Plenty even though the industry was largely defunct elsewhere.

It seems likely that whaling survived here until the mid-1920s because it was a seasonal sideline to agriculture. This is not to say it was undertaken with anything less than total commitment. Any whale unwise enough to stray close to shore near

Maori whalers working at
the try-pots, Te Kaha, 1919.

(WHAKATANE DISTRICT MUSEUM & GALLERY
COLLECTION, B161-2)

the townships of Maungaroa, Te Kaha, Omaio or Maraenui during the months of August to October was guaranteed a hard time. Lookouts on the hilltops signalled sightings to workers in the fields below. Fires were lit: first on one hilltop and then on others in swift succession as the whale made its way along the coast. The maize and kumara fields were instantly deserted amid a headlong stampede to the shoreline to launch the sleek rowboats — perhaps simultaneously from several marae. The pursuit could be both arduous and time consuming. A whale could easily tow whale-boats as far as the volcano of White Island that bellows ominously over 50 kilometres offshore. Indeed it is said that an Omaio boat once hooked on to a whale and disappeared over the horizon for more than a fortnight. Eventually the crew returned to find their tangi under way.

There is much more to the legend of whaling in these parts. The name *Hangutuwera,* for instance, is translated as 'Burnt Lips', a reference to a whale chase begun during a ceremonial feast. To eat on board a whale-boat is strictly tapu so the whalers hastily gobbled hot kumara on their way to the boat, scalding their lips. And then there is the legend of Kopiritoto, the training rock that lies halfway between the tides just below Kaiaio Marae. Here young whalers learned to take good care of both themselves and their boat as they carried it across a rock encrusted with razor-sharp mussel shells. It was hard schooling indeed but just part of the life-long lesson that nothing which happens at sea is accidental. Mishaps mean a job has not been done properly. For sheer bravado, there is the legend of harpooners standing full square on a whale's back before plunging the spear deep into their victim with due ceremony and solemnity. Whales, like the sea itself, were treated with respect even at the moment of death. They were the god-given harvest from the garden of the deep.

The whale harvest was divided with the strictest protocol. Sheers and try-pots were set up on the beach below the marae. At Maungaroa the place is still marked by the old storehouse that once held both wool and whale-meat in season. Whalebone was made into implements and furniture or used for carving spears or mere (clubs) for display. The meat was divided so that everyone in the tribe received a share. The oil was sold and the cash used to finance many communal projects including churches, schools and marae. It all added up to whaling communities quite unlike any others in the colourful history of the industry in New Zealand — ones rich in culture, community and spirituality.

LATER SOUTH ISLAND VENTURES

Waikouaiti Whale Fishing Company

In the deep south of the South Island whaling lingered on in various places well after the heady catches of the 1830s and 1840s were over. In 1869, for instance, local Maori started the Waikouaiti Whale Fishing Company, operating out of Waikouaiti and Otago Heads. Whale stocks had hardly recovered from previous overfishing, however, and the venture failed. Their whale-boat *Maori Girl* is now in the Otago Settlers Museum, Dunedin.

Stewart Island

Much later, Norwegian whalers settled in to their Kaipipi shipyard at Prices Inlet, Stewart Island. They had little in common with earlier times, however. The Norwegians were into big-time whaling. The mother ship, the 13,000-ton *Sir James Clark Ross I*, fished Antarctic waters along with its five whale-chasers. Stewart Island represented a pleasant oasis at which to repair the storm-battered whale-chasers over the winter months, while the mother ship and most of the crew made the long journey home.

A slipway, a large workshop and a variety of domestic buildings were erected at Prices Inlet and were fully operational by 1928. It was a bad time to be whaling, for the price of whale oil slumped dramatically during the Depression. After just four years the shore base was abandoned. Many of the buildings were dismantled over the next few years but a few reminders of its brief lifespan still linger on in the form of the slipway, some rusting ironwork — and a few Norwegian surnames scattered among the population of Stewart Island and Southland.

2
TIMBER

'It was a pitiful war … an executioner's warrant to pick out the eyes of the forest,
to slay and ruin the rest, and then go elsewhere.'
GUY H. SCHOLEFIELD, 1909

In May 1772 the ships of Marion du Fresne's expedition to the South Seas took refuge in the Bay of Islands, looking for replacement spars following a battering in a storm. Suitable kauri was felled and with the judicious use of block and tackle on the steep grades the logs were laboriously hauled from the forest almost to the shoreline. There, when on the top of a small hill and within sight of the sea, the logging party received word that du Fresne and other members of the expedition had been massacred, and probably eaten, during a visit to a nearby village. The timber was swiftly abandoned and the loggers scurried back to the security of their ship. The spars are said to have then lain undisturbed, and in fair condition, for the next 70 years. It was a sobering early chapter in the dramatic story of the New Zealand logging industry — a tale that rarely lacked an element of physical danger and was frequently clouded in controversy.

Over the next 70 years the European presence in Aotearoa was too small to seriously affect the vast forested areas. Although Polynesian burning is thought to have reduced the indigenous forests substantially during the previous millennium, there were still an estimated 14 million hectares of native trees — including timber species such as kauri, kahikatea, rimu, matai, rata, totara and beech — majestically clothing great swathes of New Zealand, especially the North Island. A few hundred explorers, sealers, whalers and missionaries could barely peck at the margins of such a vast natural resource. They were, of course, the thin end of the wedge. By the opening of the twentieth century the native forests had been halved by either felling or deliberate burning.

TIMBER — NORTH ISLAND

1. **Great Barrier Island.** Access is by air from Auckland Airport or by boat from Wynyard Wharf on the Auckland waterfront.

2. **Kauaeranga Valley.** Consult DOC Field Centre, Kauaeranga Valley, near Thames for details of access to driving dams. Phone 07 867 9080.

3. **Matakohe** is 140 km north of Auckland (SH 1, then SH 12). The Kauri Museum is in Church Road. Phone 09 431 7417.

4. **Ongarue** is just off SH 4, 24 km north of Taumarunui.

5. **Orua Bay** is at the top of the Awhitu Peninsula, 40 km north of Waiuku.

6. **Otaki Forks** is 19 km inland from Otaki on the Kapiti Coast. Take Otaki Gorge Road.

7. **Piha** is 40 km west of Auckland city centre, via Titirangi, Scenic Drive and Piha Road. The mill site is at the top of Glenesk Road. For Karekare turn left before descent into Piha. Consult the Arataki Visitor Centre, Scenic Drive, for advice on the area including walking tracks to driving dams. Phone 09 817 4941.

8. **Pukemiro.** The Bush Tramway Club is approximately 10 km west of Huntly along Rotowaro Road.

9. **Putaruru.** The Timber Museum is on SH 1 just south of town. Phone 07 883 7621.

10. **Waiuku.** The *Jane Gifford* has her home base opposite the Kentish Hotel.

11. **Whatipu** is 44 km west of Auckland city centre via Titirangi and Huia.

12. **Whitianga** is on the east coast of the Coromandel Peninsula 68 km from Thames by road. Ferry Landing is a short boat trip across the narrow harbour entrance.

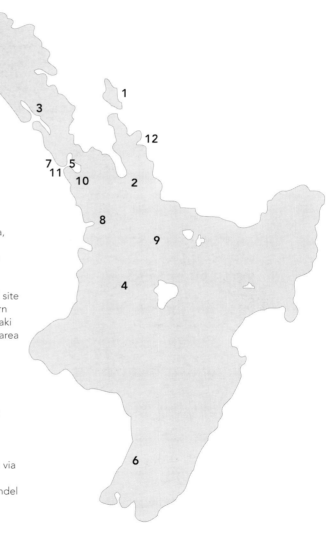

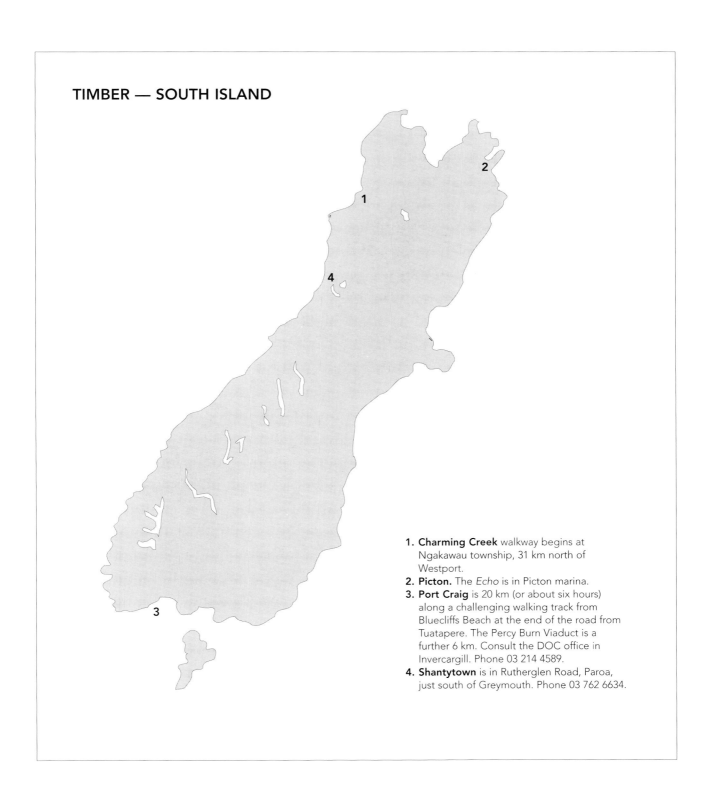

TIMBER — SOUTH ISLAND

1. **Charming Creek** walkway begins at Ngakawau township, 31 km north of Westport.
2. **Picton.** The *Echo* is in Picton marina.
3. **Port Craig** is 20 km (or about six hours) along a challenging walking track from Bluecliffs Beach at the end of the road from Tuatapere. The Percy Burn Viaduct is a further 6 km. Consult the DOC office in Invercargill. Phone 03 214 4589.
4. **Shantytown** is in Rutherglen Road, Paroa, just south of Greymouth. Phone 03 762 6634.

By the mid-1790s the timber export trade had started in a modest way with the brig *Fancy* carrying away a cargo of spars much needed for the top masts of the British naval fleet, whose other sources of supply were rapidly diminishing. The spars came from the banks of the Waihou River in the Hauraki Gulf and were probably kahikatea and of only limited durability. Nevertheless ships soon returned for more. At the turn of the century the *Plumier* took on a load of spars but became stuck on a sand bar with seemingly little hope of assistance in such a distant outpost of the Empire. Amazingly, the *Royal Admiral,* also looking for spars, almost immediately sailed round the point to her rescue. Sadly that was the end of the *Plumier*'s good fortune. En route to deliver the timber to market in China she was seized in Guam by the old enemy, Spain. The *Royal Admiral,* however, successfully delivered her cargo to the British navy and there is the possibility that it was New Zealand's contribution to victory at the Battle of Trafalgar in 1805.

The burning of the *Boyd* and the slaughter of her crew while on a mission to gather spars at Whangaroa in 1809 then proved a serious deterrent to further exploitation. But little could deter the missionaries of the time. The Rev. Samuel Marsden's brig *Active* carried spars from the Bay of Islands to market in Sydney at the time of the opening of the first mission stations. By 1820 HMS *Dromedary* was scouring the Northland coastline equipped with the means of serious timber hauling: a team of five pairs of bullocks. After many tribulations the *Dromedary* found her cargo at Whangaroa and the epoch-making oxen ended up ploughing the straight and narrow at the mission station at Kerikeri.

Also in 1820, HMS *Coromandel* visited the peninsula that now bears her name, intent on harvesting local kauri; this visit was long thought to have resulted in one of our earliest items of industrial archaeology. In his history of the New Zealand timber industry, *Kauri to Radiata* (1973), Thomas Simpson recorded a conversation with two Coromandel old-timers in the 1920s. They confirmed the existence of a constructed canal on the outskirts of the township and suggested it had been dug by the men of the *Coromandel* to float kauri down to the harbour. Sadly there is now no physical evidence of a canal, though a map made in the 1850s by Charles Heaphy does show one in this area. The current local view is that though the canal may have been used to transport logs, it is more likely to have been an attempt to drain the land. In either case it is thought unlikely to have been dug as early as 1820.

Very little technology was involved in the timber export trade at this time. At best logs were merely squared-off for ease of stacking and security on the long journey to market. Domestically, however, value was being added to timber products as isolated pockets of skilled pit-sawyers began processing wood for house construction and shipbuilding. Port Pegasus on Stewart Island thrived as a pit-sawing centre in the 1820s. During the 1830s the shores of the Hokianga Harbour were a hive of activity. One vessel built there, the *Sir George Murray*, was a substantial ship of 394 tons and greatly admired by a writer for the *Sydney Gazette*, even though 'she is built entirely … at the uncivilised islands of New Zealand'.

EARLY SAWMILLS

There had to be a sea change in the primitive economy of New Zealand to transform timber into a major industry. On the supply side there was a drastic need for mechanised milling to materially enhance the production of sawn timber. In turn, increased demand could only come with population growth. Both constraints were rapidly removed from about 1840 onwards.

Thompson's Mill, Catlins (1898) was typical of many hundreds of small mills around the country: open-sided, supported by rough timber posts, probably with a corrugated-iron roof, and a horse-drawn wooden tramway.

Surprisingly, the establishment of New Zealand's first water-driven sawmill actually slightly predates the Treaty of Waitangi. Dacre and Browne's mill at Mercury Bay on the Coromandel Peninsula dated from 1838. Managed by Gordon Browne, it was situated in 'a secure little cove' at the mouth of the Whitianga River, according to the missionary the Rev. W.R. Wade. He also recorded that a wharf had been built from local stone 'which was really a creditable piece of native workmanship'. In addition, a small vessel was on the stocks and a 'sawmill was erecting'. Sadly the original Whitianga mill did not last long. For Browne himself it proved the nadir of a chequered commercial career. He had previously dabbled rather unsuccessfully in timber and shipbuilding in the Hokianga, the Firth of Thames and Mahurangi. Matters deteriorated rapidly at Whitianga and he was soon reporting a 'frightful' imbalance on his accounts. By 1840 Gordon Browne was thought to be quite incapable of conducting business affairs. He was certified insane and died in 1842.

Browne left his mark, however. The wharf at Ferry Landing on the east side of the river is still much as the Rev. Wade recorded and has since been trodden by the feet of millions of holidaymakers. It was built to last from huge rectangular blocks hewn from the nearby cliff, leaving its rock face with a 'most grotesque' appearance.

Timber milling was to be the mainstay of Mercury Bay for fully 80 years after Gordon Browne's death. Ferry Landing also housed the mill built in 1862 by the Mercury Bay Timber Company. Cramped between the hillside and the harbour it was vulnerable to flooding by spring tides and also littered the foreshore with sawdust and waste slabs. A larger site, capable of handling the vast footage of timber now being cut in the region, was established across the harbour in the early 1880s. One of the most productive mills in the country, at its peak it employed two shifts of 70 men. A short distance along the beach the mill's waste-wood fire burned almost continuously for the next 40 years, a navigational aid to shipping but a potential disaster for the mill in a strong easterly wind. Yet the mill survived until 1922 when the kauri of the area was finally worked out. The machinery was shipped to the company's mill on Great Barrier Island. On the last working day the handle of the steam whistle that had summoned the workers for decades past was tied down with a rope. Its disconsolate final call echoed around the harbour for more than an hour.

Following Gordon Browne's venture other sawmills soon opened. On the northern shores of the Manukau Harbour at Mill Bay a steam mill powered by a

Cornish beam engine was established in 1842 but proved as ill fated as the nearby settlement of Cornwallis. Wellington had several early mills, including one owned by Edward Catchpool that was also driven by steam. Another mill was attempted on the Porirua Stream in 1842 but sensibly abandoned when a belligerent Te Rangihaeata raised the question of land rights. The millers relocated to the Kaiwarra Saw Mill near the present-day junction of Kenya Street and Crofton Road, Ngaio.

From then onwards the number of sawmills grew steadily in line with population expansion. The ready availability of water supplies ensured that the majority continued to be powered by waterwheels.

DEMAND FOR TIMBER SOARS

From the 1860s onwards, New Zealand's population exploded, powered firstly by the gold rushes and then by Vogel's expansionist immigration policies. The miners' need for wood for pit props and flumes was second only to their insatiable demand for water. During the initial mad rush to the West Coast, for instance, demand briefly exceeded available supply. Amazingly, sawn timber was imported from Australia to one of New Zealand's most densely wooded regions. A little later railways used previously undervalued wood, such as matai, for sleepers. Simultaneously, the burgeoning urban centres, especially in the North Island, gobbled up wood for housing.

By the early 1880s there were well over 200 timber mills in New Zealand, the vast majority now steam powered. Despite an inevitable slackening of pace during the subsequent recession, the number of mills had doubled by 1907 and electricity was being used in the most modern. Many mills remained modest affairs employing just a handful of men. Others were much more substantial. The Kauri Timber Company's mill in Fanshawe Street on the Auckland waterfront and the Taupo Totara Timber Company's mill at Mokai each had around 300 hands.

At this time New Zealand's sawn timber output was estimated at 432 million

No early sawmills are left in New Zealand though Endean's Mill, Waimiha, built around 1928, is an authentic throwback to the heyday of the industry. The boiler, shown end-view, was fired by waste wood and worked until 1960. In the right foreground is a belt-driven planer. The mill finally closed in 1995.

super feet per annum, a figure not reached again for another four decades. The Auckland region alone was yielding 190 million super feet per annum. The European presence had unmercifully cut a massive swathe through the native forests. Looking back from the perspective of 1909, Guy Scholefield summed up the process in his *Evolution of New Zealand*:

> It was a pitiful war … an executioner's warrant to pick out the eyes of the forest, to slay and ruin the rest, and then go elsewhere. … It was a reign of unbridled rapine and licence.

There were differing perspectives of course. To the new immigrant farmer, dirt-poor and without a return ticket to the Old Country, bush clearance was a matter of survival. Without it there would have been no dairy or meat industries. For the inhabitants of the burgeoning towns and cities it provided the wherewithal for new homes. For many thousands of unskilled labourers the timber industry meant jobs. For the economy it was a godsend. After the initial euphoria of the gold rushes, timber became a major export.

TACKLING TIMBER TRANSPORTATION

The transformation of timber milling into a major industry needed many more technical advances than just efficient sawmills. The problem was not the cutting of timber, nor its milling, but its transportation. In his *New Zealand: Its Advantages and Prospects as a British Colony* (1842) Charles Terry told of the major operation entailed in shifting a giant kauri from high on a ridge on the Coromandel Peninsula. When newly felled the tree had a length of over 45 m, a circumference at its base of around 7.5 m.

> It had to be dragged up and down two ravines, at nearly an angle of 45 degrees, through the woods, and then for nearly a mile across a mangrove swamp, to the borders of a creek.

There they awaited a flash flood to move the monster to the harbour.

> This operation requires skill and dexterity and is generally performed by the natives, who run along the banks, and are continually in the stream, to prevent the timber from being driven ashore, or direct across the creek.

For the remainder of the century great ingenuity, much bravado and considerable capital were expended in order to alleviate — but never wholly resolve — the problem of transport. Rolling roads, blocks and tackle, improvised capstans and bullock teams were all employed in the early days. Chutes of ever-increasing length and sophistication were commonplace. They varied from a few saplings laid lengthways down a hillside to timber-lined monsters lubricated with water and designed for years of work. One at Tairua on the Coromandel was over 2 km long. Sometimes giant logs gathered such speed as to be completely out of control. At the opening of the Foster Brothers' Mill at Herekino, North Auckland, an official photographer was positioned at the bottom of the chute to record the auspicious occasion. It had rained overnight and the chute was in fine fettle for a record run. The log gained such momentum, however, that it smashed straight through the mill with the photographer fleeing for dear life. There is no photographic record of the event.

Timber jacks and log-haulers

From the 1870s and 1880s onwards the bushman's best friend, the timber jack, was in common use. Weighing around 30 kg, this was a portable man-powered machine that proved essential for manoeuvring logs over short distances, such as onto mill skids, rolling roads, chutes and tram bogies. Over the years timber jacks were manufactured in tens of thousands, notably by A. & G. Price, of Thames.

Stationary log-haulers — basically wood-fired boilers powering a winch and rope — became an industry staple. This technological advance had been delayed only by the development of flexible wire cables. New Zealand's first stationary log-hauler was probably manufactured by Jabez Hay & Company of Invercargill in 1888. Within a generation horses and bullocks had largely disappeared from the bush, a thankful release from a life so tough that many animals could be worked for only four hours per day and even so died prematurely. Steam haulers were to come in many shapes and sizes over the following years, providing steady work for numerous engineering companies around the country, such as Dispatch of Greymouth, Judd of Thames, Johnston of Invercargill, Fraser of Auckland and Davidson of Hokitika. Later, giant 90-ton Lidgerwood haulers could reap a relentless harvest over great swathes of forest.

Trams and lokeys

Bush tramways were developed for the longer haul. Initially they were relatively modest affairs with wooden rails possibly coated with steel on the curves. Later they extended deep into the bush with all the grandeur of viaducts, inclines, cuttings, spirals and branch lines. Ellis and Burnand's bush tramway ran into the hills from Ongarue for over 35 km and included a rough-hewn engineering masterpiece, an elegant, curved hardwood viaduct over 100 m long and 28 m high. In the central North Island the Taupo Totara Timber Company's line extended for 81 km with 28 km of branch lines. It included a 73-m-long single-span bridge built over the Waikato River at Ongaroto in 1903. Constructed entirely from totara, it was showing its age after a quarter of a century, sagging and groaning on the passage of each heavily laden train. The company could not afford to replace it, so in the true spirit

Patriotic opening ceremony of the Siberia Bush Tram, Northern Wairoa.

(Yvonne Coles Collection)

of Kiwi ingenuity each load of sawn timber halted at the bridge. The fireman and any passengers dismounted and walked across. Then the engineer set the throttle to low and also got off, leaving the locomotive to slowly chunter over the Waikato unattended. At the other side of the river the fireman jumped aboard and stopped the train. The bridge was finally replaced in 1931 and the line worked on until 1944.

A unique breed of locomotive, the small, slow but powerful 'bush lokey', was developed. New Zealand's first, a tiny Chaplin vertical boiler 0-4-0, was imported from Glasgow by William Brownlee for his Kaituna Valley tramway as early as 1871. Initially it performed poorly on existing wooden rails. The closure of the nearby Dun Mountain mineral railway proved fortuitous, however. Brownlee bought some of the metal rails and his little engine worked happily until 1885. From then onwards a vast variety of lokeys dutifully trundled along the tramways of New Zealand. New

Camera-conscious canine poses in front of an early Price bush locomotive on a tramway near Raurimu.

(ALEXANDER TURNBULL LIBRARY, NATIONAL LIBRARY OF NEW ZEALAND/TE PUNA MĀTAURANGA O AOTEAROA, 71728½)

Zealand Railways' underpowered tank engines — all they could afford in the early days — were pensioned off and proved much more at home in the bush. In the twentieth century powerful, long-lived Climax and Heisler engines were imported from the United States. Home-made models of varying durability and individuality were produced by Dispatch Foundry, A. & G. Price, J. Johnston & Sons and G & D Davidson. Like all steam locomotives they were invariably held in deep affection by the men who laboured on them. Later they were much sought after and cherished by enthusiastic conservationists.

In the 1920s rail tractors were introduced which could go where no lokey had gone before. Adapted from the hugely successful Fordson F farm tractor, they were cheap, light and noisy, and could climb gradients as steep as 1 in 6 and successfully negotiate the tightest curve. It took several years' experimentation but in 1924 Trails of Southland developed a successful design based on the transmission of power to the bogie carrying the log, thus greatly increasing adhesion. Very soon there were six competing designs on the market.

In total there were over 500 bush tramways throughout the country with a mileage comparable to that of New Zealand Railways, though they did not all operate at the same time. The last did not close until 1982. It was just 400 m long, across a swamp in the forest near Okarito, on second-grade rimu tracks. Except that it was powered by an old Ford Prefect engine, little had changed in over 100 years.

Driving dams

Most commonplace, destructive and wasteful of all were the kauri driving dams. The sheer size of the kauri is compensated, from the bushman's viewpoint, by the fact that the logs float. Waiting for a convenient flash flood could be a tedious business, however. From the mid nineteenth century onwards, dams were specially constructed to flush kauri seawards in an elemental surge. Initially the dams were simple one-off constructions. Soon trapdoors were fitted and they became reusable, often in swift succession down the entire length of a river and its tributaries. Driving dams were immensely destructive, both of the river valleys and of the logs themselves, however. Wastage of up to 25 per cent was commonplace. Sometimes logs went straight through the collecting booms and out into the ocean. A few were reported washed up on the beaches of South America.

TIMBER MILLING SITES

Searching out the industrial heritage of the nineteenth-century timber industry can be an arduous task. Of necessity the early mills were mainly temporary structures, just unpainted wooden sheds with at least one-and-a-half sides open to the weather and a gabled roof sheathed in ubiquitous corrugated iron. Typically this housed just a boiler mounted on a concrete base, twin circular saws, a flat-top bench and a breast bench. When the local timber was worked out the mill and its machinery were often moved to the next valley, or burned to the ground. Abandoned chutes, tramways and inclines rapidly reverted to nature. Even the great kauri-built driving dams rotted away in time. Log-haulers, lokeys and rails were fair game for local scrap merchants, professional and amateur. Just occasionally, however, even typical small-scale logging firms left a few clues to aid inquisitive future generations.

Awhitu Peninsula

One example of a typical small-scale milling operation was the sawmill established around 1860 by the Panormo family near the beach at Orua Bay, on the tip of the Awhitu Peninsula. The grand design was to build a couple of earth dams across a swamp to trap water between one hillside of the valley and a narrow rock outcrop behind the beach. The back-breaking manual labour paid off. There was sufficient water to power a wheel and millions of feet of kauri were processed, including that to build a cutter, the *Stormy Petrel,* which ferried timber across the Manukau Harbour to the port of Onehunga. The dam walls are still in evidence in the middle of the valley leading to the holiday baches of lovely Orua Bay.

The neighbouring area also provides an object lesson in the transient nature of small-scale kauri logging. Another mill was soon built at Wattle Bay. Not only did this require the construction of a tramway and a wharf but also a tunnel had to be dug through a hillside to the workable bush. Within five years or so the kauri was exhausted, the mill relocated in a nearby valley and the entrances to the tunnel blown up.

Close at hand the road names are enlightening. Roe's mill was in Boiler Gully for a time but eventually the boiler exploded. Roe moved on, the abandoned boiler was left as a local landmark for many years until recycled, but the road name lives on.

45

Tram Gully was Roe's next stop. There an 11-km bush tramway carried logs down to the harbour by gravity. They were then rafted to Onehunga.

Waitakere Ranges

Almost directly across the Manukau Harbour from Orua Bay, Nicholas Gibbons began making inroads into the kauri of the Whatipu Valley in 1867. Logs were hauled from his mill along a horse-drawn wooden tramway to a wharf established in the lee of Paratutai Rock at the mouth of the harbour. It was the start of a network of tramways and inclines that were to intermittently work the western valleys of the Waitakere Ranges for the next half century.

Paradoxically, given the proximity of the booming Auckland market and the availability of water transport, timber here proved difficult to exploit profitably. The eastern valleys of the Waitakere Ranges had presented a relatively straightforward logging operation, with Henderson's Mill and then Swanson's Mill prospering from the 1840s and the 1850s respectively. The timber of the west, however, was guarded by high ranges on one side and the wild surf and shifting sands of the harbourless coastline on the other.

Shortly after it opened, Gibbons' Whatipu tramway was joined by another line running up the coastline to mills at Pararaha and later Karekare. Using little more than picks, shovels and sledgehammers, men gouged the tramway out of solid cliff faces a few metres above high-water mark. Inlets were bridged in a makeshift manner, cuttings excavated and a short tunnel blasted through an obstructive spur. A small locomotive, with an upright boiler and a funnel that was collapsible so as to negotiate the cliff overhangs and the tunnel, was pressed into service. By the time the entire operation closed in the recession of the mid-1880s, much of the timber of the Karekare region had been hauled down to the wharf at Paratutai Rock. The rails were then taken up and reused in a firewood venture in the Huia Valley. The old locomotive proved unsaleable, however, and for many decades rusted away on Karekare Beach where it is now thought to be buried under several metres of sand, an inglorious end for one of New Zealand's first indigenously built locomotives. It seems likely that it had been assembled by Fraser and Tinne in 1872 and that it had previously worked the short-lived Grahamstown & Tararu Tramway along the Thames waterfront.

For the next 20 years the remaining stands of kauri around Karekare, Piha and Anawhata were undisturbed. By about 1907, however, the rest of the timber at the head of the Karekare Stream was being logged by an Auckland-based dentist, Dr Frederick Rayner. Married to a Chicago heiress, Rayner was a man of substance, style and considerable entrepreneurial vigour. His American Dental Parlour on Auckland's Queen Street revolutionised local dentistry by opening for 11 hours a day, six days a week, employing five dentists. He is said to have offered painless free extraction — provided the patient bought dentures. Rayner lived a leisured lifestyle in a mansion on the slopes of Mt Eden, but certainly knew a bargain when he saw one.

Under the new regime horse-drawn wagons of sawn timber were hauled along the sands at low tide to the wharf at Whatipu. After a time the mill was relocated to the flat land at the junction of the Piha and the Glen Esk streams in what is now Stedfast Park. Then for a few years the extraordinary mishmash of west coast log hauling grew to its full glory, a tale well told by David Lowe in *The Piha Tramway* (1974).

Up to six loads of timber per day were hoisted over the 300-m hill between Piha and Karekare by a log-hauler situated near today's Te Ahuahu Road. With a gradient of 1 in 4.5 up from Piha and 1 in 2.5 down to Karekare, it was a spectacular operation. Then, for a time, wagonloads of timber wound an uncertain path southwards down the coastal beaches to Whatipu, weather permitting. West coast weather often did not permit, of course, and ships might wait impatiently and expensively at Paratutai Rock for days. It all made for a tedious and costly amount of timber handling: cut tree; haul to driving dam in Piha watershed; await suitable driving conditions; drive to holding dam near mill; transfer to mill; haul milled timber over Piha-Karekare hill; transfer to wagons; await tide and weather; transport to Whatipu wharf; load onto ships bound for Onehunga or Australia.

Soon a decision was taken to reopen the 1880s tramway along the rugged coastline. A tiny, five-ton, four-wheel locomotive, recently declared redundant by Seifert's Miranui flax mill in the Manawatu, was purchased and rechristened *Sandfly*. Even such modest horsepower, operating on a three-foot (914-mm) gauge and mainly steel-faced wooden tracks, improved the situation markedly. Later the haulage hiatus at Karekare was resolved by a rail link on a 5-m-high trestle across the beach between the incline and the tramway.

Sandfly negotiates the
tramway to Whatipu.

During the First World War the timber of the Piha Valley was rapidly depleting.
A tramway was built down the valley from the mill and then northwards along Piha
Beach to connect with an incline over the hill to Anawhata. By this time the milling
operation had been bought from Dr Rayner by New Zealand Railways, his main
customer, so the line was built to a standard 3 foot 6 inch (1067-mm) gauge, worked
by a tank engine, A 196. To bring everything neatly into line, the old Karekare–
Whatipu tramway was refitted to New Zealand Railways standard and *Sandfly* was
carted off to the Newmarket workshops to be re-gauged. Now New Zealand Railways
had an integrated rail/incline system stretching about 15 km along the west coast
from Anawhata to Whatipu.

The system availed them little, for logging here was always at the mercy of the
weather. Once rainfall was so heavy that the driving dams burst. The resulting surge
of water flooded the Piha Valley and with it the mill. Gale damage to trestles, bridges
and the towers of the log-haulers was a continuing problem. Sand piled high over the
tracks with such frequency that gangs of men were employed to scoop it away. At
other times drought temporarily decommissioned the driving dams, holding up production. Matters were not helped by the enlistment of men for the war effort and the
slow realisation that some Anawhata timber was of poor quality due to wind damage.

By the time the Piha mill closed in 1921 it had processed 14 million super feet of timber, but had rarely been at full capacity. New Zealand Railways showed a loss on the venture. Dr Rayner, however, reportedly did well, having retained cutting royalties to the timber when he sold the mill.

The mill was dismantled and transported down the tramway to Whatipu. The mill site at the top of Glenesk Road is now a Boys' Brigade camp. A lone puriri tree, identifiable on old photographs of the mill, was spared the axe and remains the focal point of the area. A relatively short walk up the Piha Valley track from the mill, the cills and parts of the wings of the Black Rock driving dam are still in place.

The alternate forces of coastal erosion and the accretion of sand dunes have ensured that most of the old tramway system has now disappeared, though here and there remnants are still visible. On north Piha Beach only the odd piling remains where the tracks once crossed the Wekatahi Stream, an area known to the millers as Mauri Creek Gardens. Around Karekare Point, at the southern end of the beach, the line of the tramway can be readily traced by rusting rows of huge sleeper nails. A little further south the old tram route passes through a 20-m-long tunnel. By the side of the southern portal lies a 5-m-long boiler, abandoned in the early 1880s when the mill at Pararaha was gutted by fire and its equipment relocated to Karekare. Everything, that is, except the boiler, which was too large for the tunnel. A sturdy example of Victorian engineering, it looks set to withstand the vicissitudes of west coast weather for many centuries to come. In the lee of Paratutai Rock at Whatipu, now a favourite fishing haunt, the old wharf has sadly all but disappeared.

Tramway across Piha Beach with Lion Rock in the background.

(E.R. WILLIAMS COLLECTION, ALEXANDER TURNBULL LIBRARY, NATIONAL LIBRARY OF NEW ZEALAND/TE PUNA MĀTAURANGA O AOTEAROA, 054898¼)

Charming Creek, West Coast

If the Piha tramway was the most windswept and precarious in New Zealand, the prize for the most stunning must go to the aptly named Charming Creek.

Ngakawau, 31 km north of Westport, seems an unlikely starting point for a memorable ecological experience. The township is dominated by massive coal-processing bins that are fed incessantly by an aerial ropeway which glides eerily down the mountainside from the opencast mine way up on the high plateau beyond the ghost town of Stockton. Trainloads of Buller coal then lumber off on their long journey to the Port of Lyttelton.

Across the tracks and behind the hill, however, the walkway follows the old tram tracks up the valley of the Ngakawau River for nearly 4 km to the timber mill built by George and Bob Watson. On the way walkers are surrounded by a shimmering array of native bush clinging to the steep sides of the gorge, including rimu, rata and beech. The river bed is littered with boulders. The Mangatini Waterfall tumbles over a sheer rock face into the river. Mosses and lichens shroud the earth. Occasional clumps of celmisia sparkle in shafts of sunlight.

Building a tramway up this narrow gorge was an exacting engineering feat but the Watson brothers were both innovative and incentivised. Substantial coal deposits as well as large stands of rimu and yellow pine awaited exploitation beyond the gorge.

Clinging to the cliff face, the Charming Creek tramway was an ambitious engineering project for the enterprising Watson brothers. It is now a walkway worthy of its name.

The Granity-based brothers had already enjoyed a degree of success with a previous tramway built in 1903. It traversed the ridge high above the north side of the river and then plunged down a steep incline to the mill site. That was hardly the optimal route and in 1912 the Watson brothers decided to tackle the south bank of the gorge.

Their second attempt slots precariously between cliff face and river, sheltering under rock overhangs in some places, crossing small bridges in others. Two tunnels were hewn from the rock; one has an interesting wiggle in the middle where, reputedly, hasty readjustments were made as the teams working from each end checked their bearings. The pedestrian swing bridge that crosses the river near the waterfall is a replacement of a replacement. The original suspension bridge collapsed under the weight of a coal train in 1934 and construction workers then laboured around the clock in all weathers to bridge the river more securely. That bridge outlasted both the mine and the mill and was eventually replaced as part of an army training exercise.

Abandoned boiler in the bush at Watson's Mill, Westland.

The tramway, which ultimately moved far more coal than timber, did not close until 1958. Consequently some of the standard-gauge rails are still in place, including the centre-braking rail deemed necessary by the unrelenting incline and the sharp curves. Little is now left of the mill that once straddled a creek, the repository of its sawdust. A pair of wood-fired boilers proved too hefty to move, however, and remain on site. Otherwise, the West Coast's regenerated bush proves an impenetrable barrier to curiosity. The house of George Watson — who managed the mill while brother Bob conducted business more comfortably from Granity — the workers' huts, the original incline up the hillside, the tramway branch lines built after the mill gobbled up the easily accessed timber, are all now just a memory.

Port Craig, Southland

By the time of the First World War the readily accessible native timber of New Zealand was largely worked out, so enterprising Dan Reese relocated the operations of the Marlborough Timber Company to one of the most distant corners of the country, the far end of Te Wae Wae Bay, Southland. Even today the site of the Port Craig mill is dauntingly remote, a six-hour hike from the road end beyond Tuatapere.

51

Dan Reese was not a man to venture forth unprepared, however. By his early forties Reese had accumulated volumes of life experience, starting when his father died, aged 50, in 1891 at the time of the long recession. Then aged 12 and the middle of nine children, Reese's higher education of necessity took the form of an engineering apprenticeship. As this was with the premier firm of John Anderson, augmented by evening classes with Professor Scott at the Canterbury College School of Engineering, Reese was never to feel at all disadvantaged.

When aged 16, Reese became one of our youngest ever provincial cricketers. He and his lifelong friend, Arthur Sims, took New Zealand cricket by storm as teenagers in the 1890s and were dubbed 'the Canterbury Twins'. They allied practice and perseverance to outstanding natural talent and never looked back. Reese was to become New Zealand's first cricketing superstar, a gifted left-arm spinner, a classical, dashing batsman and a lissom fielder. In an age when New Zealand was firmly entrenched in cricket's backblocks, Reese gained worldwide recognition.

Cricket was pursued merely for pleasure and comradeship a century ago; it certainly did not pay the bills. Reese worked his passage to England and then travelled the world as a marine engineer. Back home in 1907, he joined his brother Tom in the family building firm and managed the Golden Bay Cement Works. Then the brothers successfully logged the Opouri Valley high in the hinterland of Nydia Bay, Pelorus Sound.

For Reese, Port Craig had two advantages — hectare upon hectare of virgin rimu and beech forest, and direct shipping access to the major ports of the region. Reese was in no doubt that with an infusion of capital, hard work and modern technology, the forests of the region could be profitably logged for decades to come. Consequently everything at Port Craig was done with a degree of permanence unusual for a timber mill.

To get the venture off the ground, an old mill was transplanted from the Opouri Valley. Then an entire, two-level, state-of-the-art sawmill was bought from the Sumner Iron Works in the United States and erected alongside the first mill on the plateau above the cliff face at Mussel Beach. On the top level were saws and workbenches; below were drive shafts and belts and the huge sawdust-burning boilers. Sawn timber was transported down a 1-in-3 timber chute to the tally yard on the beach. No port as such existed at Port Craig, or elsewhere on that remote coastline, so rock was quarried from the cliff face and a breakwater constructed with a wharf in its lee. When the breakwater caused the wharf to silt up, timber was transhipped by punt to ocean-going vessels anchored at sea. This costly process was soon improved in a unique manner. A huge timber-framed tower was built at the end of the wharf and slings full of timber were loaded by a flying-fox mechanism. Visiting ships' captains were initially apprehensive but with the vessels secured by rope to the shore and anchored on huge concrete blocks placed on the seabed, the system worked beautifully.

Little expense was spared out in the bush either. Port Craig's tramways, which ran for nearly 15 km parallel with the coastline, with nearly 10 km of branch lines, were built to a standard to make New Zealand Railways envious. Four impressive viaducts were constructed and a 17-man Lidgerwood steam hauler and a skyline cable pulled timber to the tramway from a wide swathe of forest.

A township quickly grew around the mill, with a school, billiard room and

The cliff-top mill at Port Craig with timber chute to the tally yard on the beach.

(SOUTHLAND MUSEUM)

library. The company store became the hub of a cashless society with the cost of purchases deducted from the men's wage packets. High prices prevailed, however, and not everyone was happy that the truck system should endure so long into the twentieth century. A unique form of partial prohibition also applied. Alcohol was traditionally banned in the bush — though benders in town of a Saturday night were legendary. With no town available for R & R, Port Craig's management feared disruptive week-long sly-grogging from the visiting ships. A system was imposed whereby the men brought whatever alcohol they liked to Port Craig but handed it over to the mill manager until Saturday — which must have been riotous.

A high price was paid for Port Craig, both financially and in human terms. It seems that Reese, a likeable and optimistic man, let his enthusiasm for the venture outweigh his business acumen. Almost everything proved disappointing. The density of usable timber was low and its quality variable. With no local market for second-grade timber, mill wastage was high, at up to 40 per cent. It was hard to attract quality labour to such a distant outpost, especially married men with families. Some of the imported technology, such as the Lidgerwood log-hauler, performed below par. Capital expenditure seemed to mount inexorably. At one time the company looked likely to sink under the burden of compounding debt. Reese desperately sought a partner and thought he had one in H.A. Massey, the timber king of Southland. Massey died before he could put pen to paper. Then Arthur Sims strode purposefully into the breach and one of New Zealand's great partnerships was rekindled. Sims, by now a force in the meat industry, bought a half interest in what was briefly the biggest mill in the land. Sims introduced new, decisive management. When prices slumped in 1928 and the tally-yard on the beach bulged with unsaleable timber, the mill was closed with hardly a day's notice. The workers and their families were hastily shipped out to Bluff. Officially opened only in 1921, Port Craig effectively closed in October 1928. After a brief, ill-fated attempt at reopening in 1930, the mill was mothballed for a decade and dismantled in 1939 and its hardware shipped out and sold.

The greatest cost had been in human life. Port Craig is named after its first manager, John Craig, who drowned (along with boatman Fred Parry) at the time the mill went into production. Capable and highly committed, Craig was anxious to retrieve a vital piece of equipment dumped on the far side of the bay in bad weather.

Caught in a squall, he was probably dragged under by his waterlogged gumboots. Less than a year later his brother James was mortally injured in an explosion while excavating a cutting for the main tramline. His burns were so severe that he could not bear to be carried and walked back to the tramway. He was then transferred by ship for a tortuous voyage to hospital at Riverton but died within days.

What is left of one man's dream lies scattered around the site of Port Craig, including a mill wall and remnants of a felled chimney. The old school is intact, however, and has been converted into a trampers' hut. Down on the beach the piles of the old wharf can still be seen nestling by the breakwater. The Lidgerwood's boiler is half buried nearby. But the lasting legacy of Port Craig is out in the bush where the four magnificent, long-lasting viaducts were slung over a succession of deep ravines — Peter, Percy, Edwin and Francis.

Peter, Edwin and Francis are all substantial bridges but the Percy Burn Viaduct, at 125 m long and 36 m high, was the largest on any bush tramway and bigger than all but one of the wooden viaducts built by New Zealand Railways. It is possibly the highest surviving timber trestle bridge in the world. The viaduct was initially manufactured, assembled and numbered at the Port Craig mill before being reassembled on site. Constructed from Australian hardwood it was built to last, unlike the majority of bush tramway viaducts. Sadly, the builder, the Chester Construction Company, was much better at civil engineering than accountancy. At £6000 the estimate was cut too fine and Edward Chester was declared bankrupt. The satisfaction of creating the premier monument to the New Zealand timber industry would have been small consolation. The Percy Burn Viaduct was refurbished in 1994.

The full story of Port Craig, a dream that died, can be found in Dan Reese's *Was It All Cricket?* (1948), an erudite autobiography of a multi-faceted man. A fine historical perspective is supplied by Warren Bird in *Viaducts Against the Sky* (1998).

Auckland waterfront

Fanshawe Street, Auckland, is now a main route out of the city over the Harbour Bridge to the commuter haven of the North Shore. On one side it is flanked by all the trappings of the Age of the Yacht — the apartments and eateries of the America's Cup village and, further along, the Westhaven Marina. Up the hill, on the other side of Fanshawe Street, the Auckland Casino and Sky Tower dominate the skyline.

Back in the late nineteenth century this part of Auckland was a vast timber yard. The shallow pool that was Mechanic's Bay was usually log-jammed with kauri. Strapped to the decks of scows or lashed in great herringbone rafts pulled by steam tugs, millions of feet of New Zealand's finest timber were hauled each year from Northland and the Coromandel to be processed in the heart of its biggest city.

Auckland's shoreline was home to several major milling operations, including the mighty Kauri Timber Company. Known everywhere by its initials, the KTC was formed in 1888 out of the embers of the enduring recession that threatened to engulf the fortunes of many in the industry. Financed from Melbourne, the KTC opportunistically gobbled up most of the great names in the timber trade — including Sir John Logan Campbell's Te Kopuru Sawmill Company, the Mercury Bay Timber Company, and many others mills in the Hokianga, Whangaroa, Thames, Great Barrier Island and elsewhere. KTC's dominance was truly remarkable. Tom Simpson in *Kauri to Radiata* (1973) stated the company had two-thirds of the entire kauri timber trade. He also provided a few statistics that read like international telephone numbers. From the year it was founded until the closure of its Auckland mill in 1942,

Log jam on the Auckland waterfront, featuring the scow *Lady of the Lake*.

(WILLIAM A. PRICE COLLECTION, ALEXANDER TURNBULL LIBRARY, NATIONAL LIBRARY OF NEW ZEALAND/TE PUNA MĀTAURANGA O AOTEAROA, 001200^1/2)

the KTC produced 1,537,826,119 super feet of sawn kauri timber, with the mill at Auckland processing 456,847,776 super feet, Te Kopuru 267,734,336 super feet and Mercury Bay 204,909,984 super feet.

KTC's Auckland mill, which employed around 300 men, was accompanied on the waterfront by many more, including Leyland O'Brien & Company, Goldie's, the Waitemata Sawmill Company, Parker Lamb & Company, Macklow Brothers and, round the corner in Cox's Creek, Cashmore Brothers. This was a remarkable concentration of timber-milling power for a place with no trees. All depended on water. Cutting trees was a tough trade; milling them was increasingly capital intensive and not without physical danger; but transport was always the key to kauri. The creeks, rivers, estuaries and harbours of the Auckland region provided a unique solution. Fortunately for such a transient, depletive industry, we are still left with a few physical reminders of the transport solutions from the days when kauri was king — not least the ubiquitous scow.

Scows — working boats

The scow was Auckland's working boat par excellence. Blessed with a flat bottom, scows could cross river bars, load at jetties even with the tide out and penetrate deep into the most unlikely-looking creek. With huge logs of kauri, kahikatea or totara buckled across her beam, a heavily laden scow entering the Waitemata Harbour under full sail was one of the great sights of the time. The fleet of large sailing scows owned by Leyland O'Brien, the *Moa*, *Rangi* and *Seagull*, were particularly renowned. The *Rangi*, however, was to tragically demonstrate the hazardous nature of such boats when fully laden in bad weather. She was lost in 1937 after developing a list off Cape Colville. Logs were jettisoned to correct this but she then heeled over the other way and capsized. The crew took to the lifeboat but four were lost in the surf. The *Moa* gained instant fame when, in December 1917, she was seized near Great Mercury Island by Count von Luckner and other escaped German prisoners of war. They sailed for the Kermadec Islands, only to be greeted by a New Zealand warship on arrival. The *Moa* was towed back to Auckland, her crew not at all amused at having flown the German flag — or at being towed into their home port.

Scows were all-purpose boats of the labouring class. They would also carry stock to market, transport tea-tree to keep the home fires of Auckland burning, or on occasion move entire timber mills from one side of the country to the other. Scows could also be deliberately beached for two hours or so after high tide, and shingle or sand rapidly loaded by means of a wheelbarrow pushed skilfully up long narrow planks. Much of Auckland was built from the sand and shingle of its beaches and from the sweat of the brow of the 'shingle pushers'.

New Zealand's first scow, the *Lake Erie*, was built by Septimus Meiklejohn at Omaha in 1873. The scows were soon considered so useful and popular that no fewer than 125 were built over the next 50 years, many by Darroch at Omaha and by George Niccol in Auckland. But the tide of technology and ecology turned against them from the time of the First World War. The last, the *Alwyn G*, left the shipyard in 1925 and many ended their trading days over the next few decades rotting away in some backwater, unwanted and unloved. By the 1970s only the *Jane Gifford* was still in business. 'Janey', built in 1908, finally retired in 1984 after a spectacular voyage towing a house out to Great Barrier Island for the local policeman. In 1985 she was gifted to the Waiuku Museum and after a long period of restoration became a pleasure craft sailing from Waiuku Wharf on the southernmost arm of the Manukau Harbour. Time has recently caught up with the *Jane Gifford* and she is again undergoing an extensive refit.

Most scows never left their home waters around Auckland. Just a few ventured south to Cook Strait, including the *Echo*, built in 1905. One of the few 'hold' scows, the *Echo* traded between Wellington and Blenheim from 1920 to 1965, with time off on loan to the United States armed forces in the Pacific Islands in the Second World War. The number of times the *Echo* was stranded, in a collision or on fire during her long career runs well into double figures, so it is a little surprising she lasted long enough to enjoy her sedate retirement on the shores of Picton Harbour.

DRIVING DAMS

At the other end of the logistical nightmare of transporting giant kauri was the driving dam. Their exact number is unknown but certainly ran into the thousands. From the 1850s to the 1930s they littered kauri country — from the hills near Kaitaia in the north, through the vast forests of the northern Wairoa, across the Waitakere Ranges to the west of Auckland and up the steep valleys of the Coromandel Peninsula.

The concept was simple. Water was released from the dam high in the hills and the logs carried in an almighty elemental surge down the valley until restrained by booms at the mill or the estuary of the river. Initially they were not reusable — everything disappeared downstream. This changed when trapdoors were added that either opened or collapsed on the tug of a tripwire. There is evidence of this as early as 1850 when Thomas Henderson's mill near the upper Waitemata Harbour was supplied by such a dam built by an immigrant from Nova Scotia, John McLeod.

The case for reuse was compelling, for driving dams were neither easy nor cheap to build. First, a temporary dam was constructed upstream and the river diverted through a specially dug water race. Secure footings were gouged in the beds and banks of the river, usually without the use of dynamite for the bedrock had to remain intact. A sizeable tree was then felled nearby to provide a horizontal 'stringer' to fully bridge the dam site. This might be 25 m long and weigh many tons. Sturdy, vertical 'rafters' were cut and manhandled into place. Planking was pit-sawn on site. The total tonnage of timber was colossal — enough in an average dam to build several houses. All this was done with little more than brawn, timber jacks, capstans and blocks and tackle — and, of course, the skill and experience of the dam builders, who almost always lacked any formal engineering training. Then, as the dam filled up, the leaks were systematically plugged, often with pukahu, the fibrous material from the foot of the kauri tree which has the useful attribute of expanding in water.

Operating a driving dam could be a tricky business. Often it was months, or on occasion many years, before a sufficient head of water built up. Then if rain came suddenly the action was intense, especially if a succession of dams had to be tripped simultaneously. A military-style operation was undertaken involving synchronised watches or perhaps a series of whistles. Anything from a few hundred to many thousands of logs might be driven downriver to the booms. One drive, or 'fresh', to the mill at Tairua was said to have totalled 10,000 logs.

Drives of anything like this magnitude were totally destructive, carrying all before them and laying bare the valley floor. There was also serious log damage, especially in the steeper valleys. Statistics from the Kauaeranga Valley, near Thames, suggest that between 1918 and 1928 over 16 per cent of the kauri felled never reached the booms in the river valley.

There could be legal problems too. It was not unknown for sharp entrepreneurs

The power of water is clearly evident as a driving dam is tripped at Anawhata, Waitakere Ranges, 1916.

to buy small sections of land along creek banks, or at otherwise valueless estuary mudflats, for the sole purpose of extracting compensation for damage caused. This could seriously compromise a logging company's investment and the livelihood of many men. Disputes were fairly common in the early days and sometimes precipitated physical violence. There was at least one court case of incitement to murder. The pros and cons could be complex but after considerable debate matters were regularised under the Timber Floating Act 1873.

A driving dam was last used near Katikati at the time of the Second World War and over the years most of the structures have either rotted or been washed away. Many early examples can now be traced only by foundation holes cut in stream beds or river banks and even these are often camouflaged by vigorous revegetation.

Fortunately, posterity has been well served in this area by the surveys conducted by Bruce Hayward and Jack Diamond in the late 1970s. As a result intrepid explorers of the Waitakere Ranges can trace the remains of the 86 timber dams that once existed there. They range through time from those of the 1850s in the Henderson and Swanson valleys, the 1860s in the Kakamatua Valley and the 1870s around Huia, to those built just prior to the First World War near Piha and Anawhata. Later still just a few were constructed in the 1920s in the Wainamu and Mokoroa valleys. Sadly, even at the time of the survey the remains presented a common tale of destruction and decay with, at best, just the cills and parts of the wings having survived.

In the Kauaeranga Valley behind the town of Thames about 70 driving dams were built between 1870 and 1924 and perhaps a quarter are left, although they have all deteriorated markedly. Tarawaere Dam (1920) is the most accessible, just a few kilometres from the valley road, up a track that criss-crosses the steam interminably. Built just above a rock ledge in the narrow valley, the dam was nevertheless over 24-m wide at the waterline and stood to a height of 8 m. Now the collapsed, rotting timbers are all that remain, but a one-third-size reconstruction built near the DOC Field Centre on the main valley road gives an excellent idea of the original structure. Other significant examples of Kauaeranga Valley dams include Jim Angel's Dancing Creek Dam at the Pinnacles Hut, built in 1924, and the Kauaeranga Main Dam built in 1921 by Ebeneza Gibbons.

Elsewhere, Great Barrier Island was one of the last major stands of kauri to be logged and consequently some of the island's driving dams are in relatively good condition, including the large dam on the Kaiaraara Stream, built by George Murray around 1926, which still has its rafters and stringers in place.

BUSH INCLINES

While driving dams are the most numerous examples of the timber industry's industrial heritage, they are not the most spectacular. That accolade probably goes to some of New Zealand's bush inclines. On Great Barrier Island the KTC operated a tram incline to Whangaparapara in the 1930s that covered an extraordinary length of 9 km in 10 sections. It has been described as one of the wonders of the logging age. An impressive forerunner, the aptly named Billy Goat Incline, worked part of Kauaeranga Valley in the early 1920s, ending years of frustration in the area.

Unsuccessful attempts had been made to log the stands of kauri behind the 200-m-high Billy Goat Falls in the 1880s. Logs had been driven over the falls only to shatter to pieces. Then a holding dam and a chute were built but the results were distressingly similar. Later came a disastrous bush fire, said to have been deliberately started by a disgruntled ex-bushman, and the area was abandoned for a generation. When the KTC logged the area between 1921 and 1926, however, it employed more sophisticated methods. The Billy Goat Incline scaled the ridge by the side of the falls to a height of 290 m over a distance of 1160 m with a steepest gradient of 1 in 2.7. A mighty Judd steam winch was positioned at the summit to lower the logs gingerly down, aided by a special mechanism on a sharp curve near halfway that helped avert disaster by feeding the cable through a series of rollers. After the logs had been lowered to a point near the current viewing platform they were rolled into the river, then transferred to the main Kauaeranga tramway and finally rafted to the Auckland mill.

61

OTAKI FORKS AND ONGARUE

Old tramway and mill sites are less spectacular than inclines but nevertheless have a lingering fascination. Good examples of relatively recent small-scale logging operations can be seen at Otaki Forks in the Tararua Range. This part of the North Island was not prime timber-milling country despite its proximity to Wellington but it was logged, perhaps more in desperation than anticipation, in the Depression of the late 1920s and early 1930s. Generally a profit could be turned on the flat areas but not when harvesting the steep hillsides. There are few flat areas around Otaki Forks.

By the time logging was in full swing at Otaki Forks the age of the rail tractor had dawned. The tramways of the area — Sheridan Creek and Waitatapia — can therefore lay claim to a few New Zealand logging records. Sheridan Creek has the steepest recorded gradient of 1 in 6; Waitatapia has the sharpest curve, an incredibly tight radius of about 5 m. DOC maintains walking tracks up both tramways. Sheridan Creek offers the reward of a Vulcan log-hauler at the top. Opposite the creek, across the Waiotauru River, Seed and O'Brien's sawmill has long disappeared but its old boiler still resides proprietarily in the middle of a lush meadow. Part-way up Waitatapia old tram rails linger on — as do stories of the day a rail tractor careered out of control down the hillside and ended at the bottom of a small lake.

There was nothing small-scale or short-term about Ellis and Burnand's logging operation at Ongarue. In its time the mill was the biggest in the country, serviced by a tramway that penetrated 35 km into the bush, running through a tunnel, by the side of a rock face, around a spiral and across the sweeping curve of the Mangatukutuku Viaduct. From the mill at Ongarue it was then but a short haul down the valley to load the sawn timber onto the main trunk line. Although the upper reaches of the tramway are said to be still penetrable by the intrepid explorer, little now remains of the great mill except for a few concrete footings in the middle of a pasture while the village of Ongarue is but a shadow of its former self.

Ongarue's glory days are perhaps best recalled by the bush lokeys that once worked the line, several of which are preserved elsewhere. They were an eclectic collection. Two of the seven Climax lokeys imported to New Zealand from Corry, Pennsylvania, worked at Ongarue at one time or another. Climax 1650, which pulled an enthusiast's special up the line near the end of the mill's life, is now awaiting

renovation at The Bush Tramway Club at Pukemiro in the Waikato. The even older Climax 1203, manufactured back in 1913, still occasionally works for its keep at Shantytown near Greymouth. The remarkable Heisler 1082, built in 1904 in Erie, Pennsylvania, is also in well-earned retirement at Pukemiro, having worked for the Taupo Totara Timber Company at Mokai for 40 years and then at Ongarue for another 21 years. This was extreme longevity even for a Heisler, whose average working life was 44 years. By way of comparison, one of the best of New Zealand's indigenous lokeys, the Price E111, managed 35 years of hard toil at Mangatapu and then Ongarue before also ending up in the loving care of the enthusiasts at Pukemiro.

Climax 1650 and Price E111, ex Ellis and Burnand, Ongarue, awaiting restoration at The Bush Tramway Club, Pukemiro.

3
GOLD
— SOUTH ISLAND

'Shining like the stars in Orion on a dark frosty night.'

GABRIEL READ

CENTRAL OTAGO — ALLUVIAL MINING

Gabriel Read's description of his first shovelful of gold from Otago's Tuapeka field on 23 May 1861 sounds rather lyrical for a gold digger. But Read was not a typical prospector. Well educated and with strong religious convictions, he rejoiced in God's gift and told the world all about it. He thought that was his duty — though being human he no doubt also pondered the substantial reward offered by the provincial government for the discovery of a payable goldfield.

For a time the world, or at least the citizens of Dunedin, chose to ignore Read's tidings. But Read persisted and they eventually came to have a closer look — thousands upon thousands of them. A little apologetically, New Zealand's first substantial gold rush was under way.

At the end of June 1861 there were about 100 people on the Tuapeka goldfield just outside the present town of Lawrence. A month later the population of the area had exploded to 2000 and towards the end of the year it peaked at over 10,000. As a consequence the second half of 1861 saw the population of Otago as a whole more than double, although the outflow of humanity from Dunedin resulted in it taking on the appearance of a ghost town for a while.

Read stayed on in Gabriel's Gully to do his bit to help soothe the social turmoil. He taught the less experienced — his 'new chums' — how to select mining sites and how to pan for gold. He sometimes arbitrated in the inevitable disputes. But friction rose as the gold rush intensified, no doubt reminding Read of the lawlessness of his early days on the goldfields of California and Victoria. Read gladly left to prospect

GOLD — SOUTH ISLAND
Central Otago

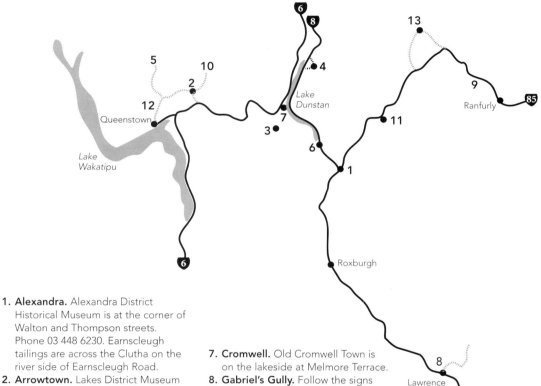

1. **Alexandra.** Alexandra District Historical Museum is at the corner of Walton and Thompson streets. Phone 03 448 6230. Earnscleugh tailings are across the Clutha on the river side of Earnscleugh Road.
2. **Arrowtown.** Lakes District Museum is at 49 Buckingham Street. Phone 03 442 1824. The Chinese settlement is at the west end of Buckingham Street.
3. **Bannockburn.** Bannockburn sluicings are 6 km south-west of Cromwell along Bannockburn Road and then right into Felton Road. On private property.
4. **Bendigo** is 23 km north of Cromwell on a loop road off SH 8.
5. **Bullendale** is a rugged three-hour tramp beyond Skippers. Skippers Road is notoriously treacherous.
6. **Clyde.** Clyde Historical Museum is in Blyth Street. Phone 03 449 2938 or 03 449 2092.

7. **Cromwell.** Old Cromwell Town is on the lakeside at Melmore Terrace.
8. **Gabriel's Gully.** Follow the signs from the centre of Lawrence.
9. **Golden Progress Mine** is in Reef Road, a loop road between Oturehua and SH 85.
10. **Macetown** is 15 km up the Arrow River valley from Arrowtown. Suitable only for 4WD vehicles, horses, mountain bikes and walking.
11. **Ophir** is just off SH 85 near Omakau, 25 km north-east of Alexandra.
12. **Oxenbridge Tunnel** is about 1 km down a rough track immediately before the Edith Cavell Bridge, 6 km north of Queenstown.
13. **St Bathans** is 61 km north-east of Alexandra on a loop road from SH 85 at Becks.

new fields for the Provincial Council. In July 1861 he made a further rich discovery in nearby Waitahuna. He later prospected fruitlessly elsewhere in Otago and in the Wairarapa before returning to his native Tasmania. There he married his cousin and took up farming but died an impoverished manic-depressive in 1894.

In the hectic final months of 1861 Gabriel's Gully was transformed into a mass of tiny mining claims, generally measuring about 7 m square. Prospectors did little more than register a claim, pitch a tent and gather bracken for a bed. Then they got on with the hard work of excavating the surface layer of mud and gravel to expose the paydirt of alluvial gold lying about 2 m below the surface. After puddling the paydirt in a tub and then washing it through a sieve and a cradle, gold was extracted — and a heap of tailings was piled high on each tiny claim. Soon it was said that the gully looked like the aftermath of a mole convention.

Only a few of the initial prospectors became seriously rich at Gabriel's Gully or

Gabriel's Gully, 1862, shortly after the start of the gold rush.

(Alexander Turnbull Library, National Library of New Zealand/Te Puna Mātauranga o Aotearoa, 096648½)

the nearby fields of Waitahuna and Waipori, for the immediately accessible paydirt was soon worked out. As usual shopkeepers, sly-groggers and the likes of Ballarat Sal and Melbourne Liz probably prospered most. Although there was further gold to be won in the gully during the rest of the nineteenth century, it involved capital-intensive methods such as stamping and sluicing and demanded vast amounts of water — never a ready commodity in Central Otago. Even as early as 1865 there were over 450 km of water races, including one from the Waipori River said to have been over 40 km long. Later the revolutionary technique of hydraulic elevating was pioneered in Gabriel's Gully.

Gabriel's Gully, the premier historic site of New Zealand gold mining, now seems unexceptional, little more than tussocky hillocks dotted with manuka and pine. A lone apple tree stands forlorn in the middle of the valley. Shadows fall seductively across Grey's Dam. Little remains of the North of Ireland Battery site or the desolate hydraulic elevator hole.

Yet a walk around the perimeter of the valley is revealing, for the topography has been transformed by a multitude of miners. The original gully floor is fully 50 m below the current level, hidden beneath the tailings of many years. The miners literally moved mountains. Anyone fossicking these days needs a lot of luck, because these tailings have already been worked over a minimum of three times.

The Dunstan

As the year 1861 wore on, the miners of Gabriel's Gully, restless for richer pickings, became increasingly willing to rush off to any supposed goldfield on little or no information. There were reports of prospectors slavishly following well-known diggers who were merely taking an evening's constitutional stroll, convinced they were on their way to the next eldorado. The miners' credulity, or desperation, knew few bounds. Once, a dotty old gent, Sam Perkins, led 3000 men on a wild goose chase across the hills of Central Otago for many days and was lucky to escape with his life when found out.

Throughout the winter of 1862 many hard-nosed prospectors, often experienced in California and Victoria, slowly worked their way inland along the inhospitable banks of the Clutha River. They kept very quiet indeed about their discoveries — if allowed to.

Horatio Hartley and Christopher Reilly made not a single peep as they dug rapaciously in a deep and remote ravine just south of the junction of the Clutha and the Kawarau rivers. Then, in August 1862, they deposited 87 pounds (nearly 40 kg) of gold dust on the counter of an astonished Dunedin gold receiver. Knowing their time was effectively up, they also agreed to reveal the whereabouts of their claim for a reward of £2000. Hartley led an official expedition back to his river beach — and could not find any gold. The Clutha, abnormally low in the bleak winter of '62, had since risen. All evidence of Hartley and Reilly's workings was now below water. Tempers were rapidly fraying and Hartley was in danger of physical abuse when he desperately plunged his spade into the river bed and came up with the glint of gold. The rush to the Dunstan was on.

Thousands of hopeful prospectors heeded the siren call. The *Otago Witness* once again reported feverish scenes in Dunedin:

> … the entire community is turned upside down. Building operations are almost at a stand; clerks, craftsmen and labourers are all gone or going to the 'diggings'. Mining tools are being turned out of every hole and corner in which they have been stowed away and are being eagerly bought at high prices … We question if the excitement which prevails in Dunedin was equalled even by that which was occasioned by Gabriel Read's discoveries.

The *Witness* then wisely advised its readers to only undertake the adventure if well equipped and provisioned.

The Dunstan was indeed hostile country. Transportation of goods from Dunedin was slow and hideously expensive. Only the sheep meat supplied by the local stations averted mass starvation. Appropriately, Mutton Town sprang up just to the south of the future town of Clyde. Timber was so scarce that it is said that gin boxes were almost as valuable as their contents because they could be readily recycled as miners' 'cradles'. Men lived in caves on the river bank and hastily erected sod and canvas shanties just about everywhere. Yet, for many, the privation was worthwhile. Within weeks the first gold escort left for Dunedin with more than 6000 ounces (about 170 kg) of gold dust on board.

The landscape of this part of Central Otago could not have changed more dramatically since the gold-rush days. For years now much of the long, bare Cromwell Gorge has been submerged by the waters of man-made Lake Dunstan. Only the occasional signpost hints at its dramatic history — the site of the original Hartley-Reilly claim near Brewery Creek; Gibraltar Rock, where rock shelters were home to the first Chinese settlers; Dairy Creek, where the Dunstan Dairy was in reality a fiery sly-grog shop.

Yet in the nearby town of Clyde — known as The Dunstan throughout the years when it was the heart of Central — solid stone buildings dating from the 1860s attest to the durability of gold money. The Corinthian-pillared Town Hall started life in 1869 as a Masonic Lodge; Oliver's Lodge and Restaurant was once Benjamin Naylor's general store. Nearby, in the building that was once the Hartley Arms Hotel (1869), the landlord, James Parks, was renowned for his hospitality but not for the variety of his cuisine. Parks kept a few hundred hens on the land by the river. The breakfast menu was eggs — poached, fried or boiled. Often much the same was on offer at lunch or dinner. Just occasionally a chicken made an appearance. The 1864 stone courthouse gives off an aura of determined permanence. The original, built of scantling and calico, blew away in a gale the previous year. Next door, the Clyde

After a change of ownership — and presumably menu — the staff and patrons of the Hartley Arms Hotel, Clyde, oblige the camera. It is now a private residence.

(Clyde Historical Museum, MF9)

Historical Museum has an exhibit guaranteed to engage even the most pedestrian imagination — a set of scales that are claimed to have weighed over 70,000 ounces of gold dust in the first three months of the rush to the Dunstan.

A feature of the museum is the old Vincent County Council Chamber, presided over by a large framed photograph of the legendary Vincent Pyke. No man in the history of Central Otago was alternately more respected and reviled than Pyke. Most positions of responsibility were his at one time or another, including goldfield commissioner, magistrate and Member of Parliament. Stout, convivial, honest and possessing the common touch, Pyke made many friends. Acid of tongue and hot of temper, he also made a few enemies. It is said that when he finally came off the fence on the issue of whether Clyde or Cromwell should be county town, he was burned in effigy by the losers, Cromwell. But throughout a long career he always remained a passionate advocate of the rights of miners and the interests of Central Otago.

Although possessing little formal education Pyke was also a journalist of talent and wrote the novels *Wild Will Enderby* and *The Adventures of George Washington Pratt*. Action-packed, with few niceties of style, they paint an authentic picture of mining life at this time and were very popular. He also found time to lead the expedition that discovered the route from Lake Wanaka to the West Coast. Pyke is also one of the very few New Zealanders to have had a county named in his honour. The story is that his political enemies suggested the idea in a fit of sarcasm — and were then appalled to find themselves taken seriously.

The Arrow and the Shotover

Shortly after Reilly and Hartley's fabulous strike at the Dunstan the quest for gold spread further into the hostile mountain ranges of Central Otago. Rumours began to fly that a mysterious figure, Fox, had struck untold riches somewhere deep in the mountain gorges near what is now Arrowtown. Hundreds of prospectors spent more time 'hunting the fox' than panning for gold. But Bill Fox, a veteran of the Californian and Victorian rushes, kept his find, on the rich alluvial river beaches of the Arrow, secret for many weeks. What's more, by a combination of native cunning and the expert use of his fists, he seems to have enforced a feudal discipline on other miners in the remote valley so that by the time they were eventually rushed, huge quantities of alluvial gold had been panned.

Almost simultaneously the nearby Shotover River provided another dramatic rags-to-riches tale. When Thomas Arthur and Harry Redfern landed at Queenstown Bay in November 1862 they lacked even the barest of necessities. Hired as sheep-shearers, on their first free Sunday they walked to the present site of the Edith Cavell Bridge and, with just a tin dish and a butcher's knife, panned four ounces of gold in the afternoon. Within a few months they had accumulated £4000 worth. No more shearing for Harry and Tom.

Such tales of fabulous riches spread instantly. Lawless Fox's — now Arrowtown — sprang into life. Not even the worst ravages of nature could deter the stream of humanity, each determined on his share of the easy pickings. Yet, in the fearsome winter of 1863 heavy rains sent huge waves of water surging down the narrow valleys and many drowned. Later, snow cut off food supplies. Dysentery, owing to poor sanitation, scurvy, as a result of dreadful diet, and rheumatism, the consequence of standing for days in an ice-cold river, took a heavy toll. Regardless, the population of Arrowtown soon hit 7000. Many of its more sturdy original buildings survive to this day.

Too soon the days of shovelfuls of gold dust were over. The young hopefuls moved on to search for alluvial gold in the Wakamarina field near Nelson and then to the West Coast. For the permanent inhabitants of Central Otago the long era of more capital-intensive gold mining — of sluicing, stamping and dredging — was about to begin.

CENTRAL OTAGO — SLUICING

Bannockburn

Sluicing was to be the most effective and popular method of gold extraction in nineteenth-century Otago, nowhere more so than at Bannockburn. Here, in one of the driest spots of a generally arid province, water was at a definite premium.

The gold-bearing gravels of Bannockburn had been deposited deep beneath layers of barren overburden by prehistoric rivers. Water, carried by races from way up in the mountain ranges, was dammed and then sold to the miners. When it finally reached the claim the water was channelled through increasingly narrow pipes. Then the resulting power-jet was directed to wash away the overburden. Often water-race owners grew far richer than the miners. Yet nothing is inevitable in gold mining. One consortium took many years to build a 32-km race from way up the Carrick Ranges down to the Bannockburn Sluicings, only to find they had only secondary rights to the water. The investors lost heavily.

Little has changed in the eerie landscape of Bannockburn since the last of the miners left nearly a century ago. Smooth-faced cliffs tower 30 m or so above valleys strewn with tailings. Isolated pillars of rock stretch skywards, monuments to long-forgotten disputes about the exact position of the corners of adjoining claims. The tops of the pinnacles mark the original ground level. The remains of paved water races and sludge channels can still be traced as they criss-cross the barren landscape. The place is like a miniature badlands backdrop for a B western movie.

On the hillside above the sluicings is the flat terrace of Stewart Town where two bachelors, John Menzies and David Stewart, built a large stone-lined reservoir in 1868. It supplied the workings below via an elaborate network of grooved channels, pipes and aqueducts made from curved and riveted metal sheets. The stone reservoir walls and the ruined cottages of Stewart Town, with their pear and apricot orchards, still survive.

There are also only limited remains of the nearby towns, for a variety of reasons. Old Bannockburn town inevitably declined in line with the exploitation of the sluicings. Many of the original buildings in nearby Cromwell eventually felt the watery embrace of the artificial Lake Dunstan. Making the best of one of the saddest episodes in the destruction of New Zealand's industrial heritage, 'Old Cromwell' has been rebuilt by the lakeside at Melmore Terrace, including an 1866 Cobb & Co store, Jolly's Seed & Grain Store and London House stables.

Sluicing was to remain a major force in Otago gold mining throughout the nineteenth century but its technology evolved dramatically in that time. Originally ground sluicing involved little more than a steady flow of water into a sluice box. Then high-pressure hydraulic sluicing blasted powerful jets at walls of gravel. Finally, hydraulic elevating was developed. First used at Gabriel's Gully in 1879 by J.R. Perry, it involved the use of high-pressure water to raise gold-bearing gravels from one level to another. Hydraulic elevating at its most dramatic was best seen at St Bathans where miners, particularly sluicing-supremo John Ewing, moved a mountain and created a lake.

The lake that was once a mountain. From 1864 onwards miners first undermined Kildare Hill and then created the huge pit that became known as 'the Glory Hole'. Now the Blue Lake has an almost ethereal beauty in the evening sunlight.

St Bathans and its Glory Hole

St Bathans, on a loop road off State Highway 85, has witnessed most methods of mining auriferous gravels during its long and colourful life. In 1864 homesick Irish prospectors sank shafts into a 120-m-high ridge between two gullies and named it Kildare Hill. When water became available from two water races, one 24 km long, from the Manuherikia River, the gravels were shifted by sluicing until Kildare Hill completely disappeared. But disposing of the tailings was an ongoing problem. Sludge channels quickly became clogged and this severely limited the depths at which the gravels could be worked. The answer was to lift the paydirt to ground level using a hydraulic elevator. The gravels were initially broken down by a standard hydraulic monitor and then fed into the pipe of the elevator and forced upwards by a combination of water pressure and a partial vacuum.

In the 1880s Ewing installed his first elevator. It lifted the gravels 6.5 m. Emboldened by success, Ewing went deeper still. By 1894 he was raising gold-bearing material 39 m in three separate lifts. There seemed to be no reduction in the quantity of gold produced, so Ewing pushed ever lower. By 1897 the total elevation was 49 m. Ewing's empire came under threat soon afterwards, however, and 'the Glory Hole' passed into the hands of a succession of companies, each of which set new records. By 1933 the Kildare Consolidated Gold Mining Company was elevating what was

73

St Bathans in the twenty-first century.

claimed to be the deepest lift in the world in two segments — one of 54 m and one of 19.5 m.

The end came in the form of a notice to cease mining from the Maniototo County Council. The workings were threatening to undermine the township. By then St Bathans was only a shadow of the town that boasted 10 hotels and a population of 1000 back in the 1860s, but the locals were justly proud of the place and were unimpressed by the thought of slipping into the Glory Hole. So St Bathans, the most lopsided of villages, lives to tell its unique history, even though these days the number of buildings exceed the number of permanent residents. The short string of venerable buildings that line one side of the main street include the old Bank of New South Wales, the public hall, the post office and the mud-brick Vulcan Hotel, where miners have imbibed since 1882, though it was originally the Ballarat. On the other side of the road, literally a few metres away, the hole that was once a hill, is 69 m deep. On a summer's evening the usually milky-blue lake shimmers seductively, as if innocent of its dramatic history.

CENTRAL OTAGO — QUARTZ STAMPING

Following hard on alluvial mining and sluicing came the third phase of gold prospecting, quartz mining. Never as important in Otago as elsewhere in New Zealand, quartz mining offered a particular challenge as it was often located on the bleakest hilltops.

Quartz, the mother lode of gold, was first mined around Wakatipu in the mid-1860s and there were mines of varying productivity across the province. Cardrona's Gin and Raspberry Mine, named after the miners' favourite tipple, had remarkably rich but patchy veins. The Golden Progress Mine near Oturehua worked intermittently until 1936 and still boasts Otago's only surviving poppet head at a small, integrated site that includes boilers, tailing dams and miners' cottages.

Bendigo

Central Otago's most successful hard-rock mine was at Bendigo. Initially thought to be just a short-lived alluvial field, Bendigo's quartz potential was first noticed by Tom Logan who, after numerous setbacks, found three partners with the necessary capital to erect a five-stamper battery powered by a huge overshot waterwheel. In just 10 days the partners — the Cromwell Quartz Mining Company — dug and crushed 238 ounces (nearly 7 kg) of gold and the second Bendigo rush was on. More reefs were quickly found. Many proved profitless and short-lived but the Cromwell Company flourished and paid substantial dividends. Yet the fate of the four original investors provides a salutary tale. One died after falling from his horse. Another lost his fortune in disastrous business ventures, including the ill-fated Bannockburn water race. The third lived the lush life in Dunedin but was eventually reduced to a pauper. The fourth returned to England, invested wisely, and died a rich man.

By 1869 a township had been laid out around the Solway Battery. Along Oxford Street Goodall's Bendigo Reefs Hotel and the Solway Hotel dispensed some of life's luxuries and the bakery, whose stone shell still stands, some of its necessities. Soon afterwards Logantown and Welshtown sprang up in the rugged hills behind Bendigo. Here ruined stone cottages still hug the hillside, side by side with mine shafts and mullock heaps. The good news in this tough environment was majestic views across the valleys towards the St Bathans Range.

Macetown

Fifteen daunting kilometres up the Arrow River from Arrowtown lie the remains of another quartz-mining settlement, Macetown. Quartz reefs were discovered here when the hordes of alluvial miners scoured the river in 1862–63, but they were exploited only from 1876. Then, until the turn of the century, up to 200 people eked out a precarious living. Mining finally ceased in the 1920s.

With access originally only by a track over a 1000-m-high saddle and with the 1800-m Advance Peak at its back door, Macetown was an isolated but seemingly contented and close-knit community. Even today access is limited to four-wheel-drive vehicles, hardy hikers and muscular mountain bikers. The rough road crosses a river of uncertain depth 22 times and intermittently clings precariously to the mountainside. In summer the track is lined with a blooming legacy of early mining days in the form of a multitude of wild roses, lupins, poppies and broom mingled with tough native matagouri. Macetown itself is shaded with poplar, hawthorn and sycamore. Only three buildings still stand, most notably the restored Needham's Cottage, home of Joseph Needham, postmaster and schoolteacher for 10 years until 1889. Then the authorities demanded he acquire the qualifications for the job and he immediately reverted to gold mining. Up the Rich Burn behind the township lie a succession of ever more inaccessible battery sites — Anderson's, Homeward Bound and remote Maryborough.

LEFT ABOVE: Anderson's Stamper Battery, Rich Burn, Macetown.

LEFT BELOW: Beyond even remote Macetown the Maryborough Company had a mine 1300 m above sea level. A five-stamp battery driven by a huge waterwheel operated from around 1879. Altitude, rough terrain and fierce winters contributed to poor returns, however. Later an infusion of capital ensured better results.

BEATING THE ODDS

All gold rushes are triumphs of optimism over environment. Prospectors to the West Coast, for example, had to endure a fearful trudge over the Southern Alps or face the hazards of the harbour bars at Hokitika or Okarito. Then they endured near starvation in a land hostile to cultivation.

The opening of Central Otago was even more dramatic. Here nature repelled all but the most hardy and determined invader. The climate is extreme. Fierce winters are matched by blistering summers. Water, the miner's friend, is at a premium. The mountains are steep and bare of the timber needed for building materials. Ravines discourage road building. None of these factors dampened the dreams of fabulous wealth, of course, but some feats of endurance by the early diggers are mind-boggling for the modern visitor.

A waterwheel and a powerhouse

Ponder, for a moment, the great waterwheel that stands outside Alexandra's museum. It is about 7 m in diameter and weighs five tons. Built in Dunedin in 1879 it lay abandoned for many years in a deep gully in the Fraser Basin, around 1700 m up the Old Man Range behind the town. In the late 1960s a number of intrepid townsfolk, proud of their heritage, commendably decided to bring it down the mountain. As well as husky Otago manpower, a tractor, a four-wheel-drive vehicle and eventually a helicopter, were recruited for the job. Yet that waterwheel — probably part of the machinery used in an attempt to open up the Alpine Ridge Reef — defied several attempts at relocation over a considerable period of time. The full story is told in *Operation Waterwheel* (1972) by Myra Hannah and reads like an Antarctic epic. If it took such dedication and determination to get the waterwheel down the mountain, it beggars the imagination to think of the grinding effort required to get it up there by bullock wagon in the first place.

Even so, shifting a single waterwheel might have seemed like a blessing to the folk of Bullendale. A three-hour trek beyond Skippers on the Shotover River, Bullendale was a daunting place to live and work. The Shotover may have been the 'richest river in the world' but its bounty was guarded by a treacherous ravine. Even today the road is narrow, winding and potentially precipitous. Placenames such as Hell's Gate and Devil's Elbow were not bestowed lightly.

Although hauling heavy equipment up to Bullendale in the gold-rush days must have been a logistical and physical nightmare, a traditional water-powered battery was in place by 1865 and worked for 20 years. Then the Phoenix Quartz Mining Company and its manager, Fred Evans, had a spectacular technological success with New Zealand's first hydroelectric generating plant. Two of the largest dynamos then made, plus two pelton wheels and over 200 m of iron pipe were dragged up Skippers. A powerhouse was built at the base of a 60-m cliff. Water flowed along races and down the tapered piping fixed to the cliff face to feed the pelton wheels, which in turn drove the dynamos. Electricity was then carried by number-eight copper wire over a high ridge to the stamper battery 3 km away. There were teething problems at the generating plant and inconsistent yields at the battery but it pounded on until 1907 and employed 200 men. The hardy souls of Bullendale enjoyed electric light before the gentry down in Dunedin.

Moving water

For sheer futile, back-breaking work, consider the attempts to master the mighty rivers of the area. Logically there should be great riches down at the bottom of nature's sluice boxes and many attempts were made to divert or dam the major waterways. On the Kawarau, at Quartz Point, the Nil Desperandum Company went to great expense to build a 240-m-long dam, only for it to be swept away in a swirling torrent in January 1866. Others put their faith in tunnelling. In 1887 William Scoles dug a 46-m-long tunnel through a razorback spur to divert the Arrow but found the bared riverbed to have been previously worked. Just after the turn of the twentieth century the Oxenbridge family showed even more determination, spending three years digging a tunnel through solid rock in order to divert the Shotover River. When they finally hit daylight they were about one metre too high. Undeterred, they built a wing dam to divert the river through the tunnel. It was washed away. Never daunted, they rebuilt the dam, installed pumps, steam engines and a hydraulic elevator. After spending a small fortune, they eventually exposed the river bed only to find it littered with evidence — from wheelbarrows to whisky bottles — of an earlier dig. Their returns were minimal. The Oxenbridge Tunnel, testament to hard work and bad luck, lies just above the Edith Cavell Bridge.

The real payback on the rivers came not from tunnelling but with steam dredging. By 1900 about 200 dredges — monoliths with all the grace of floating freezing works — were scouring the river beds of Otago, especially the Clutha. The largest floated on 40-m pontoons, scooped silt from a depth of 15 m and had huge elevators able to dump tailings high on river banks. There they will remain for evermore, most conspicuously on the Earnscleugh Flat opposite Alexandra.

The Chinese in Central Otago

For sheer tenacity in the face of a hostile environment — this time human — consider the history of the Chinese community in Otago. The first Chinese immigrants arrived in February 1866, actively solicited by the provincial government and the business community to replace the outflow of miners to the newly opened fields on the West Coast. Many miners tended to carry a baggage of racial discrimination from the Australian fields, however, and the reception accorded the Chinese was often less than rapturous. The *Tuapeka Recorder* commented that there was 'nothing in their general demeanour that could be called downright repulsive'. Over the years the ingrained racial prejudice hardly changed and the Chinese were never allowed to assimilate into European society. They lived in separate communities and fostered traditional pastimes such as fan-tan, built joss houses and organised secret societies known as tongs.

Main Street, Round Hill, Southland, in the 1890s. Sluicing continued here for many years, attracting one of the largest Chinese communities on the goldfields.

(SOUTHLAND MUSEUM)

By 1871, the peak for Chinese immigration to Otago, there were over 4000 Chinese throughout the mining towns of the province and many more in Southland. Although they remained in a minority in most places, in Bannockburn their numbers equalled Europeans, while in Nevis they were a majority. An informal network of Chinese stores was established, supplied by merchants in Dunedin, the most prominent of whom was Sew Hoy whose family was to remain in the city through six generations and whose business premises still stand in Stafford Street. Always the Chinese fossicked assiduously, often successfully reworking heaps of mining spoil long abandoned by the original miners.

Arrowtown Chinese Settlement, an archaeological reconstruction.

Mostly the Chinese were single men intent on staying in New Zealand just long enough to acquire modest wealth — perhaps £100 or so, around 20 years wages in Kwantung Province (now Guangdong) in south-western China from where most originated — and then returning home. This plan often remained unfulfilled, of course. The less fortunate, or less thrifty, sometimes lingered in their hovels long after the gold deposits were exhausted. Alexander Don, the missionary, recorded their plight:

> … most of the men are very old and infirm and they just live on from day to day, eating little, sleeping much, without God and without hope.

Few Chinese brought their wives to New Zealand and their homes were simple and austere, making the most of whatever local material was freely available. They were particularly adept at walling in the caves or the overhanging rock faces of ravines. Elsewhere tiny huts were often built from schist slabs held together with mud and roofed with metal sheeting. Around Lawrence flattened gas cans and rice sacks were popular while at Waipori sun-dried mud bricks were in vogue.

Until it disappeared, Cromwell had a fine example of the Chinese community that flourished on the edge of town for nearly 50 years until about 1920. Here around 40 men lived in huts on small plots of land where pigs and chickens were raised and fruit trees cultivated. The enclave had a market garden, shops, gaming houses and a brothel for a time. In Arrowtown there is an archaeological reconstruction of the

Chinese settlement that developed from 1869 onwards. The Arrowtown reconstruction, begun in 1983, has transformed a few scattered and sunken flagstones into a distinct community. Ah Lum's store, originally built in 1883 and modelled on traditional structures found in the Canton delta region, is perhaps the finest of Otago's Chinese relics and required relatively little work. Other tiny dwellings — usually one room with no plumbing — such as Ah Gum's, had to be rebuilt from the foundations. Fortunately the conservationists have been able to draw on the curiosity of nineteenth-century visitors equipped with photographic equipment to allow Arrowtown, the sole survivor of over 20 Chinese communities, to once again come to life amid the willows, poplars and hawthorns of the historic river bank.

WEST COAST GOLD

'San Francisco itself did not rise so fast,
Melbourne not much faster …'
SIR CHARLES DILKE

On the sandspit at Hokitika there is a replica of the schooner *Tambo*. It serves as a memorial to all the ships wrecked and the lives lost in the mad scramble to pan gold on the Coast in the few years from late 1864 onwards.

Getting ashore in those days was truly perilous, especially from sailing ships. There was a collision or grounding every 10 days or so in the period 1865 to 1867. After a short time the shoreline must have been a daunting sight for new immigrants. Wrecks dotted the beach — the *Montezuma*, the *Sir Francis Drake*, the *Titania* and the paddle steamer *New Zealand* were but a few.

Yet the prize could be well worth the risk. In those initial frantic few years the West Coast's gold production of over 1.3 million ounces (valued at around $NZ850 million at the prices prevailing at the time of writing) rapidly outstripped even that of Central Otago. What's more, much of it was alluvial gold and easily won by the first arrivals. Yet access to the Coast was a major problem. The Southern Alps and the dense bush were near impenetrable barriers. For those with the money to pay for the passage it was best to take a chance on the shifting river bar.

Within two years Hokitika exploded from a mere name on the map to one of New

Zealand's largest towns and, briefly, its busiest port. Revell Street, hacked through the bush and the sand dunes by the founding fathers in late 1864 and named after the goldfield warden Big Bill Revell, was said to boast over 80 hotels at its rip-roaring peak. Most were hastily thrown up from little more than scantling and calico, but there was also an abundant supply of raw material on the beach just waiting to be recycled for more permanent use. It did not go to waste. By Christmas 1865 the local Wesleyan Church was supported by a ship's bow and the region's first sawmill, on Gibson's Quay, was powered by a salvaged boiler.

Early alluvial fields
Initially most of the tens of thousands of souls who poured over the bar in 1865–67 headed for goldfields being opened at an amazing rate in the inland river valleys. The first commercial discovery had been made in early 1864 at Greenstone Creek, a branch of the Hohonu River. Local Maori unearthed gold dust when seeking greenstone and a small rush resulted — though Maori successfully fooled Pakeha prospectors for a short time by hiding their lucrative diggings and going through the motions of gold panning in another, barren area. Soon Greenstone was overrun with diggers, of course. Then many further fields were opened, including Totara River, Waimea Creek and Kaniere.

A 70-km stretch of the coast from approximately the Grey River in the north to the Ross Flat in the south was now alive with diggers. They swarmed from Central Otago, where production was in decline, from the Wakamarina near Nelson, which had proved a flash in a gold pan, and from Victoria where the Ballarat and Bendigo fields were undergoing the inevitable transformation into large-scale, capital-intensive industry. For many a miner, baulking at the thought of working for wages and still yearning for the thrill of the gold chase, the Coast now offered the latest promise of instant riches.

Many of these early alluvial fields certainly provided quick and plentiful pickings for lucky individuals — and then petered out within a few years. But the small sluicing companies of the Coast were to continue as the backbone of the New Zealand gold industry for many years. As late as 1884 the West Coast still produced half New Zealand's total gold, despite the opening of the Thames field and continued production in Central Otago.

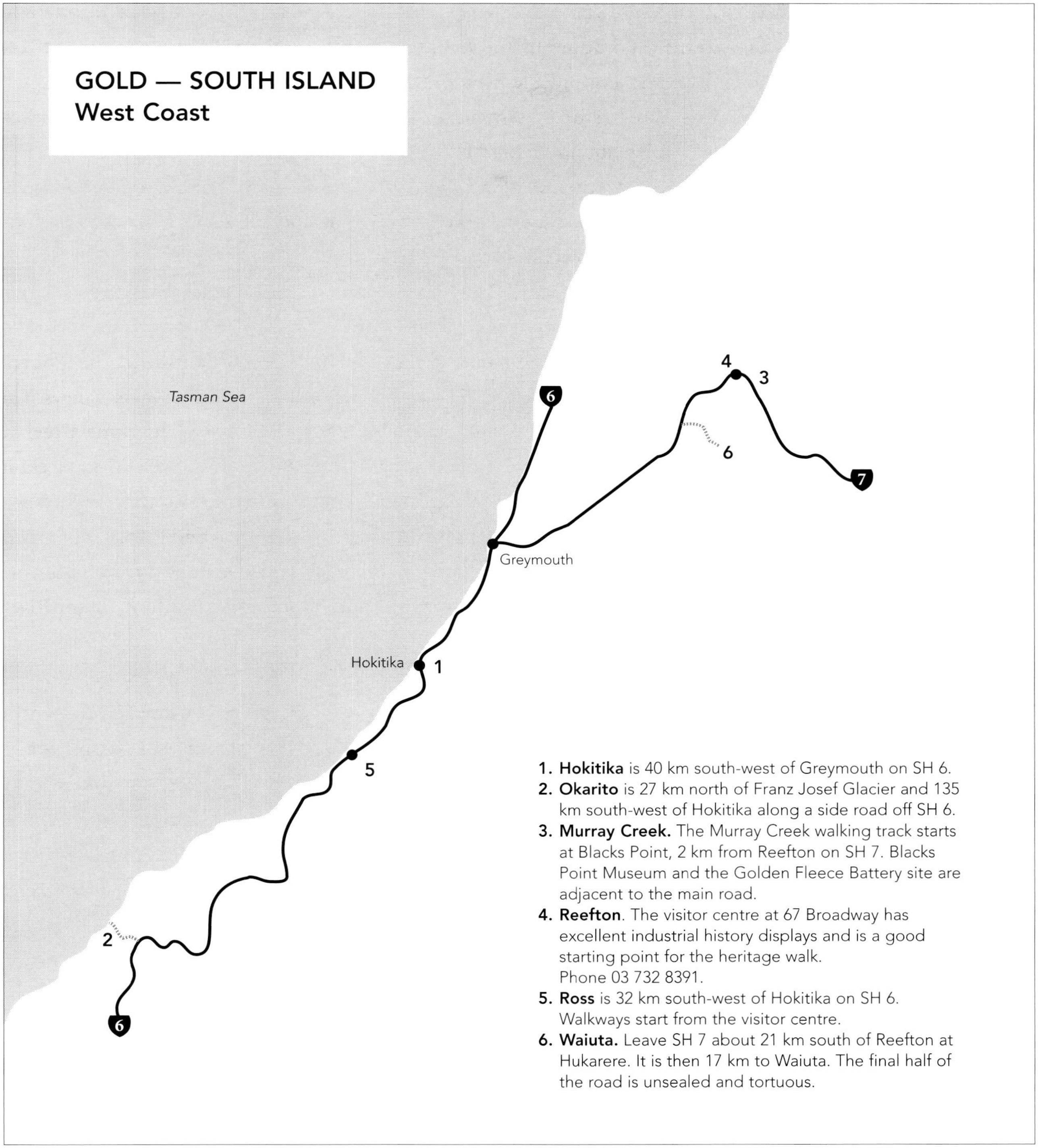

GOLD — SOUTH ISLAND
West Coast

Tasman Sea

Greymouth

Hokitika

1. **Hokitika** is 40 km south-west of Greymouth on SH 6.
2. **Okarito** is 27 km north of Franz Josef Glacier and 135 km south-west of Hokitika along a side road off SH 6.
3. **Murray Creek.** The Murray Creek walking track starts at Blacks Point, 2 km from Reefton on SH 7. Blacks Point Museum and the Golden Fleece Battery site are adjacent to the main road.
4. **Reefton.** The visitor centre at 67 Broadway has excellent industrial history displays and is a good starting point for the heritage walk.
   Phone 03 732 8391.
5. **Ross** is 32 km south-west of Hokitika on SH 6. Walkways start from the visitor centre.
6. **Waiuta.** Leave SH 7 about 21 km south of Reefton at Hukarere. It is then 17 km to Waiuta. The final half of the road is unsealed and tortuous.

Ross

Ross provides a good example of one such area that worked on and on. Even in the early twenty-first century the hum of heavy machinery can still be heard from the town's opencast mine. What's more, fossickers are encouraged to try their luck, and not just as a gimmick. All that is required is plentiful patience and a willingness to observe the well-signed rules: stick to the active stream bed; all natural and historic features to remain undisturbed; use only non-motorised, hand-held tools such as picks, shovels, pans and riffle boxes.

From the start of mining at Ross, in the winter of 1865, the deposits on Jones' Flat were strictly for well-equipped miners with a view to the longer term. These auriferous gravels were often deep underground and substantial shafts were needed. Other, surface-bound, alluvial gravels could only be worked by hydraulic sluicing. Both methods required a vigorous supply of water to power pumping machinery and sluicing guns. Fortunately, unlike Central Otago, this was the West Coast's most abundant resource. Soon water races, tunnels and wooden flumes criss-crossed the valley.

The old water races of Ross, now shrouded in a blanket of verdant vegetation — ponga, manuka, rimu, macrocarpa, pittosporum, montbretia and fuchsia — can be

By choice gold miners ensured essential water supplies by digging water races around the contours of hillsides, but deep ravines sometimes had to be crossed on rough-hewn wooden trestles. The fluming at Jones Creek, Ross, was built as early as 1866.

(Alexander Turnbull Library, National Library of New Zealand/Te Puna Mātauranga o Aotearoa, F38866½)

followed around the contours of the hills near town. All this is regrowth, of course, for the original bush was rapidly hacked down for pit props and flumes. Sadly there is now no trace of the 170-m-long, 40-m-high flume that was slung across Jones Creek in the 1860s, an engineering feat of some magnificence for so young a community.

Okarito and Five Mile Beach

The early West Coast diggers did not realise that as they stumbled ashore or plodded the beaches — the only highway in those days — they were walking over a fortune. For many prospectors, educated in the art of sniffing out gold on the fields of California, Victoria or Otago, the possibility of the beaches of the Tasman Sea offering rich and easy pickings was beyond their imagination. But rivers flowing in torrents down the western slopes of the Southern Alps had swept exceptionally fine gold dust out to sea. Then currents and tides had left rich but frustratingly scattered deposits on the black-sand beaches.

Remnant of the Jones Creek water race, Ross.

The dawning realisation of the fortune underfoot came one day in late 1865 when three men arrived in Hokitika with about 50 kg of gold. The locals were more than politely interested in the location of the claim — which they eventually pinned down as a beach just south of Greymouth. For a brief period all the beaches of Westland were systematically turned upside down — most profitably those around and to the south of Okarito.

Today Okarito is a gentle, soporific place. With the Southern Alps rising dramatically to its rear and a long, lazy lagoon on its doorstep, it is the dreamy and untroubled home of a few dozen souls. On a typical Westland day the varying grey hues of sea, sand and sky mingle and merge one with another and the world is at peace. Only a close inspection of the obelisk in the centre of the township gives the game away. It is inscribed to the pioneers whose courage and perseverance founded and settled Westland. Certainly when they founded and settled Okarito they did so with amazing speed and determination.

Before October 1865 Okarito was a lagoon fringed with native flax, graced by flocks of white heron. By early 1866 the area had been transformed into a town, a sort of civilisation for several thousand prospectors. Briefly, Okarito became the third port of the Coast despite its treacherous, shifting sandbar. Tradesmen camped out overnight to bid fancy prices for small retail frontages on the main street. For a time Okarito ripped and roared with the best, with communal strife between Irish Republicans and Unionists a speciality. Yet within a year or two the black sands had been thoroughly worked over and Okarito was in rapid decline. From then onwards it just spluttered along on the back of timber and flax mills.

Much of the action took place a little further down the coast, especially at Five Mile Beach. Here deposits were so rich that rival claims were marked out with plumb lines so as not to miss a single grain. R.C. Reid, a gold buyer, recorded that on one trip he almost immediately ran out of bank notes when a group of miners offered up two billy cans crammed with fine gold dust. Briefly, the town of Five Mile stretched for about 3 km along the sand dunes.

One of the more mindless gold rushes took place around these parts. Albert Hunt had a Midas-touch reputation. Word got around that he had struck it rich near Bruce Bay. Pursued by the greedy and the gullible in their thousands, Hunt headed south down the beach and was physically threatened if he tried to turn back. A town sprang up with all the usual trappings of the instant goldfield — hotels, barmaids and grog shops. Hunt eventually lost the mob in the rainforest some miles into the interior. Several miners perished and the rest were not best pleased. In some of the worst violence in New Zealand's gold mining history (by and large New Zealand's gold-fields were well ordered, thanks in part to the quality of government wardens) the mob accused the tradesmen of Bruce Bay of being in league with Hunt and wreaked a terrible vengeance on their premises.

REEFTON — THE MOTHER LODE

Reefton is an uncomplicated, well-organised place. Even the name is straightforward. In Australasia a gold-bearing quartz lode is known as a reef. A town with reefs aplenty should obviously be called Reefton, though it was also known as Quartzopolis at times.

The mother lode at Reefton runs in a frustratingly fragmented fashion for about 30 km along and around the valley of the Inangahua River. Many mines were to be dug in this area and a few were to prove as bountiful as their names were colourful: Keep-it-Dark, Hopeful, Just-in-Time and the Wealth of Nations (proprietor, inevitably, one Adam Smith). The last-mentioned mine lived up to its billing partly

because its manager was a paragon of common sense in an industry not famed for such. After a few fruitful years this mine 'lost' its reef in 1881. The tailings had been carefully stockpiled, however. They were reworked to provide sufficient cash flow to allow the search for the reef to continue. This was a tortuous business but they struck lucky again in 1893 and, together with its sister shaft, the Energetic — also well named for it reached a depth of around 700 m — the Wealth of Nations worked on until 1927.

Wealth of Nations Battery, Murray Creek, Reefton.

(BLACKS POINT MUSEUM)

The town of Reefton

Reefton itself was the service centre for the hard-rock mines of the area. It was a lucky community in that the major mines and batteries were situated in the gullies and hillsides out of town and the relentless rattle of stampers was far less oppressive than in Thames, for instance. From the earliest days it had an aura of permanence utterly at odds with alluvial shanty towns. The reefs were only going to give up their bounty reluctantly so Reefton settled in for the long term. Within just a few years churches, lodges, shops and public buildings had been erected that survive, often little changed, to this day.

The courthouse is a fine object-lesson in the strong community spirit of Reefton. In his first report on the town, in 1872, Warden Charles Broad complained of the absence of a courthouse. A small hotel room had been pressed into use and was usually packed to the gunwales for the registration of leases and the settlement of disputes. Tempers frayed in Reefton's sizzling summer heat. Yet, within a year the Warden's Court — which settled all disputes, criminal and civil — was meeting in a stately new building. Over a working life of almost a century it is said that the number of criminal hearings was much below average, so steadfast was the quartz miner, particularly the large number of chapel-going Cornishmen.

On the other side of Bridge Street the Oddfellows Hall (1872) is a reminder of the mutual aid such friendly societies provided in the days of rampant phthisis, the symptoms and consequences of which are similar to tuberculosis. The quartz dust thrown up by the 'widow maker' rock drill could rapidly cripple or kill, and initially only 'the Lodge', or similar organisations, could help with doctor or funeral bills. Eventually, Parliament outlawed the 'widow maker' in favour of water-jet rock drills, partly as a result of dramatic lobbying by Mark Fagan, secretary of the Inangahua Miners' Union. In 1919 he and other union leaders literally dumped the problem on Parliament when they organised a dry-rock drilling demonstration in the basement of the House. Members were impressed and the more expensive water-fed drills became mandatory. By that time, however, Reefton had lost several hundred miners to phthisis. Mark Fagan, born in Victoria, phthisis victim and life-long advocate of health and safety issues, was to go on to be a minister in the 1935 Labour Government and Speaker of the Legislative Council.

Around the corner from the Oddfellows Hall, the Reefton School of Mines was a relative latecomer on the scene. Yet it probably had a greater impact on the town than any other single building.

In 1885 the Minister of Mines, William Larnach, employed the enthusiastic and popular James Black, Professor of Chemistry at Otago University, to tour the nation's goldfields imparting the finer points of geology and assaying. The government had a vested interest, of course, in that much of its revenue came from the duty on gold. More efficient recovery techniques would boost the coffers. Audiences were large and enthusiastic and in his wake Schools of Mines mushroomed in most of the major mining centres, though many proved as short-lived as the goldfields they served.

By dint of local subscription and a pound-for-pound subsidy from the central government, a fine building was erected in Reefton, which on a later visit Black mistook for a church. Later, additional rooms were added, including a furnace room and a library. The school did not close until 1970, long after its major North Island counterpart, Thames.

Over all those years the Reefton School of Mines turned out hundreds of men highly qualified in the varied techniques of mining. As well as mine manager's certification, which was made compulsory under the 1886 Mining Act, the school taught a variety of subjects — everything from pumping and winding to managing a dredge.

Moreover, not only gold was on the curriculum for Reefton's remit was also to extend to coal and ultimately uranium.

It would be a mistake, of course, to think of Reefton as a town waxing rich solely on the wholesome virtues of mutual aid and education. In the 1870s especially, the townsfolk, in common with the citizens of Thames, indulged in wild and unprincipled gambling in the shares of local mining companies. Prices could change rapidly as 'scrip mania' swept along the verandahs of Broadway, often on the back of gossip or chicanery, such as the 'salting' of worthless claims with a sprinkling of gold-bearing quartz. At times almost the entire town was in a speculative thrall. It was said that even a Scottish minister of the Kirk once lost everything he possessed in wild speculation.

Murray Creek

The major sources of the real mining action were on the northern perimeter of the Inangahua field around Larry's Creek and in a small area of Murray Creek, which runs down the steep mountainside to the Inangahua River a few kilometres south-east of Reefton.

Murray Creek is a cornucopia of gold-mining heritage (not to mention coal, mined here until well after the gold was exhausted). From the moment when Patrick Kelly first struck the reef in 1870 a total of over 200 gold-mining claims were pegged out in an area no more than 3 km by 2 km. Within three years of his discovery seven stamper batteries were functioning. The heavy equipment was often installed only after amazing tales of physical endeavour. For instance, it took six weeks to haul the Ajax battery and boiler the 2 km or so up the valley from the river. The Energetic Mine — known locally as the slaughterhouse — was less distant but its equipment was dragged by block and tackle at a heartbreaking rate of 20 m per day. The good news for today's goldfield heritage buffs is that there was no way some of this was ever going to be removed.

Down by the riverside the story is different, of course. This was the logical place to site a battery complex and three of the most profitable — Golden Fleece, Wealth of Nations and Keep-it-Dark — are located there in quick succession. Sadly they were also easily accessible for scrap recyclers.

On the Golden Fleece site, at Black's Point, a swift tutorial in quartz-mining history is on offer. The battery site itself — the dam and the concrete foundations of cyanide tanks and the stampers — is half hidden by vegetation. There is also an excellent museum on all aspects of mining in the old Methodist Church nearby. Yet most revealing of all is the old Morning Star Battery which has been relocated on the battery site and restored to working order. The process of quartz crushing — a sort of heavy-handed applied kitchen technology — is revealed. First feed quartz rock into mortar box and pound with huge metal stampers amid ear-shattering cacophony. Spill resulting slurry onto rectangular vibrating table. Hope heavier gold and silver particles collect on one side and amalgamate with mercury. Scoop into revolving berdan to crush a little more with huge metal balls. Heat the amalgamated lump to vaporise mercury to be condensed and reused. Pour bullion into crucible and heat. Pop down to Bank of New Zealand in Reefton.

Waiuta

Like the famous recipe for jugged hare, of course, the difficulty lies in first finding the quartz reef. The miners of Reefton pursued their errant, fractured reef manfully over many years, coming up with the last major strike on the birthday of King Edward VII, 9 November 1905, way up in the hills well to the south of town.

The discovery of the 'birthday reef' was in many ways a typical digger's dream. Four unemployed Reefton miners had spent a month prospecting the Blackwater area on a government-sponsored scheme. They had no luck and were about to return to Reefton when Jimmy Martin scraped his heel in some gravel during their lunch break and revealed the glint of quartz.

Rashly, but not untypically, the original quartet sold out almost immediately to a speculator, P.N. Kingswell, for a relative song: £500 each was good money for unemployed miners but Kingswell and his syndicate almost immediately flicked the claim on to Consolidated Goldfields for £30,000. Even at that price the company had bought a bargain.

The mine proved easy to open up and by 1910 was employing 274 men and paying a 15 per cent dividend. Over a long life the Blackwater Mines Ltd went on to produce three-quarters of a million ounces of gold. It was the third most productive in New Zealand after Martha at Waihi and the modern opencast pit at Macraes, East Otago.

The Blackwater Mine at Waiuta was an object lesson in the intelligent use of local geography in gold production. Quartz was not winched up the 563-m shaft but hauled in tubs along horizontal adits that reached daylight as the hillside dipped sharply down to the Snowy River. There the stampers and the cyanide vats transformed quartz ore into gold. The flaw in the system was the increasingly long distances that men had to push the tubs in the steamy, putrid atmosphere. This was resolved in the mid-1930s by sinking another shaft, the Prohibition, on the hillside to the north of town. This eventually delved 879 m, one-third below sea level and New Zealand's deepest. Ore was lifted to the surface at the Prohibition and for a time transported by an aerial ropeway directly across the Blackwater Mine site to the Snowy River. Eventually a state-of-the-art processing mill was built at the Prohibition mine.

Blackwater mine, Waiuta.

The end came suddenly for Waiuta, though no gold mine lasts for ever and there had been a decline in production and employment over the previous few years. By 1950 the amount of ore milled was less than half that of a decade earlier and employment was down to just over 100 men. No dividend had been paid for six years. On the other hand, there were grounds for hope. A new level — number 17 — had just been opened and the miners had reported a quartz reef of amazing quality that 'shone like a jeweller's shop'.

Then, on the evening of 9 July 1951, a blockage created irreparable ventilation and pumping problems. It was impossible to breathe in the mine and too expensive to reopen it. Mining was abandoned almost overnight. Within days the fabric of the town was being dismantled and offered to all bidders. On 20 July an advertisement in the *Grey River Argus* invited tenders for the purchase and removal of:

> Lot 1, Miner's Hall, Lot 2, contents of such hall … including 60 soft padded theatre seats, Lot 3, Library and Office, Lot 4, One Krupp-Ernemann 35mm picture projection unit …

The closure was especially hard on folk who owned their own homes. Overnight they were virtually worthless. The only compensation was £10 relocation expenses.

Houses were trucked down the rough metal road that squirms its way to State Highway 7 at Hukarere as miners desperately sought work elsewhere. Luck was on their side in that the primary economy was in the midst of the Korean War boom. Work was also found for some on the construction of the Cobb and the Roxburgh dams.

The wholesale collapse of the community may be gauged from the school roll. In July 1951 it totalled 55 children. By September it had slumped to 25. By the year-end it was down to eight — five of whom were the children of the two teachers.

Today only a handful of buildings remain in Waiuta but the town walk readily evokes memories of a proud, productive and cohesive community:

o Mine buildings and the boiler house chimney, once over three times its present height.

o The mullock heap — mine spoil that stretches 100 m or so beyond the mine shaft but was rolled flat and true for use as a bowling green, complete with neat privet hedge, now outlandishly overgrown.

o Nob Hill, where management lived behind a high hedge of native trees. (There were limits to social cohesion; the early mine managers, usually brought out from England, demanded a little social exclusivity and even had their own tennis courts.)

o Incubator Alley, which once housed five families with 54 children between them. Inevitably it led from the hospital to the school.

o The recreation ground, laboriously levelled using mine waste. The goal posts remain erect, seemingly expectant of a rival footy team emerging up the twisting, metalled road. The field's surface would now be too rough though for the ladies' hockey matches: 'Home Brewers' versus 'Froth Blowers'.

o The Empire Hotel, known as Waiuta's third gold mine until the 1947 'beer strike' when miners here, and elsewhere, successfully stood firm against an increase in the price of a pint from six to seven pence.

o Nearby Lighthouse Hill, whose house lights guided many an inebriate home, for the town had no street lighting.

The full story of our most intriguing ghost town is told with warmth and clarity in *Waiuta, the Gold Mine, the Town, the People*, edited by Gerard Morris (1986).

4
GOLD
— NORTH ISLAND

'A great rush set in … Auckland was excited.
Hundreds of empty houses were taken down and rebuilt at Thames.'
REV. JAMES BULLER

THAMES

Totara Pa provides a marvellous vantage point — the glimmering Firth of Thames to the north-west, the hills of Coromandel to the north-east, the pastures of the Hauraki Plains to the south. Dreamy landscapes, but there has been much more to see over the centuries. A microcosm of New Zealand history unfolded beneath this once near-impregnable fortress.

From this legendary stronghold Ngati Maru puzzled over the sighting of Lieutenant James Cook's *Endeavour* when she anchored in the estuary in November 1769. Two generations later early Christian missionaries passed by. In 1821 Hongi Hika's 2000-strong war party rampaged down from the north. Despite Hongi's men being armed with muskets, the three-day assault proved fruitless. Then Hongi treacherously sued for peace and retreated round a headland. He returned at night to overwhelm and slaughter Ngati Maru.

Today the view from Totara Pa remains as stunning as it was when Hongi shattered the peace, but it should not be confused with the original panorama. Then the narrow plain just below was mudflat, peach grove and a few raupo huts. The hills were sheathed in primeval kauri and kahikatea. Now those hills are covered with regrowth pine, poplar and manuka and the plain and foothills house the town of Thames.

The makeover started in late July 1867. Auckland politicians were alarmed at the recession gripping the city following the withdrawal of Imperial troops at the end of the New Zealand Wars and the transfer of the seat of national government to Wellington. The severity of the situation was noted by the Rev. James Buller in the *New Zealand Wesleyan*:

> There was utter stagnation. Trade languished; property was valueless; bankruptcy was common. Crime trod upon the heels of poverty. The Provincial Government was burdened with the support of multitudes; skilled artisans were breaking stones on the road .... The country was devastated; the town was ruined; the people were demoralised.

A deal had been struck with the local chieftains for mining rights to an area between the Kuranui and Hape creeks. Maori drove a hard bargain. The price was quite high for the times and the area tiny — just four square miles excluding a small enclave in the centre. But the Provincial negotiators — James Mackay and Daniel Pollen — were desperate to alleviate the city's unemployment problem and also probably working on fairly hot information.

Within days a major find was made at the Shotover claim on the Kuranui Creek. Thereafter, any Maori watching developments from the heights of Totara Pa might well have thought Pakeha even crazier than usual. 'A great rush set in,' wrote Buller, 'Auckland was excited. Hundreds of empty houses were taken down and rebuilt at Thames. Capital was unlocked; the country farms deserted.' The twin towns of Shortland and Grahamstown, soon to amalgamate as Thames, were to balloon to a population of around 12,000 within four years. The hillsides were denuded of vegetation, pock-marked with mine shafts, dotted with poppet-heads and dissected by tramways. On the narrow plain dozens of stamper batteries crushed quartz and near deafened the townsfolk. Giant pumps with huge chimneys drained mine shafts that eventually delved depths of 300 m. An initial mishmash of miners' tents and huts was rapidly rationalised into wide streets with an amazing variety of hotels, grog houses and 'places of entertainment'. All this in the wild pursuit of a yellow metal with no value in traditional Maori society but which had become the single most potent driving force in the economy of the European settlers.

The quartz of Thames did not yield its gold easily. Geologically much younger than the gold-bearing structures of the South Island, the quartz of the Coromandel Peninsula was tough to mine and then had to be pounded into submission. There was little place here for the craggy independent digger panning and sluicing for alluvial

GOLD — NORTH ISLAND
Coromandel

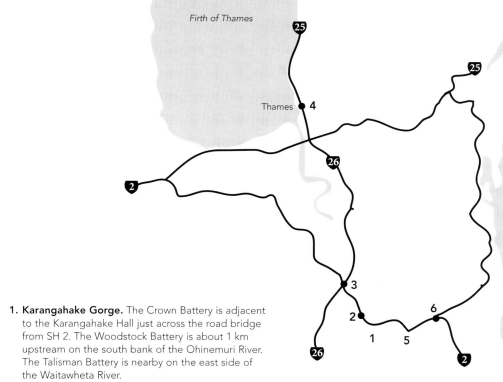

Firth of Thames

Thames

Pacific Ocean

1. **Karangahake Gorge.** The Crown Battery is adjacent to the Karangahake Hall just across the road bridge from SH 2. The Woodstock Battery is about 1 km upstream on the south bank of the Ohinemuri River. The Talisman Battery is nearby on the east side of the Waitawheta River.
2. **Mackaytown** is 6 km south-east of Paeroa on SH 2.
3. **Paeroa** is 33 km south of Thames.
4. **Thames.** Many historic mine sites, including the Shotover, the Moanataiari Tunnel, and the Golden Crown, are clustered together by the main road at the north end of town. The Thames-Hauraki pumphouse and quadrants are in Bella Street. Thames School of Mines is on Cochrane Street. Phone 07 868 6227. Totara Pa is 2 km south of the town.
5. **Victoria Battery.** Follow the signs from Waikino Railway Station on SH 2.
6. **Waihi.** Goldfields Steam Railway is in Wrigley Street. Phone 07 863 8251. The Cornish pumphouse is behind the Information Office on Seddon Street and overlooks the modern mine.

Steel quadrants from the steam-operated Thames-Hauraki Pump, Thames.

gold. Many a dream of scooping a shovelful of gold from a creek bed died a swift death in Thames. And lots of the early arrivals were certainly dreamers — they were the unemployed of the streets of Auckland rather than hardened diggers.

Many of the hard-rock mines of Thames rapidly became legends in the industry. Pockets of the Shotover reef assayed at a fabulous 250 ounces of gold to the ton. This was the stuff of eldorado. Capital was raised to mine and crush the ore and the owners, Hunt, Clarkson, Cobley and White, became wealthy men.

The pattern was set for the growth of Thames. Auckland and British capital flowed in and each newly found reef was expertly exploited. For six days a week, 24 hours a day, a rhythmic metallic clatter echoed around the town. Visitors could not sleep. Respite came from midnight Saturday to midnight Sunday. Then it is said some of the locals could not sleep. While most folk struggled on regardless — picking and hewing, pushing and shovelling — those with shares in the right mine at the right time grew rich. Sometimes it was a matter of patience as well as luck. After plodding along hopefully, in 1870 the Caledonian Mine hit the richest concentration of gold of any quartz deposit in New Zealand. At times the density of gold in the quartz was so great that the precious metal was said to be clogging up the stampers.

For a short time the mine was producing about a ton of gold per month, which was unheard-of in an industry that usually measured output in ounces. Yet by 1872 the bonanza had passed and the Caledonian shares plunged. Then in the late 1870s the Alburnia and Moanataiari mines each hit the jackpot after years of unspectacular graft. As late as 1904 the Waiotahi Mine — known disparagingly as the Old Men's Home — suddenly produced only slightly less gold than in its previous 32-year history. By that time, however, the Thames field was virtually worked out, although a few mines lingered optimistically.

The town of Thames

In the century or so since serious mining ceased in this tiny, rich rectangle, the town of Thames has flourished as a commercial and residential centre. Naturally enough, much of its industrial heritage is no more than a distant memory.

On the northern edge of town signboards reveal the site of the original Shotover Mine and the nearby Long Drive, the claim of Alfred Newdick, who missed out on his mate's Shotover bonanza because he arrived late. Next door the Moanataiari tunnel was begun in the 1870s and eventually penetrated 2 km into the hillside — a subterranean highway from which other shafts and levels were dug. Nearby, however, part of the Golden Crown Mine workings remain open as a tourist attraction, complete with stamper battery.

There is little trace of the town's colossus, the Big Pump. Thames' mines encountered major drainage problems from the early 1870s onwards and the Big Pump was their saviour. At the back of the town, however, there is the Thames-Hauraki pumphouse, built a generation later when the Queen of Beauty shaft was deepened to 300 m. With 10 huge boilers and a chimney over 30 m high it was then said to be the largest single pump at a New Zealand gold mine. Eventually the deeper levels flooded, the mine closed and much of its gear was auctioned, but the 4-m-high quadrants remain as tangible evidence of the scale of the pumping operation.

Water was always a problem in the early mining industry — too much below ground, too little above. With about 50 stamper battery sites pounding away and a burgeoning population, a water race was completed in the 1870s from way up the Kauaeranga Valley behind the town. With open-cut ditches, tunnels and fluming up to 25 m high, it cost a small fortune — £80,000 — but it fed the stampers and supplied the needs of the people of Thames until 1945. The stone intake structure is near Hoffman Pool and a wastewater control gate can be seen near the Kauaeranga Valley Field Centre.

Water is one thing, beer entirely another. Once Thames probably had more than 100 public houses, to use the term loosely. The worst were no doubt pretty shoddy but the best still live on in stately splendour, greatly adding to the character of the town. On Pollen St the elegant and much-photographed Brian Boru is actually a 1905 replacement following a fire but it still provides a fine example of the style of the better hotels in the larger towns of the era. The Cornwall Arms is equally distinguished and now functions as a club. The Lady Bowen graces the corner of Albert and Brown streets, having been barged down the Firth of Thames from Auckland at the height of the boom in 1868. Sited near the town jetty, she was renamed the Wharf, then the Park and finally the Lady Bowen before settling for an elegant retirement as a private residence.

Immediately across the road, but no longer with us, was the up-market Pacific Hotel and its partner the Academy of Music where top-flight musicians entertained 'the elite of the world'. For those of a pecuniary disposition — most of the town — Scrip Corner was directly opposite. Here, under the verandahs of the boardwalk, the real action took place as stockbrokers traded mine shares with a ferocity that would shame many a latter-day derivative or futures dealer. Expectation, supposition and rumour, and just occasionally hard fact, was the currency of the day. The shares in a lucky mine could reach dizzy heights, the record reputedly being the purchase of a single share in the aptly named Wild Missouri claim for £3000. But when a mine lost the reef, or was rumoured to, worthless pieces of paper were tossed into the estuary. Either way the Pacific and the Wharf did good business.

The enduring town icon is surely the School of Mines. Founded in 1886 during the flood of enthusiasm that followed James Black's lecture tour, the buildings are partly the 1868 Wesleyan Sunday School and partly later additions. Courses were held in chemistry and metallurgy, assaying and mineralogy, surveying and mathematics, engineering and foundry work. Practical aspects were catered for by a two-stamp battery, which could be hired on a user-pays basis, roasting furnaces, setter, berdan and a pelton wheel fed by the town's water race.

Almost from its formation, however, the School of Mines was something of a

misnomer. Mining in Thames had been in decline for some years. By the outbreak of the First World War only 159 miners were employed in the town and only a minority of students were taking courses that would result in a mining career. Diversification with an ever-increasing emphasis on engineering was the price of survival and the School of Mines became the de facto Thames technical college. The school closed in 1954 when its long-time Director, Hugh Crawford, retired.

This view of the Thames School of Mines has changed little in over 100 years.

OHINEMURI — A 'DUFFER'?

Thames was a disappointment for many independent diggers who soon turned their gaze longingly to the Maori lands to the south. Chief Te Hira guarded his lands and mining rights jealously, however. By and large the government respected his wishes and kept prospectors at bay. A few renegade diggers went prospecting anyway, of course, and returned with stories of potential riches. True to tradition, the tales of eldorado multiplied with each additional telling.

By early 1875 Te Hira yielded to persuasion and a little subterfuge (involving debt repayment) by Commissioner James Mackay. When notice was given that the new field would open on 3 March diggers converged on Paeroa and then on the hastily improvised canvas settlement of Mackaytown. They trudged along with an 'elasticity of step, an intelligent twinkling of eye and a radiant hopefulness beaming from the features of all' according to the *New Zealand Herald*.

At 10 am that Wednesday morning they had to wait no longer. The licences required to register a claim were handed out to the eager throng under the watchful eyes of the Commissioner and a posse of police. A gun was fired across the valley. The air filled with the dust of a thousand pairs of feet as prospectors scrambled over the scrubby field in pursuit of fortune. They jostled and fought, eager to stake the best claims on Karangahake Mountain, about 5 km away. Some worked in relay teams and some were on horseback, all the better to first peg out a claim, licence in hand. A correspondent wrote:

> Away they dashed, up hill, down dale, over the creeks, until a second relay was met with and like grim death they sped on to the locality of the prospector's claim.

Inevitably there were many disputes. It was forecast that:

> … the result of today's proceedings will be a god-send to the lawyers inasmuch as there are many areas of ground pegged off for which several parties lay claim.

Yet, by and large, the predicted violence was absent.

Within hours a steady trickle of stragglers headed disconsolately back towards Mackaytown and all points north. Within a week this had filled out to an exodus. The diggers proclaimed to anyone who would listen that the Ohinemuri field was a 'duffer'. There were dark mutterings that the folk who had irresponsibly excited the miners' hopes 'should have their ears cropped'.

Certainly all expectations of alluvial gold had been immediately quashed. There were signs of gold-bearing quartz reefs but even these did not outcrop as readily as in Thames. The gold was deep within Karangahake Mountain and its low-grade refractory ore even defeated the first companies set up to exploit it. Not until the 1890s, with the development of the cyanide process of extracting gold from quartz, which involved massive capital expenditure, was any serious money made.

Inevitably Mackaytown never recovered from such a difficult birth and is now just a few tidy houses by the side of the bustling State Highway 2. It is a modest memorial for a substantial personality. James Mackay, 'The Thames Autocrat', was the stuff on which empires were built. Large, fearless, tenacious and handy with his fists, he could also be patient and tactful when necessary and was fluent in the Maori language. He was an ideal instrument of government land policy. Mackay successfully negotiated the purchase of most of Marlborough and the West Coast for the Crown at amazingly modest cost. Later he received the surrender of the Lower Waikato and Hauraki areas after the New Zealand Wars. As warden of the Collingwood and the Thames goldfields, he ruled with an iron hand. A popular hero in his heyday, Mackay's reputation has suffered latterly as the whole process of land acquisition has been more closely scrutinised. Ironically Mackay went bankrupt over a failed land deal in 1880. Despite receiving a small government pension in later life, he died in poverty in Paeroa in 1912.

From Mackaytown State Highway 2 hugs the banks of the Ohinemuri River through the spectacular Karangahake Gorge up to the town of Waihi. Here lay riches beyond the wildest dreams of generations of diggers. The quartz of Waihi did not yield its bullion quickly or easily but eventually output exceeded all other New Zealand goldfields combined.

SUCCESS AT WAIHI

Robert Lee and John McCombie first saw the glint of quartz at Waihi in February 1878. They were to suffer all manner of tribulations over the next four months. Initially they had to return to the nearest settlement, Waitekauri, to be grubstaked, but nearly drowned fording a stream on the way back. Then they found they could not remove the spoil from their tunnel so had to manhandle a wheelbarrow through the bush. A struggle followed with a group of Maori women who protested that the hill was a burial ground and tried to entomb the miners in the tunnel. Threats that Lee and McCombie would be carried out of the district lashed to poles like pigs ensured that only one of the pair worked — the other kept watch. Eventually Lee and McCombie had their ore assayed. The results were inconclusive. Substantial capital would certainly be required. McCombie and Lee went prospecting elsewhere.

Shortly afterwards it was the turn of William Nicholl to see the glint of quartz on this odd, conical hill. A short distance from McCombie and Lee's tunnel he struck a quartz reef and named it after his half-sister Martha. For the next 15 years or so mining was marginal due to the poor recovery rate and the high sulphur content of the low-grade ore. All was transformed, however, by the development of the cyanide process in the 1890s. From then onwards the London-based Waihi Gold Mining Company dominated the area and by 1905 employed 1400 men. Mine workings were eventually to extend down to more than 500 m. Such depths necessitated effective water pumping. The answer, the 1904 Cornish Pumphouse, now resplendent in Virginia creeper, remains as an icon to mining in the town.

Success at Waihi came at a cost. Times were tough at Martha with rock falls, phthisis and fingers lost in the batteries. The hardest memories come from the industrial dispute of 1912. On Black Tuesday, 12 November, Fred Evans, a stationary engine driver and a 'Red Fed', became New Zealand's first fatality in an industrial dispute.

The strike had grown increasingly bitter over the previous six months as the Waihi Gold Mining Company reopened the mine using 'scab' labour. The 'Red Feds',

Black Tuesday, 12 November 1912, and a crowd gathers outside the Miners' Hall, Waihi, following the shooting of a policeman and the death of a striking miner.

(BRIAN MCCLINTOCK COLLECTION)

led locally by Bill Parry, steadily lost control to more militant elements. The Massey Government and the police in turn reacted aggressively. At one stage 10 per cent of the nation's police force was stationed in Waihi and 60 leading strikers were jailed.

Amid increasing violence, a fight on the steps of the local Miners' Hall resulted in a strikebreaker, Thomas Johnston, being shot in the knee, probably by Evans, and a policeman in the stomach. Evans was hit and kicked and later died. Both Johnston and the policeman recovered.

Eventually the strike was broken and violence unequalled in New Zealand history erupted as strikers and their families were hounded through the streets. Evans was given a large, union-organised funeral in Auckland and was buried in Waikaraka Cemetery where his grave is a place of annual remembrance. Thomas Johnston, who was strike-breaking because he faced ruin due to his failed Auckland market garden, was later committed to a mental institution. Bill Parry went on to be Minister of Internal Affairs in the Labour Government of 1935.

Martha Mine, Waihi.

(ALEXANDER TURNBULL LIBRARY, NATIONAL LIBRARY OF NEW ZEALAND/TE PUNA MĀTAURANGA O AOTEAROA, 19299¹/₂)

Victoria Battery

With a little organisation it is possible to return down the Karangahake Gorge from Waihi in style, by steam train. Swaying gently behind the Goldfields Steam Railway's 1938 Peckett loco (ex Dominion Portland Cement, Whangarei), the trip is pleasantly evocative: wood panelling, imitation red leather seats, narrow upward-sliding windows, reversible seating, art deco lighting. Notices from yesteryear sternly prohibit train-buff pleasures such as leaning out of windows, quitting the train while in motion or 'EXPECTORATING on the floors or mats'.

Pleasure was the last thing on the minds of the directors of the Waihi Gold Mining Company back in the 1890s, of course. Just a little into the gorge from the present Waikino Station (which is in fact the relocated Paeroa Station) they built the Victoria Battery to take advantage of water power. The railway carted quartz ore from the Martha mine. Soon to be the biggest in the country, with a capacity of up to 800 tons of ore per day, the Victoria Battery occupied a wide spur of land that slopes down towards the Ohinemuri River — an impressive feat of industrial vertical integration.

Initially the ore was roasted in eight wood-fired kilns at the top of the site in order to aid crushing. But the kilns, which have recently been excavated, gobbled up to a hectare of wood per day and were soon abandoned for better technology. Then

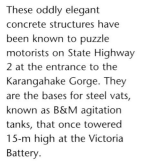

These oddly elegant concrete structures have been known to puzzle motorists on State Highway 2 at the entrance to the Karangahake Gorge. They are the bases for steel vats, known as B&M agitation tanks, that once towered 15-m high at the Victoria Battery.

primary crushing plants reduced the ore to small lumps. Two hundred stampers, rhythmically falling in sequence 100 times per minute, pulverised the rock to dust. Rotating tube mills, partly filled with abrasive chalk flints, then ground the dust to a very fine powder with the consistency of flour. A succession of Vee boxes, settling tanks, leaching vats, B&M tanks and vacuum washing plants dissolved the precious metal in a cyanide solution and then combined it with zinc to form a heavy black slime. This richly impregnated sludge was then carted back by rail to Waihi where it was heated in a furnace to become molten gold.

The Victoria Battery continued in production with ever-decreasing productivity until as recently as the mid-1950s. The concrete battery foundations are still intact, littered with metallic detritus of gold mining. Down by the Ohinemuri the remains of the B&M tanks seem oddly ecclesiastical in appearance. The steel cyanide tanks once towered 15 m above these foundations. By their side the vast concrete tailrace spewed waste into the river, an official sludge channel. Towards the back of the site there is the powerhouse built when the Waihi Gold Mining Company converted the battery to electric power, utilising its newly constructed Horahora hydro scheme.

From the Victoria Battery a walkway follows the line of the old Paeroa–Waihi railway 7 km down to Karangahake. The track eventually divides and to the right disappears into a narrow, kilometre-long railway tunnel. Started in 1901 and lined

'Portable' tube mill, Victoria Battery, Waikino.

with two million bricks, the tunnel was in use until 1978 when a more direct route was opened via the Kaimai Tunnel. The gradient is surprisingly steep (1 in 50) — hard going for engines, even in pairs. Sometimes the driver and fireman just let rip full throttle and crouched on the cab floor with their faces wrapped in cloth. Passengers who forgot to shut the windows had a memorable journey. Sometimes the Ohinemuri River used the tunnel as a shortcut.

Woodstock, Talisman and Crown batteries

Leftwards the track loops round the hill to the confluence of the Waitawheta and the Ohinemuri rivers. Here the Waitawheta Gorge forms a natural cross-cut into the quartz reefs of Karangahake Mountain. Adits speared into the hillside and the quartz was carted away to one of three substantial battery sites by aerial ropeway or horse-drawn tram. The foundations of the Woodstock Battery lie close to the track, those of the Talisman Battery are a little way into the bush. Even though they are crowded onto confined sites, these two batteries totalled around 90 stampers at the turn of the twentieth century. When the exceptionally lucrative Talisman Mine closed just after the First World War it had recovered well over three million ounces of bullion.

Around a further bend in the river the multi-tiered, 60-stamper Crown Battery hugged the hillside. New Zealand Crown Mines has an important place in our industrial history. In 1889 it successfully field-tested the cyanide process for the patent holders, the Cassel Company. The results were so good — the recovery rate on low-grade refractory ores of around 90 per cent was almost twice that of dry grinding — that very soon the cyanide process was adopted throughout the Karangahake and, indeed, in other gold-mining areas in New Zealand and overseas. Crown Mines immediately went on a modernisation spree, building the battery near the current Karangahake Bridge in 1893. Crown was prosperous for only a short time, however, with flooding at the mine a persistent problem.

Across the river from the track that was once the tramline joining the Woodstock and the Crown batteries lies the settlement of Karangahake. Once home to 1374 folk, it is now just a few houses on the hillside. Most were demolished or removed when the batteries closed after the First World War. But the old school on the hill still guards the entrance to the historic gorge as the traffic of State Highway 2 thunders by.

5

RAILWAYS

'Let the country but make the railroads
and the railroads will make the country.'
HENRY PEASE

Pease's words echoed around the world throughout the years of the Industrial Revolution. In his native Britain the major urban areas were swiftly linked with one another from the early 1830s onwards and economic growth gathered pace as never before. In the United States the opening of the vast interior by the rail was to be a feature of the Age of Steam. In India, the advance of rail helped a small colonial power to rule over a vast subcontinent.

New Zealand, however, was not natural railway country. Often mountainous, bisected by deep ravines, even the plains were criss-crossed by wide, fast-flowing rivers. Much of the country was blanketed in thick forest. Between the two islands was the greatest barrier of all, Cook Strait. The making of railroads was not going to be easy.

Nor did the pattern of colonisation aid railway development. The major settlements of Auckland, New Plymouth, Wellington, Nelson, Christchurch and Dunedin were so remotely placed relative to one another that the natural means of communication was by sea. The politics of colonisation were also a hindrance. Great tracts of the central North Island were to remain no-go areas for railway surveyors for many decades. Not until 1908 did the Main Trunk line finally link Auckland and Wellington.

Despite these obstacles, the early European colonists were keen to join in the transport revolution. They were accustomed to rail travel. Indeed, they had probably journeyed to their port of embarkation by train. Once here, the miserable quagmires that passed for roads were a further spur to railway development. Consequently, as

Most early railways were built by little more than muscle and shovels. This cutting was being constructed as part of the Catlins branch line in the early 1890s.

soon as population growth allowed, tracks began to be laid — but in a distinctly New Zealand fashion.

In New Zealand, railways initially had a very limited, localised role. They were small-scale operations linking a port, or sometimes just a jetty, to its hinterland. There were several such speculative ventures in the 1860s, all in the South Island. The question of pride of place as to the first commercial railway has been the subject of much debate, however. When conducting the research for this book, for instance, two separate noticeboards were encountered, each proclaiming a unique heritage. One at the start of the Dun Mountain Walkway in Nelson reads 'New Zealand's First Railway'. Over 400 km away a plaque on a stone pillar near the site of the Ferrymead Wharf and Railway Station, Christchurch, loudly proclaims exactly the same message: 'New Zealand's First Railway.' As it happens, both may be incorrect.

A great deal depends on semantics — what exactly constitutes a railway? It is a question open to a variety of interpretations, for railways have taken many evolutionary forms over the centuries — from modest early wooden-railed tramways that hauled minerals by man or horsepower, to the modern-day bullet trains that

RAILWAYS — NORTH ISLAND

1. **Auckland Railway Station** is on Beach Road.
2. **Carterton Railway Station** is west from SH 2 along Belvedere Street.
3. **Frankton Junction.** The railway settlement is just west of the railway station along Rifle Range Road.
4. **Hapuawhenua Viaduct** is along a walking track off the mountain road from Ohakune Junction.
5. **Kawakawa Railway Station** is at the west end of Gillies Street.
6. **Lower Hutt Railway Station** is in Hutt Road behind a shopping complex.
7. **Makatote Viaduct** is 11 km south of National Park adjacent to SH 4.
8. **Makohine Viaduct** is 5 km south of Ohingaiti by SH 1.
9. **Manganui-o-te-Ao** is just south of the Makatote Viaduct adjacent to SH 4.
10. **Onehunga Railway Station** is now at 38 Alfred Street, Onehunga.
11. **Papatoetoe Railway Station** is on the railway embankment just off St George Street.
12. **Rimutaka Incline.** For Cross Creek take Western Lake Road south-west from Featherston for about 10 km and then a footpath of about 3 km from the car park. The Fell Engine Museum is in the centre of Featherston, 64 km from Wellington. Phone 06 308 9379.
13. **Raurimu Spiral** is 36 km south of Taumarunui just to the east of SH 4.
14. **Shannon Railway Station** is near the centre of Shannon on SH 57, 33 km south-west of Palmerston North.
15. **Tangarakau.** Take the side road at Tahora, about halfway between Stratford and Taumarunui on the challenging SH 43.
16. **Wellington Railway Station** is in Bunny Street.

RAILWAYS — SOUTH ISLAND

1. **Blenheim Railway Station** has recently been moved about 100 m from its original site on SH 1.
2. **Christchurch.** Lyttelton Railway Tunnel: Station Road, Heathcote. Ferrymead Historic Park: Bridle Path Road. Phone 03 384 1970.
3. **Dunedin Railway Station** is in Anzac Avenue.
4. **Nelson.** Dun Mountain Railway walkway starts in Upper Brook Street, Nelson.
5. **Oamaru Railway Station** is in Humber Street just off the town centre.
6. **Picton Railway Station** is near the Ferry Terminal.
7. **Wangaloa and Coal Point** are 20 km south-east of Balclutha on the coast beyond Kaitangata.

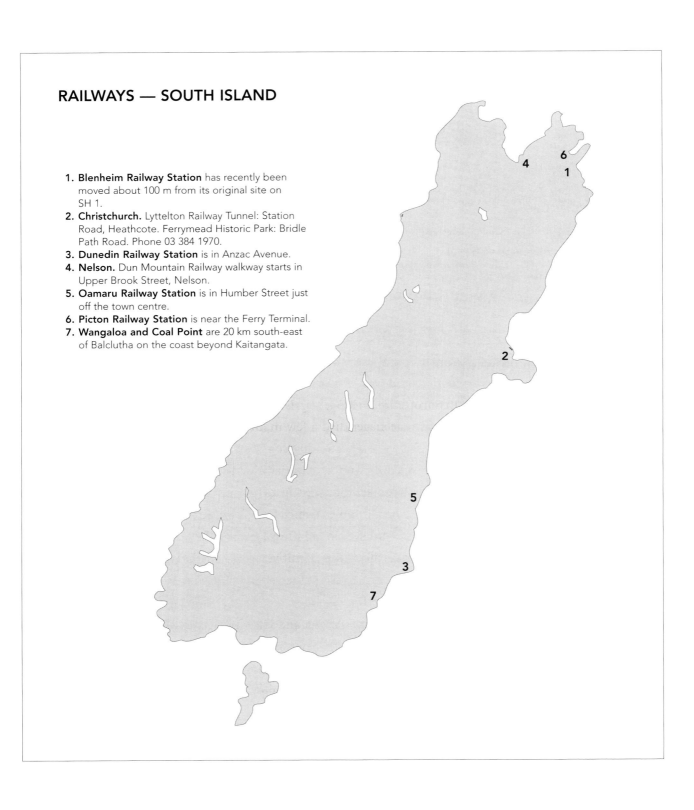

shoot silently across the plains of Europe or Japan at 200 kph. A further complication is that the South Island in the 1860s was a hive of railway or tramway activity, mostly unbeknown to each other or to any central authority. It may yet be that some other contender for the title of first railway will emerge from the mists of time, possibly from the logging or quarrying industries. For the moment, however, we must turn to a small coal mine on a windswept hillside on the coast of South Otago.

Clutha Coal Mine Railway

James George Lewis certified to the Otago Provincial Council that his Clutha Coal Mine Railway was completed on 15 July 1861. A modest affair indeed, at just 1.5 km it was mainly worked by horses on iron rails but also had a self-acting incline that lowered loaded wagons towards the wharf on the north bank of the Clutha River and drew the empties up.

The story of the Lewis Coal Mine and its railway has been painstakingly researched by Jim Dangerfield and is an object lesson in the toil and tribulation encountered by early New Zealand entrepreneurs. Lewis was already a successful mine owner of late middle age when he emigrated from Shropshire in 1854, largely for the sake of the health of his son, James George junior. The teenager died a few months later. After an unsuccessful attempt at brick-making Lewis began mining coal near Wangaloa with a view to shipping it to the embryonic city of Dunedin. Initially he had trouble convincing buyers of its quality. Then he became embroiled in disputes with the lessor, the Otago Provincial Council, which was in some financial plight. When his long-awaited metal track and fittings arrived from the United Kingdom they did not meet specifications. Always there was the discomfort of a primitive, isolated, windswept dwelling — and also the unanticipated arrival of another child when Lewis was 60 and his wife 48.

Just when Lewis was getting coal production up to speed, and with his tramline almost complete, Gabriel Read struck paydirt at Tuapeka. Lewis's workmen wanted to head for the gold diggings immediately. He talked them into finishing the tramline first but they upped and left the very next day. The traditional ceremony on opening a tramline or railway in England — the drinking of a wagonful of punch — was sadly missing. It seems likely that Lewis's brainchild was little used over the next few months. Not only was there no labour to work it, with Dunedin deserted his market had also disappeared. Lewis effectively became a mine caretaker. When normality returned the Lewis Coal Mine worked with only intermittent success until about 1874. Transport was an ongoing problem. The fickle winds and currents at the mouth of the Clutha played havoc with sailing ships. A round trip to Dunedin could take six weeks. Once there horse-drawn drays had to work in the harbour mud. When Dunedin really developed as a market for coal it was the nearby mines such as Green Island that benefited. Later, when the steam railway reached South Otago, the much more successful Kaitangata Mine was opened on the other side of the hill.

Dun Mountain Railway

When the Dun Mountain Railway, Nelson, opened on 3 February 1862 things were very different. It was the occasion of large-scale festivity as befitted a much more substantial operation — a brass band, flags and bunting, speeches, feasting and a ball. The narrow (0.91-m) gauge line, built primarily to transport chromite (chromium ore) from the Dun Mountain Mine to the port of Nelson, was a considerable engineering feat. Clinging to the contours of steep hillsides, it drops from a height of 875 m over a length of 21.5 km. For long distances the grade is around 1 in 18. There are over 700 corners that vary from a gentle radius of 200 m to a distinctly sharp 20 m. Inevitably the Dun Mountain Railway was worked by gravity and horses. It would have been impossible for contemporary steam locomotives to operate on such demanding gradients and curves. Wagons of chromite descended at a sedate 6 kph under the control of a brakeman who was under pain of dismissal if this was exceeded. Even so, the risk of derailment remained high and additional wooden checkrails were installed on the sharpest corners. Then the empty wagons were slowly hauled back up the incline by two hard-working horses.

Initially the economics of the Dun Mountain Railway looked extremely attractive. Chromite was fetching about £10 per ton in England where it was used as a dye in the textile industry. After mining costs of just over £3 per ton, and total transport expenditure of a similar figure, the company seemed set for a profitable future.

Problems soon set in. The price of chromite plummeted when the American Civil War led to sharply reduced cotton exports and many Lancashire mills were forced to close. In addition, synthetic dyes were coming onto the market as a by-product of the distillation of coal gas. Reserves of high-grade ore, previously assessed as substantial, began to run out. The deposits that remained were poor quality and patchy at that. Perhaps the final straw came when labour costs rose as men departed for the newly opened Wakamarina goldfield. The Dun Mountain line struggled on for a while, working part-time hauling lime and wood, but finally closed in 1866. Its assets were sold at auction a few years later.

All was not lost for the citizens of Nelson, however. The Act authorising the line had insisted that a passenger service should be operated on the flat land between the city and its port. To the modern mind there is a nice sense of the ridiculous in the stipulation that this section of line must not use a steam locomotive. In reality it was the only part that could have done so. The 'City Bus' was, therefore, a horse-drawn, 40-passenger carriage and probably New Zealand's first urban tram service. Services commenced on 3 May 1862 and were to prove a nice little earner for a succession of proprietors. For a time it was even something of a tourist attraction. Nothing similar to the City Bus operated in the other major urban centres, although some West Coast mining towns had horse-drawn trams and Thames had a steam-powered tramway along the waterfront in the early 1870s.

Naturally nothing remains of the old City Bus system that passed along Brook Street, Hardy and Waimea (now Rutherford) streets and then along Haven Road to the port. Up in the hills behind the city, however, on the walkway that now follows the path of Dun Mountain Railway, a small notice records the bus timetable: every 30 minutes at a fare of threepence during daylight hours, sixpence after dark. Unusually, but perhaps logically, patrons paid after the journey was completed. The City Bus service continued until 1901. No longer a tourist drawcard, it was also technologically obsolescent — by this time Dunedin was operating the country's first electrically driven trams. Nelson, the first New Zealand city to have a tram, was also the first to dispense with one.

No doubt on a literal definition the Dun Mountain line constituted a railway: '… a track carrying vehicles guided by flanged wheels'. Moreover, its Act of Parliament proclaimed it to be one. It was also a public utility carrying the fare-paying public as well as chromite. Yet in many regards it was in part a traditional mineral tramway, in part a horse-drawn urban tramway. It was to be the advent of steam railways — following the opening of George Stephenson's Stockton to Darlington railway in

1825 and the Liverpool–Manchester Railway in 1830 — that changed the face of industrial Britain and, a little later, that of New Zealand. For the coming of the revolutionary power of steam transport we must look south to the Christchurch suburb of Ferrymead.

THE AGE OF STEAM

The Ferrymead Railway

The Ferrymead line was a steam-age railway in all regards. The gauge was a little odd at 1600 mm but that probably resulted from the availability of suitable trains and carriages. Its lifespan, at just over four years from its opening on 1 December 1863, seems odder still, but it was only conceived as a stopgap measure. Canterbury was only a little over a decade old but ultimately had more grandiose plans. The province was growing rapidly on the back of wool exports but problems with port facilities were threatening to stifle activity. The choice was stark in those early years. Traders either risked their goods on the Sumner Bar or tackled the steep track over the Port Hills. The long-term solution was the Lyttelton Railway Tunnel.

William Sefton Moorhouse, Canterbury Superintendent and the prime mover behind the tunnel, turned the first sod, at the Heathcote end, on 17 July 1861. At 2.6 km and with a cost of about £240,000, it was a bold undertaking for so young a province. The first train ran through the tunnel just over six years later. The social and economic impact was immediate. On the next public holiday 3000 people, a large proportion of Christchurch's population, are said to have journeyed by rail to picnic on the harbour. More significantly, freight rates from port to city fell dramatically. Lyttelton Railway Tunnel is one piece of early railway heritage that remains in use to this day and is a fine testament to both colonial self-confidence and Victorian engineering skills. Its impressive portals are best viewed from the old railway platform off Station Road, Heathcote.

Between times, the *Pilgrim* and her sister locomotives plied the track from the city station in Madras Street to Ferrymead as a stopgap yet revenue-yielding measure. With the opening of the tunnel, however, the spur to Ferrymead was redundant and was last used commercially in July 1868. New Zealand's first steam-operated main line to open became its first branch line to close. Other than a bronze commemorative plaque (at Ferrymead) little remains today of our earliest excursion into steam-powered public-service railways. The railway buff has to search diligently around the entrance to one of New Zealand's premier industrial museums, Ferrymead Historic Park, for a few clues. Just downstream there is modest reward in the form of the piles of the original Heathcote River wharf, where ships that had braved the bar discharged their cargo onto the railway.

Oreti Railway

Following hard on the tracks of Canterbury, Southland was an early entrant to the Age of Steam. The Oreti Railway was opened in October 1864, an unsuccessful attempt to reach the Otago goldfields from Invercargill. Sadly, even an opening excursion was a bit of a fiasco. A heavy shower made the wooden rails slippery and the picnickers were stranded at Makarewa. The ill-fated line does have one claim to fame, however. In August 1863 the *Lady Barkly* made a demonstration run on a short section of track on Invercargill wharf and so predated even the *Pilgrim* as New Zealand's first operational steam locomotive. The *Lady Barkly* later served on the Invercargill–Bluff Railway (1867) and ended her working life as a sawmill engine in a place that still bears her name just north of Winton.

Lady Barkly was the first locomotive to raise steam in New Zealand. She is seen here outside the manufacturer's works in Ballarat, Victoria, about 1861. The man on the left is probably engineer William Errington, who went on to a distinguished career in Thames and Auckland, including the installation of Western Springs pumping station.

(SOUTHLAND MUSEUM)

North Island lines

In the North Island progress was tardy. An attempt to build an Auckland to Drury line in 1865, to supply troops fighting in the Waikato, was soon abandoned. A horse-drawn wooden tramway was built at Kawakawa in the Bay of Islands in 1868 following the discovery of high-quality coal on the hill behind the current town centre. Originally covering just a few kilometres to a landing place at Taumarere, the line was converted to steam operation in 1871. Later extended to the deep-water port of Opua, it was not closed by New Zealand Railways until 1985. Subsequently operated as the Bay of Islands Vintage Railway, it steamed enthusiastically into the early twenty-first century but then suffered an operating hiatus, hopefully temporarily. In classic New Zealand style the tracks run straight down the middle of the main street of town, much to the delight of tourists.

A NATIONAL RAIL NETWORK TAKES SHAPE

All this was progress of a sort but it was to take the visionary, if financially reckless, drive of Julius Vogel to etch a recognisable rail network across the landscape of New Zealand. Vogel, born in London but essentially a product of the Victorian goldfields, was basically an adherent of private enterprise. He was prescient enough to realise, however, that private capital was not up to the task of financing major railroads in New Zealand in the 1870s. The payback for the community would be over the long term. Only government could shoulder the risk of such heavy investment. In his 1870 financial statement Vogel, the Colonial Treasurer, proposed a national network of 2500 km of low-cost, standard-gauge railway as the most efficient way of opening up the country. Parliament was amazed by the broad sweep of his vision — and the amount of debt to be incurred; '… many of the members held their breath for a time as he rolled out his millions of gold …' reported the parliamentary correspondent of the *New Zealand Herald*.

The first government-owned railway in the North Island was opened between Auckland and Onehunga in 1873, quickly followed by a Wellington–Lower Hutt line in 1874. The smaller provincial towns were also keen for their share of government largesse and railway lines soon stretched inland from a variety of places including Napier, Nelson, Picton and Foxton.

Because the railway boom of the 1870s was financed by borrowed money, track, stations and engines were lightweight, inexpensive and (hopefully) durable. F Class locomotives fitted the bill precisely. F185, built by Dubs of Glasgow in 1878, started work on the Bluff to Hurunui section of the rail network in the following year. It was retired from full-time work at the Taupiri Coal Company in 1972. Beautifully restored in 1996, F185 still steams at The Bush Tramway Club, Pukemiro.

Inter-provincial rivalry was often intense at this time and frenzied political lobbying was matched by sharply honed press comment. In the case of New Plymouth, for instance, the government's decision to finance the short line from the city to Waitara followed hard on Premier William Fox's gruelling 18-hour coach journey along the wretched roads of the region. The Waitara line — surveyed in 1872 and commenced in August 1873 — was not much appreciated elsewhere but it proved to be just a modest start on more ambitious plans to connect with the rest of the country. Finished a little behind schedule in September 1875, it was soon extended to Stratford and Hawera and a through service to Wellington was possible by 1886. For a few years around the turn of the twentieth century the steamer service from Onehunga to New Plymouth and then rail to Wellington was the favoured route between Auckland and the capital. But the line also contributed another of New Zealand's quaint but sometimes lethal urban traffic nightmares, crossing New Plymouth's main thoroughfare, Devon Street, at right angles. 'It was to fray tempers and ruffle dignity' wrote local historian A.B. Scanlan. Despite a speed restriction of

117

under 10 kph, warning whistles and a man with a red flag in the centre of the crossing, horses were alarmed and occasionally humans killed until the line was re-routed in 1907.

Overall, Vogel's dream was realised surprisingly quickly. In early 1879 New Zealand's first Main Trunk line, from Christchurch to Invercargill, was opened. By the early 1880s around 1900 km of track had been laid down throughout the country.

The Rimutaka Incline

New Zealand's rugged topography continued to place great demands on the ingenuity and skill of Victorian railway engineers, however. This was particularly evident in the construction of the railway linking Wellington and the Wairarapa. Here engineers had to contend with the formidable barrier of the Rimutaka Range. The northern side of the hills was always going to be a severe test of engineering ingenuity, for the line drops at a gradient of 1 in 15 between the Summit Tunnel and the settlement of Cross Creek.

Three Fell engines grind their way up the 1-in-15 Rimutaka Incline in the early 1900s.

(BRIAN McCLINTOCK COLLECTION)

118

Such a dramatic incline was beyond the scope of conventional steam engines and a solution was found in a system patented by an English engineer, John Fell. The Fell engine was really two engines in one. Horizontal wheels beneath the frame gripped a raised third or centre rail and supplemented the normal traction wheels. By this means each locomotive could haul 66 tons — the equivalent of three carriages of passengers — up the incline, albeit at a very pedestrian pace.

The Rimutaka Incline, opened in 1878, was an extraordinarily labour-intensive and time-consuming system — and also one of the great achievements in New Zealand's railway history. Four locomotives (a 'four-up') spaced at regular intervals were often required to haul a full complement of passengers or freight up the hill. This necessitated four drivers, four firemen, four brakemen and a guard. Sometimes a 'five-up' was pressed into service. The engines were changed three times. An A Class locomotive hauled the train from Featherston to Cross Creek at the foot of the incline, where it was replaced by the Fell engines. At the summit the Fells were decoupled and another A Class engine completed the noisy, smelly, three-hour journey to Wellington. Nevertheless this was a vast improvement on the previous trek of two or three days by horse-drawn wagon.

Hauling was only half the problem. Braking on the downward journey could be scary as the hot metal brake pads of the engines and the brake vans shot a fusillade of sparks into the air. Yet remarkably few lives were lost during the Incline's 77-year service, although two carriages were tipped down an embankment into Horseshoe Gully in 1880, killing three children. But the smoke-belching Fell engines were not environmentally friendly beasts and life on the footplate was tough. Near asphyxia often threatened as the Fells ponderously ground their way through three dreary tunnels. For animals in open stock wagons the journey was sometimes fatal.

Rimutaka's Fell system was not unique. The first, over the Mount Cenis Pass between France and Italy, was quickly superseded by the Mount Cenis Tunnel. The equipment was then used briefly in Brazil. The Rimutaka system, however, enjoyed remarkable longevity, to the extent that it became something of an embarrassment to New Zealand Railways and an increasing inconvenience to the folk of the Wairarapa. Nevertheless the Fells were allowed to chug on gamely until the opening of the Rimutaka Tunnel in 1955. Such an extended lifespan spawned near permanent settlements along the incline.

Foundations of the engine sheds at Cross Creek.

Cross Creek at the foot of the incline was once home to about 30 railway families, many of whom stayed for several generations, belying the township's reputation as the Railway Department's equivalent of a Siberian salt mine. The township had a school and its own swimming pool for the truly hardy. Now it is a ghost town as surely as those of the mining and logging industries. Best preserved is the locomotive depot — whose concrete foundations are probably indestructible — which originally had a two-road engine shed and rail sidings for 46 wagons. By the end of the nineteenth century capacity had been doubled, particularly to cope with the heavy stock haulage numbers in summer. Then the incline worked well into the night and a railman was quoted as saying 'the wives didn't mind the shift work … it gave them a spell away from us'.

Up at the summit station near-Siberian conditions really did prevail, with over 2 m of rain each year and wind speeds intolerable even for seasoned Wellingtonians. Passengers were advised not to alight from the train. Elsewhere, tunnels, embankments, bridges and remnants of equipment can still be seen from the Rimutaka Incline Walkway. Down in Featherston H199, built in 1875 and the world's last remaining Fell engine, is in well-earned retirement in a purpose-built museum. The first of six H Class engines to work the incline, H199 was initially assembled and steamed by the Avonside company in England and then stripped and shipped to Wellington in mid-1876 as 8000 separate parts. She was then reassembled by engineers who had never seen the complicated Fell machinery before and seems to have worked first time. H199 then set to work laying the track for the Rimutaka Incline. Seventy-nine years later, after a lifetime's hefty work, H199's last job was to uplift the rails when the incline closed.

THE NETWORK EXPANDS

Vogel's vision gathered momentum throughout the rest of the nineteenth century. By 1900 there were 3300 km of government-owned railway in 10 separate sections. These were augmented by a few private lines, principally the Wellington & Manawatu Railway and the New Zealand Midland Railway that attempted unsuccessfully to link Westland and Nelson with Canterbury.

The dream of opening up the country had been at least partly achieved but throughout this time a steady eye was kept on the cheque book. The Spartan American philosophy of railroad building prevailed, rather than the more luxurious European model. Available money was spent on operational capacity and efficiency. Little was lavished on passenger comfort or on aesthetic appeal.

Railway stations

Stations are an example of the emphasis on operational rather than aesthetic considerations. They were utilitarian in the extreme, often little more than lean-to weatherboard structures with corrugated-iron roofs. Most had a closed street frontage with access possible only from the platform. Design was standardised and categorised to minimise cost. The New Zealand Railway classification has been recorded by J.D. Mahoney in *Down at the Station* (1987). The smallest were little more than a shed for shelter. Pioneering rural communities — Clinton, Feilding and Drury for example — qualified for a Class 5 station whose central lobby had an office on one side and a ladies waiting room on the other. Slightly up-market Class 4 stations boasted a few ornamental posts and arched windows and were allocated to larger places such as Palmerston and Blenheim. And so the pecking order progressed. Class 3 were bigger, probably gable roofed and might also contain a post office and a storage room. Class 2 — Oamaru and Napier were good examples — were roomier still. Class 1 stations were big city terminals where much greater originality of design and ornamentation was allowed.

Unsurprisingly, only a few Vogel era stations have survived. The exceptional L-shaped Onehunga Station dates from 1873. Relocated a little way down the tracks from its original site it now serves as the headquarters of the Railway Enthusiasts Society in Alfred Street. One of the more elegant, at Papatoetoe, was built in 1875 when the line from Auckland to the Waikato was extended as far south as Mercer. Two rooms were added in 1914 but otherwise the structure is original. Papatoetoe Station closed to passengers in 1987 but lingered on for another decade as an increasingly dilapidated mid-track shelter for commuters. Then the station was threatened with demolition and only saved by the dedication of local enthusiasts. At the very end of the twentieth century it was moved to a new site on the nearby railway embankment. As befits its venerable status, two chimneys are being rebuilt, brick by numbered brick, the floor renovated and repolished and the exterior restored.

Originally sited near the corner of Princes Street and Onehunga Mall, Onehunga Railway Station (1873) has been moved down the tracks to Alfred Street.

Carterton Station dates from 1880 but has been restored to its appearance around 1900. Waitakere Station was also built in 1880, originally as the local post office. It was later augmented and did sterling service for the best part of a century before being retired to Auckland's Museum of Transport, Technology and Social History (MOTAT) where it is accompanied by Mt Albert's 1914-vintage signal box. Shannon (1893) has also been added to over the years, reaching its present form in 1936. Nevertheless it has a special place in railway history as the only survivor from the privately owned Wellington & Manawatu Railway Company.

It took George Troup to put a little style into the New Zealand railway station. Born in 1863, the fifth of nine children, Troup personified the Victorian virtues of dedication, loyalty and a ferocious Protestant work ethic. Troup's father died when he was aged 10 and his mother and sisters worked as seamstresses while George served an apprenticeship and attended evening classes. Following his mother's death, Troup joined New Zealand Railways in 1886 and remained with them until retirement in 1925, rising from draughtsman to designing engineer.

Troup was perhaps lucky that the years from the late 1890s onwards were economically prosperous and money was available for improvements to railway

structures. To luck and hard work George Troup added flair and an eye for elegance. In the 10 years from 1898 Troup was responsible for at least 16 wooden railway stations that were among more distinguished buildings of their time. There was still a degree of standardisation — this was the Railways Department after all — but now the new classifications of 'A', 'B' and 'C' were refined and embellished with modest flights of architectural fancy.

The standard design featured mock Tudor-style half-timbering under Marseilles tiled roofs. Multi-post porches, bays and canopies pleasingly filled out the basically rectangular buildings. A touch of frivolity was added in the form of decorative gable ends and the occasional turret. Suddenly image rather than mere utility had arrived at New Zealand Railways. Sadly, only about half of Troup's provincial stations are still standing. His first, Oamaru (1900) has a graceful porte-cochere entrance. Lower Hutt is one of the best preserved, although it is well hidden these days by a multi-purpose shopping development. Picton is much altered and now serves as a café and ticket office. Blenheim is substantially in its original condition, though recently relocated.

In this immensely creative period Troup was also responsible for the design of eight viaducts in Hawke's Bay and Taranaki and for two major buildings — one of national importance, the other worthy to rank among the great railway stations of the world.

The New Zealand Railways Head Office in Featherston Street, Wellington, brick built with Oamaru stone decorations, was demolished in 1982. Together with Troup's other masterpiece of Dunedin Railway Station, it earned Troup the title of 'Gingerbread George'. Dunedin remains as one of the glories of New Zealand architecture. Built from basalt quarried near Ranfurly and adorned with Oamaru stone facings, externally Dunedin Station was a confident statement of the unchallenged place of railways in Edwardian society. Inside all is opulence. The entrance-hall floor is a vast mosaic of tiny porcelain squares. Stained-glass windows depict stream locomotives. Royal Doulton cherubs add an ethereal touch.

Twentieth-century transport technology advanced on unsuspected lines, however, and trains eventually ceded pre-eminence to cars and planes. Dunedin Station was left functionally abandoned with just the daily *Southerner* and the private Taieri

Masterpiece of George 'Gingerbread' Troup, Dunedin is undoubtedly one of the great railway stations of the world.

Gorge Railway for company — a palace bereft of its original purpose. Today, Dunedin Station shines out as a masterpiece even in this, the most architecturally pleasing of New Zealand cities.

Troup, forceful and plain-spoken, retired in 1925. He then served a term as Mayor of Wellington and was involved in numerous major construction projects, including the second tunnel through Mt Victoria, the airport at Rongotai and the National Art Gallery and Dominion Museum. Sir George Troup, also long-time chairman of the Bible Society, was most deservedly knighted in 1937 and died in 1941.

Raurimu Spiral

By the time of George Troup's architectural triumphs of the early 1900s, the major problem of the rail network was nearing solution. The North Island Main Trunk (NIMT) had been a dream for decades. By the 1880s the route north had reached Marton and the line south from Auckland had been extended to Te Awamutu. The final link, however, faced extremely rugged terrain and was slowed by protracted land disputes and indecision over the route to be taken.

Here the intrepid figure of John Rochfort enters our narrative. To survey the missing link, Rochfort overcame considerable personal danger — he was held up at

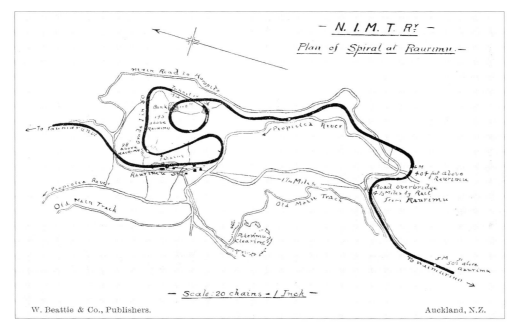

The Raurimu Spiral was an elegant solution to a railway engineer's nightmare — how to overcome an unavoidably steep rise in rugged, bush-covered country. The inspired creator was Robert West Holmes.

gunpoint three times and then imprisoned near Ohakune by Maori. Yet few things ever came between John Rochfort and the task in hand.

Rochfort had been trained by autocratic Isambard Kingdom Brunel, who accepted pupils only sparingly. Any young man passing successfully through the hands of the most indomitable spirit of the great age of Victorian engineering was not going to lack self-confidence and perseverance.

Rochfort emigrated to New Zealand in 1851. Almost immediately he became the first recorded European to walk from the Central Plateau to Hawke's Bay via the Ruahine Range and nearly died in the attempt. Soon, bored with New Zealand, he tried his luck on the Victorian goldfields. There, after suffering diarrhoea for eight days, he decided to walk the 160 km to Melbourne for treatment. He did this in three days despite a huge ulcer on his foot.

After returning to New Zealand Rochfort undertook a succession of surveying tasks that would have quickly exhausted and defeated lesser men. As one of the early European explorers of the West Coast, he indicated the possibility of the huge coalfield at Denniston. Then he laid out the town plan of Greymouth. By 1871 he was surveying the route of the Rimutaka Incline. There were numerous other projects but between 1883 and 1887 came his tour de force — that missing link in the Main Trunk line.

Rochfort's plan to solve this problem was a remarkable achievement through rugged, uncharted territory but it was to be much debated over the next two decades and eventually needed some modification. Rochfort's grades of no steeper than 1 in 70 were proved impossible by subsequent surveys. These adopted a maximum grade of around 1 in 50, the steepest then thought commercially feasible on a trunk line. Eventually, Robert West Holmes, a senior Public Works Department (PWD) engineer, presented a shorter and cheaper solution to the single most intractable of the many problems — a textbook example of a spiral that helped conquer the sharp 215-m rise between Raurimu and National Park.

The Raurimu Spiral incorporates a complete circle, three horseshoe curves and two tunnels and increases the travelling distance between National Park and Raurimu from 5.5 km to 11.5 km, thus achieving an average grade of 1 in 52. A train travelling south initially does a 180-degree horseshoe and then heads north. Two near 90-degree curves then turn the train back in a southerly direction. Two tunnels and a complete circle follow and the train continues southwards. If the train is long enough it is quite possible for the front and the back to be heading in different directions at the same time.

The Raurimu Spiral may be viewed from a special observation platform by the side of State Highway 4. A scale model details an outline that is only partially visible on the heavily wooded hillside. The only guaranteed way to grasp the ingenuity and sheer volume of the earthmoving that went into creating the Spiral is to relax in the observation car of the Auckland–Wellington train. The Spiral is worth the fare on its own.

King Country viaducts

The King Country did not yield easily to the steam age and as well as the Raurimu Spiral it contains some of the finest achievements of New Zealand's railway engineers, especially a succession of spectacular steel trestle viaducts. Most were designed by Peter Seton Hay. The University of Otago's first Bachelor of Arts in 1877, Hay joined the Public Works Department as a young man and slowly climbed the management ladder. By the time of his premature death in 1907 — as a result of pleurisy and pneumonia contracted while masterminding advanced engineering works in such a hostile environment — he was engineer-in-chief. A brilliant mathematician, he also selected the route of the future Otira Tunnel and conducted a report into New Zealand's hydroelectric potential that was to be the basis of future development.

Construction on Makohine, the southernmost viaduct, was started in 1896 under a co-operative contract system. The government, particularly Premier Seddon, distressed by the shoddy work of contractors on many previous public works and unhappy with the hefty tenders submitted, determined to act as its own site manager, buying in materials and supervising gangs of workmen in a system of co-operative piecework. Makohine proved to be an unlucky enterprise, however. Heavy rains caused landslides, one engulfing a worker's home and killing his family. There were also supply problems from strike-bound companies in the United Kingdom. Eventually a workshop was set up on site to fabricate the steelwork. Even though working hours were extended by the provision of electric lighting (probably the first on a building site in New Zealand), the viaduct was not completed until 1902. Despite these trials and tribulations, there has been no faulting the workmanship of Makohine,

127

The original Hapuawhenua Viaduct near Ohakune, 286 m long.

although it was later necessarily strengthened to take the strain of the huge K Class locomotives. Otherwise Makohine — 229 m long and 75 m high — has proved remarkably durable as well as being a visual distraction to drivers thundering down the hill on State Highway 1 in the valley below.

After Makohine other viaducts were built in swift order, notably Mangaweka, once the longest but demolished some time ago, and the elegantly curved Hapuawhenua. Further north, at a height approaching 800 m above sea level, there is one of the most dramatic. The Makatote Viaduct consists of five trestle piers holding a 262-m length of track some 79 m above the stream bed. For its construction the Public Works Department reverted to the use of an experienced contractor, J & A Anderson of Christchurch. But Andersons also had a multitude of problems with floods, landslips and the supply of components. Over 1000 tons of steel were transported from its Christchurch foundry by rail and then carted by dray over rough pumice roads. A 110-m-long fabricating shop was built and powered by steam, electricity and a water turbine. A partner in this well-established firm lived on site and roughed the frontier lifestyle with the construction workers for the duration of the contract.

Makatote was opened in July 1908 and the North Island Main Trunk became operational shortly afterwards — but not without an early example of a political photo-opportunity. That year the American 'Great White Fleet' toured the Pacific to consolidate its sphere of influence. Members of the government determined to travel to Auckland to greet the fleet — and to do so by train. A temporary track was laid at Manganui-o-te-Ao, just north of Ohakune, which proved sufficiently sturdy to carry the government entourage between the completed sections, albeit at a snail's pace. After the temporary political showpiece, the last spike completing the North Island Main Trunk was eventually driven by Premier Sir Joseph Ward at Manganui-o-te-Ao, on 6 November 1908. An obelisk by the side of State Highway 4 marks the event.

THE NETWORK NEARS COMPLETION

Even after the two halves of the North Island Main Trunk were linked, the saga of New Zealand railways was far from complete. For example, Westland and Canterbury were not connected until the completion of the Otira Tunnel in 1923. At 8.5 km, it was at the time the longest railway tunnel in the British Empire. The line across the sparsely settled bush of Taranaki, from Stratford to Okahukura near Taumarunui, was not commenced until 1901. Even so it was to be the ultimate stop-start affair and not completed for over 30 years due to financial problems and the First World War.

By 1920 the line had reached Tahora, about 75 km east of Stratford. There it remained for all of five years until local pressure led to a resumption of activities. The final leg was destined to be tough going while several lengthy tunnels were constructed. The Public Works Department settled in for the long haul by constructing the township of Tangarakau on the flat land at the confluence of the Tangarakau River and the Raekohua Stream.

Life with the PWD — Tangarakau
Tangarakau was a fine example of the many Public Works Department settlements inhabited by New Zealanders while railways and power plants were built, though it was bigger than most. At its peak the town had a population of 1200, with a main street that was a clutter of commercial and social facilities, railway marshalling yards and single men's huts. Elsewhere the homes of married couples without children — known locally as 'seedless raisins' — were grouped together. Other houses were built

129

near the school and recreation ground that produced two All Blacks in their limited lifespan. To the outside world Tangarakau had a rough reputation, especially in Stratford, but in later years hundreds of former residents happily returned to reunions, recalling the warmth and camaraderie of the township.

Tangarakau proved to be an efficient industrial complex. The electric tramway previously used to build the Otira Tunnel was moved there, linking the town and the tunnels. A powerhouse provided power to the tramway and electric lighting to houses and shops. A coal mine was opened nearby and trucks were hauled by cable along a trestle across the main street to the loading bins. Ballast was transported along the railway from Mt Egmont/Taranaki and bricks to line the tunnels and cuttings were brought from Okahukura.

After the railway was completed in 1932 the town went into rapid decline, even though the local coal mine lasted a little longer. The Public Works Department workers moved on to other projects and their houses were sold off for timber or moved elsewhere. Today, little remains of the bustling industrial and residential complex that briefly enlivened the backblocks of eastern Taranaki.

Railway housing

Workers' housing was an ongoing problem for New Zealand Railways. A number of railway settlements, generally a row of haphazard houses facing the railway line, existed from an early date in order to meet the industry's requirements of shift work, long hours and frequent changes of location. In 1919 it was decided to mass-produce inexpensive rental housing to a variety of designs by George Troup. Ten planned communities were established throughout New Zealand, the largest being Frankton, Hamilton. A factory, modelled on American methods of prefabrication, was established adjacent to the Frankton settlement and worked from 1921 to 1929. Timber was shipped down the Main Trunk line from the forests of the Central Plateau, processed into individually numbered parts and hauled off to building sites around the rail network, such as in Taumarunui and Te Kuiti. Though small, the homes were efficiently planned to allow furnishings to be readily removed when railmen changed location.

Following the drastic redundancies of recent years, many railway houses have been sold off and entire communities disestablished. Frankton, however, is the largest settlement still substantially intact, though the links with the railway have been severed. There are well over 100 pre-cut houses lining one side of Rifle Range Road and most of Pukeko, Kea, Weka and Kaka streets. Small and neat, they are distinctive and pleasing with a limited number of designs recurring in a regular pattern. The nearby house-fabrication factory, a substantial building about 150 m long, was nearly lost through vandalism and fire at one stage but is now home to a number of businesses, including a firm engaged in the restoration of old houses. The sawmill and drying kilns, however, are but distant memories in the scrubland and old railway sidings that lie between the factory and the Main Trunk line.

Auckland and Wellington termini

Not until the end of the Second World War was the final link forged in the national main trunk route with the completion of the Christchurch–Picton section. Just prior to this two of the more monumental pieces of railway heritage were built, Auckland and Wellington stations.

Auckland Station, constructed in 1930 to a design by Gummer and Ford, is a magnificent edifice tragically misplaced. After covering 685 km along the length of the North Island, the North Island Main Trunk ends about a kilometre short of its logical destination in the heart of the city. The missing link probably did much to deter Aucklanders from using their rail network, which at best is a modest thing when judged by the standards of comparable cities. So a remarkable building was gradually used less and less over the years. Its grandeur, it has been said, was soon out of all proportion to its utility. Never has such an imposing booking hall, such ornate cornices and parapets, and so much marble and cast bronze, been enjoyed by so few commuters. Today Auckland Railway Station is used for New Zealand's most elegant student accommodation.

For many years Wellington had two railway stations, Lambton and Thorndon, respectively serving the state-owned line that ran along the waterfront and up the Hutt Valley and the private Wellington & Manawatu line that went via Johnsonville and Paekakariki to Palmerston North. At one point they used the same track. Even when the Wellington & Manawatu line was bought by the State in 1908, both stations were retained, neither being big enough to cope individually. A new combined station was proposed from early in the century but this involved expensive land reclamation and was also delayed by the First World War. Work finally began in 1933 on what was to be a monolith by any standards, housing both the rail terminal and the offices of the Railways Department. The building originally had a total floor space of about one and a half hectares, with 250 rooms and over a kilometre of corridors. The fittings were luxurious for a time of otherwise grim austerity: marble walls in the booking hall and dining room, walnut panelling in the waiting room. The fifth floor had a nursery that opened out onto the rooftop.

Wellington Railway Station has had its architectural critics but it has many things going for it. It is conveniently situated in the governmental and administrative centre of the country and has always been heavily utilised by commuter traffic. A massive classical frontage gives off an impressive aura of dependability and permanence. The eight Doric columns provide a symbolic city gateway.

There was only one major problem when it eventually opened, with much pomp and ceremony, on 19 June 1937, and it was one shared by the entire railway system. The following week Union Airways operated the inaugural flight between Auckland and Wellington. A transport revolution was under way that was to shunt rail firmly into the sidings.

6
COAL

'Oh toil-worn men, lift up your eyes.'
HARRY HOLLAND

The drive up the gently wooded Grey River valley past the sleepy towns of Dobson and Stillwater is part of the tourist route to the grandeur of the Southern Alps. Distracted by ecological splendour, it is easy to miss the lone brick chimney on State Highway 7 just 11 km from Greymouth.

The chimney stands as a marker for one of New Zealand's premier industrial sites. It is also a stark sentinel to our worst mining disaster.

In the second half of the nineteenth century the chimney was part of the thriving, integrated Brunner industrial complex. Back then the valley was defoliated by steam and smoke, the river black with coal slag. Mine shafts, coke ovens and brickworks crowded the narrow river banks. Rough-hewn houses squeezed in as best they could.

Coal was first recorded here in 1848 by the explorer Thomas Brunner but it took the enterprise of Matthew Batty, 'Collier from Bolton', to open the first mine, at the behest of the Nelson Provincial Government in 1864. Although Batty's timing was excellent, for the gold rushes led to an increased demand for coal from steam ships using West Coast ports, his occupancy was to be small scale and short lived. The lease was not exploited with maximum effect until it passed to the Brunner Coal Mining Company under the guidance of Martin Kennedy in 1874.

Initially coal from the Brunner Mine was transported down to the river mouth by horse-drawn barge, a major constraint on production. The Grey River could be hazardous, often rising with alarming speed and swamping the mine facilities on several occasions. By 1876, however, transport was greatly improved when a railway was built along the valley's south bank, parallel to the existing main road, with a suspension bridge across to the main part of the complex on the opposite bank. The

Brunner has been called the cradle of New Zealand industrialisation. Certainly from the mid-1860s onwards the Grey River valley was as crowded and polluted as any in the 'Old Country'.

Brunner Mine was soon the most productive in the country. Within a few years several additional mines — mainly adits spearing horizontally into the hillsides — had been opened. Their names reflected the origins of many of the miners: Tyneside, Wallsend, Pig and Whistle and Coal Pit Heath. By 1888 the combined Grey Valley mines were responsible for 30 per cent of New Zealand's total production.

Simultaneously, the ancillary industry of coke-making was developed to use the surplus slack coal. The original twin rectangular coke ovens date from around 1867 but an early mine manager thought them no good for 'they are bilt on such a bad principle that they are allways folling in' (sic). They were superseded by a row of six state-of-the-art beehive ovens. This was soon expanded to 12 and then, optimistically, to 24. These ovens supplied a variety of industries, including the smelters of Australia and New Caledonia, the hop kilns of Motueka and the foundries of Christchurch and Wellington.

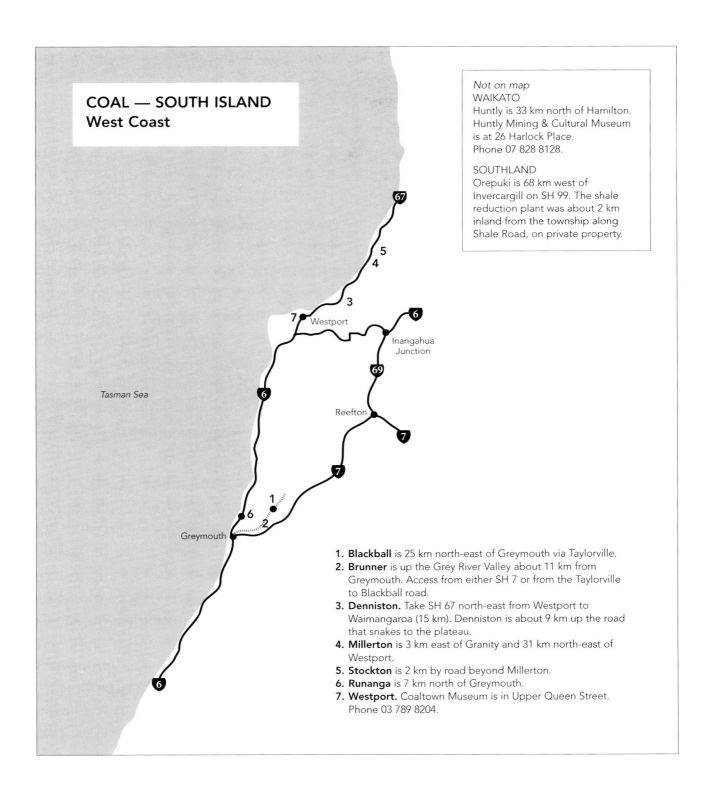

COAL — SOUTH ISLAND
West Coast

Tasman Sea

Not on map
WAIKATO
Huntly is 33 km north of Hamilton.
Huntly Mining & Cultural Museum
is at 26 Harlock Place.
Phone 07 828 8128.

SOUTHLAND
Orepuki is 68 km west of
Invercargill on SH 99. The shale
reduction plant was about 2 km
inland from the township along
Shale Road, on private property.

1. **Blackball** is 25 km north-east of Greymouth via Taylorville.
2. **Brunner** is up the Grey River Valley about 11 km from
   Greymouth. Access from either SH 7 or from the Taylorville
   to Blackball road.
3. **Denniston.** Take SH 67 north-east from Westport to
   Waimangaroa (15 km). Denniston is about 9 km up the road
   that snakes to the plateau.
4. **Millerton** is 3 km east of Granity and 31 km north-east of
   Westport.
5. **Stockton** is 2 km by road beyond Millerton.
6. **Runanga** is 7 km north of Greymouth.
7. **Westport.** Coaltown Museum is in Upper Queen Street.
   Phone 03 789 8204.

Brick-making was also undertaken in order to profit from the fireclay mined together with the coal. This was a fairly informal operation in the 1870s but brickworks were built in the 1880s. With kilns, drying sheds and an engine house all squeezed between the Brunner Mine entrance and the coke ovens, Brunner was a cauldron of integrated industrialisation. Additionally, the homes of several thousand hardy souls spread down the valley.

Disaster strikes

Then, at 9.30 on the morning of Thursday, 26 March 1896, disaster hit the mine when smoke and fumes 'resembling a huge cannonade' belched from the mouth of the pit. All 65 men and boys working up to a mile underground perished. The Press Association reported:

> Some of the bodies were so mutilated and torn to pieces that they have to be identified by the wearing apparel. One man was identified by the cap he wore, being that of the Salvation Army design. The belt of another was taken to several homes for recognition …

Others died while hopelessly trying to fend off the choking firedamp — one man with his head in a bag, another with his whole body shrouded in canvas.

About a third of the fatalities were young men, often working with their fathers, for family ties were close in Brunner. The married men left behind 37 widows and an average of four dependent children each. There were also many elderly folk deprived of their only means of support. Amid the horror there was the occasional good luck story: the miner who slept in that fateful morning; another, desperate for work, had not been selected for the shift. On the other side of the ledger, Robert Duncan wanted to stay home because his wife Jessie was about to give birth but with a family that already numbered eight he could not forego the income. In the Hunter family, emotions were cruelly jumbled. Joe should have worked but gave up the shift to his brother William, father of 12.

On a day of national mourning most of the casualties were buried in nearby Stillwater Cemetery, 33 in a communal grave. The funeral procession, headed by six bands from various local mining communities, was estimated to exceed 6000 and took half an hour to cross the Stillwater Bridge.

Speculation abounded as to the cause of the tragedy. Eventually, the Royal

Final resting place of many of the victims of New Zealand's worst industrial accident, at the Brunner Mine on 26 March 1896.

Commission's finding was that 'a blown out shot' had been ignited by persons unknown. The proceeds of a national disaster appeal provided some relief for the numerous dependants, who also took legal action against the mine owners. With the company in financial strife and after a protracted and expensive legal process, compensation from this source was also modest. It was reported that one widow received £75, together with a legal bill for £55.

The Brunner Mine worked for a decade following the disaster. Other local mines remained open longer, allowing the coke ovens to smoulder on until the mid-1930s. Then, for a time, it seemed that much of this unique chapter in New Zealand's industrial history would remain enveloped by the resurgent West Coast bush. Thanks to the hard work of local enthusiasts and the New Zealand Historic Places Trust, however, much is now saved for posterity.

The original mine entrance and the twin coke ovens by the river's edge are the earliest relics. Elsewhere, the foundations of the coal screens, bins and engine-house recall the period of peak prosperity between 1874 and 1906. Only scattered remnants of the brick-making activities remain — parts of the grinding shed and pug mill, drying rooms with hypocaust floors and the kilns.

Enough is left of the beehive coke-making complex to readily visualise the

137

The original coke ovens, Brunner.

mechanics of a simple, economical but environmentally devastating process. The ovens were two-thirds filled with coal via an overhead rail system that fed the central charging hole in the roof. Side doors, often sealed with clay, controlled the entry of air, ensuring only partial combustion. Exhaust fumes escaped through the charging hole with alarming consequences. Contemporary photographs show almost total environmental devastation on the nearby hillsides. Simultaneously the red glow of the ovens lit the night sky along the valley.

BLACKBALL REGION

As the Brunner coal mines entered into terminal decline, other mines opened in the Grey District. Blackball, on the eastern slopes of the southern Paparoas, just a few kilometres to the north of Brunner, came on stream in 1893 and was to have a long, productive and controversial life. By the time it closed 71 years later, 5.5 million tons of coal had been mined.

As was common on the Coast, transport was the initial problem at Blackball. Initially this was resolved by an aerial tramway slung down the middle of the town's Stafford Street, over the bush-clad hillsides and across the Grey River to the railway branch line at Ngahere. Two suspension cables, supported by 73 pylons, carried up to 138 tubs that could deliver up to 400 tons of coal per hour.

The 'aerial' was never trouble-free, however, and closed when a branch railway was built to the mine in 1909. Today a few pylons are still hidden in the bush and another has been rescued as an icon for the town at the turn-off from the main road. Stafford Street is now leafy and well groomed but must seem mysteriously wide to the visitor unaware of its history.

Beyond Stafford Street the road leads up the gentle incline, past the mine manager's elegant house, ironically now used as a community centre, and then dips over the brow to the mine site. The chimney stack of the mine's boilerhouse, built of Brunner bricks, stands starkly on the hillside. Other chimneys, deep in the forest, were part of the mine's ventilation system. At the mine entrance there is now only a jumbled mass of metal and concrete that is slowly but surely being camouflaged by the regenerating bush — as is the case with much of the industrial archaeology of the West Coast. But it is not too difficult to trace the scheme of things back in the days when coal was king. Coal was brought to the surface in tubs and winched into large bins beside the present road. Railway sidings in the narrow valley below allowed the ubiquitous Q Class wagons to be filled and then marshalled by gravity. Again, most of this has gone but the skeletal concrete remains of the mine's bathhouse — a hard-won prize — remain by the roadside. The railway continued for a further 2 km up a valley steep enough for a centre rail to be incorporated to aid braking. Up there on the brink of the mountains the coal bins of the Roa Mine were once the largest on the Coast. They were dismantled years ago but sufficient is left of the mine buildings and the railway to make the walk up the hill, past the tailraces and tunnels of the gold-mine era, well worth the effort.

Chimney stacks in the wilderness, a mine head engulfed in undergrowth and the ruins of the old bathhouse are about all that's left of the Blackball Mine. Blackball's place in the social history of New Zealand is much more enduring, however.

Blackball's political hotbed

Blackball, however, is much more than the scattered physical heritage of a coal mine. For a time the town stood firmly at the centre of the often torrid but compelling history of New Zealand's industrial relations. Blackball first hit the headlines, and pricked the nation's conscience, in 1908. Then the local miners took on the mine owners and the prevailing Industrial Conciliation and Arbitration Act over the right to a half-hour lunch break — or 'crib' — rather than a truly miserable 15 minutes. The highly politicised dispute — led by 'Fighting Bob' Semple from the nearby Runanga, Patrick Hickey, previously prominent in disputes up the Coast at Denniston, and Paddy Webb, like Semple previously blacklisted from the Victoria coalfields — had its roots in the generally appalling conditions of the time. Company housing was cramped and unhealthy; there was no bathhouse and miners returned home dirty and often sodden; and the mine itself was subject to spontaneous combustion and flooding.

At lunchtime on 27 January 1908 the manager of the Blackball Mine stood over Hickey with a stopwatch. Hickey pointedly refused to return to work after the statutory 15-minute break and was taken to court. Hollow laughter broke out when the judge adjourned the case for an hour-and-a-half lunch break. Fifteen minutes' crib time proved a difficult principle to defend against a mining community as firmly united as Blackball in 1908. After an 11-week strike both employer and government adopted a more conciliatory attitude and the miners were awarded a 30-minute lunch break, an eight-hour day and the reinstatement of the dismissed men. The strike action had undoubtedly violated the industrial law of the time, however, and the union was fined £75. With the union's funds depleted, the fine was collected by bailiffs raiding the chattels of individual miners. When the goods were auctioned, however, it is said that only one bidder materialised for each lot and the total raised was a mere 12 shillings and sixpence. The furniture was returned to the homes of the town. Later the fine was paid by instalments.

For a generation afterwards Blackball remained a hotbed of New Zealand socialism. The strike leaders of '08 were to go on to prominence in the formation of the Labour Party in 1916. In the same year Blackball once again stole the headlines as the centre of opposition to the 'capitalist war' after conscription had been introduced. A few years later the town was briefly the headquarters of the New Zealand Communist Party at a time when the Russian Revolution appeared to offer a new dawn for left-wing idealists.

By the time of the 1930s Depression, however, the social cohesion of Blackball was unravelling. In 1931 another months-long strike savagely split the community between traditional unionists, who wished to share the available work equally, and 'tributers' brought in by the owners to work a section of the mine at an agreed price. On 1 June 1931 the dispute reached a flashpoint as an estimated 1250 unionists marched through the town from a meeting at the Union Hall and pelted tributers' homes with stones. The community strength of Blackball was lost for ever. The eventual nationalisation of the mine in the 1940s must have brought a wry smile to many a face.

The town of Blackball

Today the backwater that is Blackball lives a relaxed, often alternative, lifestyle. Much of the town's physical history has gone, not least the Miners' Hall, lost amid vocal protest in 1981. Other icons of the past have been reduced to vacant blocks of land.

Mettricks Hotel, the adjacent dancehall and the Co-op store were burned down in 1925. The Single Men's Huts, highlighted in a report into the miners' inadequate housing conditions, are just a distant and unlamented memory. Yet, other, more pleasant memories linger in a town that once boasted an envious social and sporting calendar. In the ball season the Druids, the Oddfellows, the Masons and the Rugby League balls vied for patronage. The Oddfellows are said to have held the record of six sittings for dinner. Three town bands — the brass, the silver and the pipe — played on feast days, especially May Day. The Rugby League team was an institution, the envy of the Coast and beyond. Great names of the game originate from Blackball — Mountford, McBride, Nuttal, McLennan, Scholefield, and many more. The shopping centre buzzed vigorously, not only with the usual bakers, butchers and dressmakers but also with two bookshops.

Despite the empty housing sections and limited work opportunities Blackball lives on, heavy with memories and still independent of mind and spirit. With such a history it could never die, as conveyed in this verse by Edward Hunter:

Blackball men fought ever to be free
and never turned a fighting comrade back.
Oh, Blackball men!

Runanga, Dunollie and Rewanui

Over the hill from Blackball, State Coal Mines at Point Elizabeth commenced operation just after the turn of the twentieth century. The nearby twin towns of Runanga and Dunollie, 7 km north of Greymouth, and the settlement of Rewanui, a further 4 km up a steep valley, sprang up and were to play a significant and distinctive part in the story of the coal industry.

Although coal is still mined privately in these parts, much of the rich industrial heritage is not now readily accessible. The most potent icon, however, still dominates the townships, though sadly it is a replacement of the original. The Runanga Miners' Hall, opened in 1908, became a centre of political activity for many years. The slogans emblazoned across the front wall shouted the message to the world: 'United we stand, divided we fall; world's wealth for the world's workers'. After a meeting in these parts, Harry Holland was asked whether he thought the struggle was worth the effort. His response was the poem 'Rewanui':

141

The recently refurbished Runanga Miners' Hall remains a powerful symbol of a colourful past.

Oh, toil-worn men, lift up your eyes!
Oh, women dry your scalding tears!
Behold the red glow in the skies
Glad herald of the golden years.
See! Just beyond the vale of ill,
The sun is shining on the hill.

You had to be an optimist — or fairly desperate — to work down a coal mine. The original Runanga Hall burned down in 1937. At the turn of the millennium a local artist repainted the façade of its replacement. The message to the world at large remains the same. Inside portraits of socialist leaders, including Semple, Hickey and Webb, line the walls of the great hall.

THE DENNISTON INCLINE

When the Denniston Incline opened in 1879 the descent from the desolate plateau above Waimangaroa was thought to be 'like going over the roof of a house'. A more appropriate analogy these days — as you teeter above the precipice and gaze down to the narrow coastal plain and then out to the seemingly infinite Tasman Sea — is

The self-acting Denniston Incline was one of the wonders of the engineering world. With wagons hurtling seawards every four minutes, it was no place for the faint-hearted.

with that perilous moment when the heart flutters at the top of a big dipper. Or, perhaps, for the initiated, it is not dissimilar to the helpless, momentary terror before plunging into a bungy jump.

The gradient at this point is nearly 1 in 1.3. After the initial plunge the Denniston Incline flattens just a little and in total descends 550 m in less than 2 km. Altogether it is a frightening, audacious, self-confident piece of Victorian engineering. No wonder it was christened the eighth wonder of the engineering world.

It needed a masterpiece to transport coal to market from this most inaccessible of sites. The existence of bituminous coal had been known ever since the ubiquitous John Rochfort tramped the coastal plain in 1859 and noted deposits by the side of the Waimangaroa River. A year later geologist Julius von Haast surveyed the desolate, damp and sometimes fog-bound plateau that rises precipitously behind the plain. Near a small waterfall he removed some moss and ice and uncovered a 2.5-m seam of pure coal. He named the valley Coalbrookdale.

Scattered small-scale mining followed but conditions for the successful exploitation of the Buller coalfield were not in place for a further two decades. Easier pickings were to be had in the goldfields of the Coast, port and railway facilities were

143

inadequate and it was also doubtful that a market existed until the increased immigration and infrastructure spending of the 1870s. Most daunting of all, an efficient means had to be found of transporting the coal down that precipitous mountainside.

By the late 1870s pieces of the jigsaw began to fit together. The government improved the Westport port facilities and built the railway northwards to Ngakawau. Simultaneously it put the heat on the small coal operators, struggling vainly to lug coal down the escarpment by conventional methods, to amalgamate or lose their licences. Then the challenge was taken up by the Westport Coal Company.

It tackled the problem head on. Engineers Young Brothers and contractors Day and Blair were engaged to build the incline. The concept did not break new ground, for inclines already existed in England, but improvements in flexible wire rope technology enabled more audacious applications, especially in logging and coal industries. It was the sheer audacity and scale of execution of Denniston, in terms of length, gradient and the volume of coal carried, that led to world renown. A whole new chapter in the exploitation of New Zealand's rich but often inaccessible coal reserves was ushered in.

Railway wagons carrying up to eight tons of coal were attached to an endless steel haulage rope controlled by enormous drums in two brakehouses — one at the top near the coal storage bins, the other in the middle of the incline. There the wagons

A rope-road carried endless loads of coal from Burnetts Face to the incline at Denniston. For parents there was ceaseless worry as children strayed on the line. For young men employed clipping wagons on and off the moving rope, there was the ever-present threat of losing fingers. For almost everyone the library on the left must have been a blessing on long, damp winter evenings. This photograph was taken in 1907.

(ALEXANDER TURNBULL LIBRARY, NATIONAL LIBRARY OF NEW ZEALAND/TE PUNA MĀTAURANGA O AOTEAROA, F8501 1/2)

were de-coupled and attached to the lower section. The beauty of the beast, of course, was that as gravity took the loaded wagons down the incline, empty wagons were hauled back up the hill by their weight.

The results were phenomenal. Up on the plateau coal could be mined with unprecedented productivity from rich thick seams and transported down the incline at a rate of one wagon every four minutes or so. That added up to 120 tons per hour or getting on for 1000 tons every working day. Total production numbers were impressive. Before the incline opened, the Westport Company's output was minimal. Six years later it was producing 190,000 tons.

Soon the company's fortunes were enhanced by an international publicity coup. When, in 1889, a sudden cyclone struck Apia harbour, HMS *Calliope*, fired by Buller coal, quickly got up steam and sailed to safety. Many ships of the German and American fleets were wrecked in the harbour. Thereafter, the Lords of the Admiralty were enthusiastic customers. In all, the Denniston Incline transported 12.6 million tons of coal over its impressively long life of over 87 years.

Such a spectacular engineering feat inevitably took its human toll. Wagons, if accidentally detached from the endless wire rope, would hurtle down the incline endangering life and limb. To this day many remain where they landed, deep in the lush West Coast bush. Fatalities were not unknown among the 20 or so workers on the incline and relatively minor injuries were commonplace. Fingers were particularly endangered, for attaching the 45-kg hook to moving wagons required both strength and unerring skill.

In the early days the incline also acted as an informal passenger railway, for until a bridle track was constructed, there was no other way up. Even then it was far easier to hop in a wagon, eyes firmly closed. Not until the turn of the twentieth century did they build the road that squirms spectacularly up the escarpment. Miners, their families and possessions, and even government officials, all travelled in the wagons. In the early 1880s a school inspector refused to revisit Denniston until a road was built. He was not concerned for the dignity of his office, solely with the threat to life and limb. He wrote:

> I do not care to trust my life a second time to a wire rope that had given way shortly before my visit.

Denniston today

The Denniston Incline closed in 1967 and slowly but inexorably disappeared under the rampant West Coast bush. No longer walkable, it is barely visible for most of its length. At Conns Creek at the foot of the incline a couple of Q Class wagons have been left as reminders of an industrious past — just two of nearly two million such wagonloads that passed that way over the years. The huge middle brake of the incline has also been saved and is now the star exhibit at Coaltown Museum in Westport.

Up in the clouds at the head of the incline much of the coal-handling infrastructure has also gone — the screening and storage bins were destroyed by fire, the aerial ropeway tower dismantled, the top incline break reduced to its concrete foundations. Yet nothing is likely to destroy the solid stone ramparts of the powerhouse built by Cornish miners well over a century ago. Around the corner, deep in the bush, they left an even finer example of the stonemason's craft, Banbury Arch. Built in the 1880s to carry a horse tramway from the Banbury Mine to the incline, the shaping and placing of its stonework was a real tour de force.

Banbury was the first mine opened to feed the incline. Of only limited capacity, it had the virtues of proximity and immediate cash flow. Later Banbury's workings broke through to much larger mines and the old tramway was used as a surface ropeway from Burnett's Face. Later still, as technology advanced, aerial ropeways and then road transport brought coal from the more distant mines to the incline.

Of the once proud township of Denniston only a few hardy souls remain. Once it was a community with everything — hotels, stores, a swimming pool and a rock-hard sports ground. Gardening, a relaxation beloved of many mining communities, particularly around Huntly, was denied to the miners of Denniston, but otherwise self-sufficiency was essential, for there was effectively no way out in the early days. Some elderly folk are said not to have left the plateau in 20 years.

When the incline finally closed, many townsfolk had little choice but to rapidly relocate to the coastal plain. With no work and over 2 m of rain per year there was little to stay for other than the magnificent view down the coastline to Cape Foulwind and beyond — on the odd clear day. So Denniston became a ghost town — but one without a graveyard. The rock up there is too tough for grave digging so coffins were transported down the incline for interment in Waimangaroa. Rumour has it that occasionally one was lost in the bush off a runaway wagon.

THE MILLERTON INCLINE

Following its success at Denniston, the Westport Company extended operations into its lease to the north. This 'would serve a dual purpose', writes Norman Crawshaw in his history of the area, *From Clouds to Sea* (1996). 'It would undoubtedly increase profits and it would prevent the government confiscating the lease and handing it over to another, possibly rival, company'.

In late November 1891 the first shot was fired in the construction of an incline from the mine at Millerton to the coast at Granity. Designed by Young Brothers — who were also responsible for much of Westport Harbour, the Brunner and Mt Rochfort railways as well as the Denniston Incline — the Millerton Incline took nearly five years to complete and was initially a severe financial burden on the company.

Although much less precipitous than Denniston, with a maximum gradient of only 1 in 4, it still exhibited many features that gobbled up the cash flow from the company's other mines. The huge 3.6-m-diameter surging wheel of the braking system alone weighed 18 tons and cost £1800.

The Millerton Incline was much less spectacular than neighbouring Denniston but eventually made an excellent return for its owners.

Major stabilisation work was required to a hillside. Enormous air compressors were built near the mine entrance. Dams were constructed to supply water for the hydraulic brakes. Cranes, pulleys, tension wheels, and 200 steel drums added to the bill. Down at Granity was the most ambitious plan of all — storage and screening bins designed to hold 10,000 tons of coal. Eventually their capacity was drastically scaled back to 3000 tons but they were still enormous, 17 m high and spanning five railway tracks. The Granity Bins lasted until 1979, when structural weakness and high maintenance costs led to their demolition.

Yet the company was convinced it was sitting on a bonanza, for the seams proved even wider and easier to work than at Denniston and by the end of the century 500,000 tons of coal had been mined.

Later, problems were encountered with the high sulphur content of some of

Millerton's coal which 'played the very deuce with the fire bars' of steam vessels. There was also a continuing fire risk at the mine. Eventually both problems were overcome and annual production peaked at 350,000 tons by the start of the First World War, by which time 600 men were employed. Millerton had proved to be the 'Jewel in the Crown' of the Westport Company. By the time the incline eventually closed, over 10 million tons of coal had been transported.

Initially many Millerton miners lived in Granity's more equable coastal climate. Few wished to venture up beyond cloud level and Millerton's recorded population in 1896 was only 39. But a fiercely independent community gradually emerged and houses spread-eagled across the contours of the plateau despite the neat grid pattern initially laid out for the town. Many remain today, scattered across a moonscape terrain where the sparse vegetation is severely stunted by the harsh climate.

STOCKTON

In 1908 the Westport Coal Company's dominance was seriously challenged by the formation of the Westport-Stockton Coal Company to mine a lease on its northern border.

Stockton seems to have been a happy testing ground for different technology — perhaps over-optimistically at times. For a few years coal was transported to the bins at Ngakawau by water in a wood and metal flume that snaked down the hillside and was much given to costly blockages. Then the Stockton Company decided that the future lay with electricity to power the haulage of coal tubs from the coalface to the top of the rope incline. In a system supplied by the General Electric Company of New York, tubs were hauled, 20 to 30 at a time, by electric locomotives attached to an overhead wire rather like those of an urban railway. Probably the first electric railway in New Zealand, it experienced numerous teething problems but the company nevertheless had an intermittently fruitful working life until being taken over by the government in 1944.

Once a settlement of 500, Stockton is now no more than a memory in the wilderness, weakened by the Depression of the 1930s and the strike of the 1950s and finished off by advancing technology. Now Solid Energy's huge opencast mine lies just over the hill and a modern aerial ropeway carries its output across the plateau and down the mountainside to the loading bins at Ngakawau. From there it is a tortuous rail journey across to the Port of Lyttelton and eventually the steel furnaces of the Pacific Rim.

SHALE IN SOUTHLAND

A kilometre or two down Shale Road, behind the township of Orepuki in Te Wae Wae Bay, a large brick farm storage building stands forlornly in a deep gully. It is all that remains of a doomed 'think-big' venture a century ago — the processing of shale to extract oil.

Early gold miners had noted outcrops of shale and brown coal in these parts and thankfully burned the tough, wood-like material to ward off the severe southern winters. In 1879 a deep shaft and a tramway had been constructed in an unsuccessful attempt to mine the shale and coal deposits. Then, in 1899, the London-based New Zealand Coal and Oil Company shocked the local community by pouring cash into a giant shale reduction complex, without it seems much in the way of prior consultation. Sleepy Orepuki was transformed into an industrial complex shrouded in sulphur fumes but thankful for 200 new jobs.

The shale works at Orepuki had an amazingly short working life, 1899–1902.

(Southland Museum)

Theoretically the scheme appeared sound enough. One ton of shale was estimated to yield 38 gallons of oil together with the useful by-product of sulphate of ammonia. Yet problems soon arose and this shooting star of New Zealand industry closed within three years, the workers hardly being given a day's notice. Reasons for the closure abounded, including a conspiracy theory involving overseas oil companies. More likely culprits were the shattered, uncertain shale deposits, the high cost of mining and the withdrawal of import duty on kerosene.

For years the abandoned works were left intact, seemingly ready to reopen at the drop of an oily rag. Later, parts of the plant were recycled for use in the local gold mining industry. Now shale in Orepuki hardly rates a mention in the history of New Zealand industry. All that is left, other than the venerable farm storehouse, are a few sepia photos in the local pub and the oddest of all memorials — the shale-covered walkways of the local graveyard.

WAIKATO COAL

The history of coal mining in the North Island has little of the dramatic impact of that in the south. No Denniston Incline plunges precipitously from the clouds to the coast; there are no ruins of an integrated industrial site such as Brunner or folk memories of industrial dramas such as the strikes that enveloped Blackball.

Yet the Huntly area of the Waikato in particular was, and remains, a bulwark of the New Zealand coal industry.

The early connection was ecclesiastical. The Rev. B.Y. Ashwell of the Church Missionary Society noted an outcrop of coal near Taupiri in 1842. Later the Vicar of Onehunga, the Rev. Dr Purchas, visited sites on the Waikato River belonging to the tribe Ngati Mahuta. By 1859 the Government Surveyor, Dr Hochstetter, was remarkably prophetic in describing the deposits of the area as 'a rich treasure preserved for generations to come'.

It took a military campaign to establish the first commercial mining in the area. In the New Zealand Wars steamboats carried troops and supplies up and down the Waikato River. The boats were fuelled from an outcrop near the river bank at the village of Kupakupa, a few kilometres south of the present town of Huntly. This, possibly the first coal seam to be systematically worked on the North Island, continued to be mined after the wars ended in order to fuel the boats of the Waikato Steam Navigation Company. Even today the seams in the gullies of this area are still being mined by a small opencast company to supply the giant Huntly power station.

The military connection was soon extended. Some of the land confiscated after the war was given to the Fourth Waikato Militia. Captain Anthony Ralph had plans to mine the area but died in 1873. His widow, Margaret, her second husband and her son went ahead with the project regardless. A tunnel was dug near the present Rayner Road and by 1876 Ralph's Taupiri Mine was extracting commercial quantities of coal. It proved a providential location for a coal mine. Not only were the deposits of fine quality but communications were uncommonly good with the navigable Waikato River, the Great South Road and, from 1877, the Main Trunk railway line to Auckland all crowded together within metres of the mine. Soon the Ralph's group opened other mines nearby. By the turn of the century a thriving township had grown around mines which employed about 180 men.

Just after 7 o'clock on the Saturday morning of 12 September 1914 disaster struck the Ralph Mine. There was an explosion deep in the workings, which by now extended under and beyond the river. Such was the force that an iron cage was blown upwards from the mine entrance in the town's main street, ricocheting into the poppet-head. The *New Zealand Herald* reported:

> The roar of the explosion … was heard and felt for miles around and a great cloud of smoke and dust, momentarily shot with flame, hovered over the main shaft …. Rescue parties worked heroically but for hours were beaten back by poisonous gases and noxious fumes. The mine was found to be on fire near the main shaft.

An inquiry found that a naked light had ignited coal dust in a disused part of the mine. There was no hope for many of the men underground and 43 died. The only good news was that it could have been far worse. Saturday 12 September was a 'Back Saturday' following pay day and only a limited shift of 62 maintenance workers was underground at the time of the explosion.

Today a branch of the Bank of New Zealand and a civic centre occupy the site of the old mine head and a small plaque is all that commemorates Ralph's Mine and that awful morning at the start of the First World War.

7
MILLS

FLAX MILLS

'If the centre shoot of the flax bush were plucked,
where would the bellbird sing?'
MAORI PROVERB

The New Zealand flax industry promised much but delivered little. No other natural resource was more easily exploited yet none proved to be more cyclical and insubstantial.

The first European excursion into the flax industry came as early as 1793 when Lieutenant-Governor King of Norfolk Island decided to solve his flax-processing problems by kidnapping a flax dresser or two from New Zealand. Sadly for King the two males who were hijacked could impart only limited knowledge, for flax dressing was women's work. The men were well treated and returned home after a few months enforced holiday and New Zealand's intellectual property rights in this area remained largely intact.

In fact Maori obtained the fibre by scraping the leaves with the edge of a mussel shell. This was extremely labour intensive. First the leaves were split lengthways. Then the edges were removed by use of the fingernails. A slit across the dull side of the leaf allowed the flesh to be scraped by the shell held firmly in the other hand. The process was repeated on the other side of the leaf. The total product was around 15 g of fibre. A skilled worker might produce 5 kg per day. The fibre was then bound in small bundles, soaked overnight in a stream and dried under cover, taking care to avoid direct sunlight which made the fibre brittle. A ready market existed with the early European traders but the exchange rate was horrific. Over 400 kg of dressed flax, perhaps three months hard labour, are thought to have equated to one gun.

MILLS — NORTH ISLAND

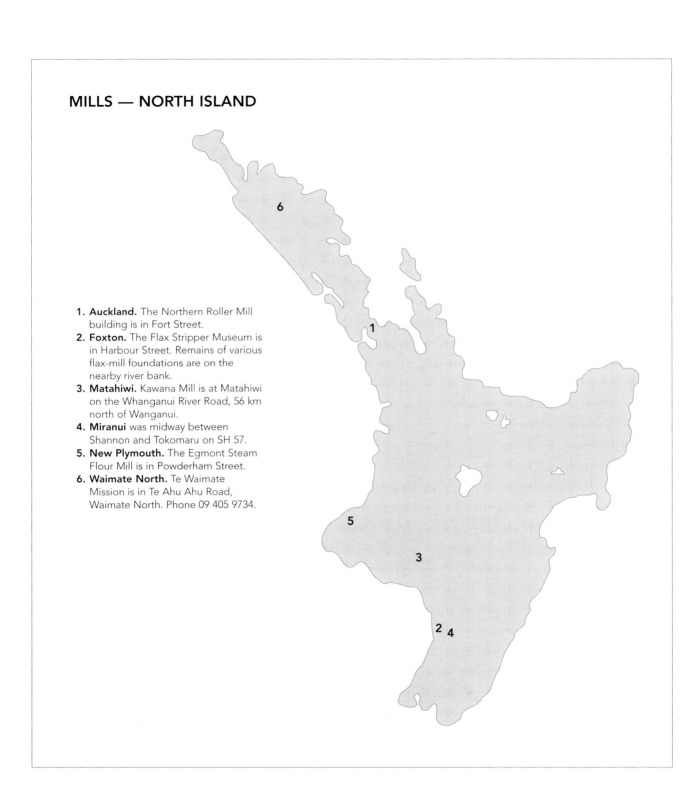

1. **Auckland.** The Northern Roller Mill building is in Fort Street.
2. **Foxton.** The Flax Stripper Museum is in Harbour Street. Remains of various flax-mill foundations are on the nearby river bank.
3. **Matahiwi.** Kawana Mill is at Matahiwi on the Whanganui River Road, 56 km north of Wanganui.
4. **Miranui** was midway between Shannon and Tokomaru on SH 57.
5. **New Plymouth.** The Egmont Steam Flour Mill is in Powderham Street.
6. **Waimate North.** Te Waimate Mission is in Te Ahu Ahu Road, Waimate North. Phone 09 405 9734.

MILLS — SOUTH ISLAND

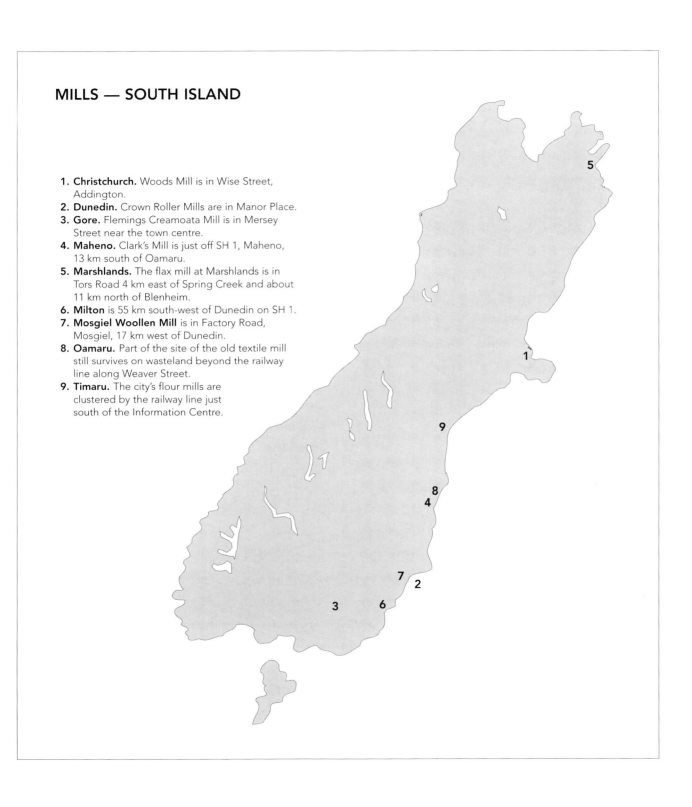

1. **Christchurch.** Woods Mill is in Wise Street, Addington.
2. **Dunedin.** Crown Roller Mills are in Manor Place.
3. **Gore.** Flemings Creamoata Mill is in Mersey Street near the town centre.
4. **Maheno.** Clark's Mill is just off SH 1, Maheno, 13 km south of Oamaru.
5. **Marshlands.** The flax mill at Marshlands is in Tors Road 4 km east of Spring Creek and about 11 km north of Blenheim.
6. **Milton** is 55 km south-west of Dunedin on SH 1.
7. **Mosgiel Woollen Mill** is in Factory Road, Mosgiel, 17 km west of Dunedin.
8. **Oamaru.** Part of the site of the old textile mill still survives on wasteland beyond the railway line along Weaver Street.
9. **Timaru.** The city's flour mills are clustered by the railway line just south of the Information Centre.

For early European settlers too, New Zealand flax (harakeke, *Phormium tenax*), was also no bonanza. Robert Williams established a flax venture at Port William, Stewart Island, in 1813 but it soon failed. By the 1830s regular exports to Australia and the United Kingdom had been established from trading ports around the coast, including the Bay of Plenty and Poverty Bay. But hand dressing was still the prevailing technique and the volume of trade was consequently modest. Mechanisation was necessary to turn flax into a paying proposition.

The New Zealand Government aided progress by offering cash rewards for the invention of stripping machines to remove the exterior tissue from the strong fibre used for making rope and cordage. Prospects soon looked rosier. A variety of machines — all based on the principle of beating the leaves between metal plates — were available by the late 1860s. Fraser and Tinne, James McIntyre and E. Gibbons and Company were all in the market. The market leaders, however, were the new emigrants, Arthur and George Price. Having tested their machine in a disused flour mill in Waipipi Road, Waiuku, the Price brothers went rapidly into production from premises in Princes Street, Onehunga that comprised a shed and converted stables. Using a home-made 6 hp steam engine, patterns manufactured from kauri, moulds fashioned from beach sand mixed with coal dust, a few lathes and a circular saw, A. & G. Price produced 100 flax-dressing machines within a year. They were compact and relatively inexpensive and could produce a ton of fibre in eight hours, which was light years ahead of traditional methods. Soon a complete flax-processing kit — including waterwheel, shafts, pulleys, three machines and a baling press — were on offer for £180.

The technological breakthrough coincided with — or perhaps had been precipitated by — a price boom in the finished product. Flax mills, some water powered, some with steam-driven strippers, sprang up in many of the country's swamps, including parts of Manawatu, Wanganui, around Raglan, Nelson, west Auckland, Canterbury and Otago. By the early 1870s the industry was booming, with an estimated 300 mills working countrywide.

Yet slump quickly followed boom throughout much of the century as the price of the competing products, jute and Manila hemp, fluctuated. Today little remains of the short-lived mills of this period. Often flax millers did no more than harvest native plants, making no attempt at fresh cultivation. A corrugated-iron shed might

Forest Hill, Southland, a
typical flax mill.

(SOUTHLAND MUSEUM)

be hastily erected on the banks of a millstream. If steam power was used, a concrete base is sometimes left as a reminder of this most transient of industries.

Just after the turn of the twentieth century, however, boom times returned as prices rose due to supply problems with Manila hemp. By 1906 there were an estimated 240 mills in New Zealand, employing over 4000 workers. Many were in the Manawatu, particularly in the Moutoa Swamp, near Foxton, and in the Makerua Swamp between Shannon and Linton.

Although much of the huge Makerua Swamp was naturally covered by a carpet of tiny flax plants, it had long been thought too low-lying for effective drainage. It took the foresight of Dr W.A. Chapple of Wellington to challenge the conventional wisdom of the day and invest heavily in a drainage scheme. Soon flax was growing to heights of over 2 m. Chapple's company sold its investment to flax millers at a most satisfactory profit.

Miranui Mill

One such purchaser was A. & L. Seifert Ltd whose Miranui Mill, built in 1907, was to be a star of the flax-milling firmament for the next generation. In an industry notorious for small-scale, short-lived mills, Alfred and Louis Seifert were an object lesson in vision and effective management. At its peak Miranui employed over 300

workers and operated nine stripping machines powered by two Tangye suction gas engines. The storage yards — raised on concrete pillars above flood level — were sometimes crammed with 400 tons of flax leaf waiting to be processed.

Nearby, the flax-bleaching paddocks covered hundreds of acres and, it has been said, looked like 'a tent town hit by a hurricane'. Far into the distance, flax fields were serviced by a tiny Bagnall locomotive on a narrow-gauge railway. Even this lightweight engine proved too heavy for the boggy terrain, however, and it was soon sold off to work the Piha logging tramway, being re-christened *Sandfly*. From 1910 onwards horses worked the Miranui tramway.

Miranui, 'the Big Mill', became a Manawatu legend that has been well documented by local historian Bob Ayson. Employment conditions for 'flaxies' set the industry standard, including comfortable bunkhouse accommodation, a dining room, reading and billiard rooms. The mill's rugby team was a force to be reckoned with and the company's annual ball, when the Druid's Hall in Shannon was decked out with streamers of flax fibre, was the social event of the year.

Yet Miranui, though periodically very profitable, also highlighted the recurrent problems of the flax industry. If the Manawatu River was not in flood then there was

At Miranui, Alfred and Louis Seifert created a 300-hand mill that became a Manawatu institution. Here fibre is being carted from the mill to the bleaching and drying paddocks.

(ADKIN COLLECTION, ALEXANDER TURNBULL LIBRARY, NATIONAL LIBRARY OF NEW ZEALAND/TE PUNA MĀTAURANGA O AOTEAROA, 065681 1/2)

the danger of fire in times of drought. Then for many years a mysterious 'yellow leaf disease' raged through the swamp, drastically reducing yields. A new flax-cutting method was tried. A success at first, it was soon found to reduce leaf size. Perennially, there were the vagaries of international prices that could fluctuate ruinously.

At times A. & L. Seifert tried alternative crops such as potatoes and once even attempted to manufacture industrial alcohol from flax leaves. The company finally closed down in the depths of the Depression, in May 1933.

Today the flax fields of the Makerua have been transformed by modern drainage schemes into prosperous dairy farms. The fleet of cyclists heading for work each morning, the screeching of the stripping machines, the stench of the waste product, the cartloads of fibre heading for the railway — all these have gone for ever. Indeed it is almost as though the industry had never existed. Travellers along the busy State Highway 57 would be hard pressed to pin down the site of the old mill at Miranui. The road, elevated above the flood plain and lined with weeping willow, runs parallel with the Manawatu River. The area between was once almost pure flax. Today only the underpass beneath the Wellington–Manawatu railway line gives a clue of the once thriving flax industry.

Foxton

Just across the old Manawatu flood plain, at Foxton, Charles Pownall opened the first mill in the 1869 boom and in total 19 different mill sites have been identified in the town. Many were built on the river bank and were serviced by punt-loads of flax leaf towed by steam tug from the Moutoa Swamp. Now only the concrete engine blocks of a few mills are still to be seen besides a part of the river that has been reduced to a backwater by the Manawatu flood control scheme.

Unlike Miranui, however, flax processing survived in Foxton in one form or another until relatively recently. In the Depression of the 1930s the government subsidised the spinning and weaving of flax woolpacks in order to compete with imported jute ones. A six-stripper mill near the site of Pownall's original mill processed both local flax leaf and that harvested in the Thames Valley, Wairarapa and Westport. For many years Foxton once again hummed to the sound of stripping and scutching and suffered the stench of the waste ponds. Later, flax was also used in the manufacture of floor coverings.

Marshlands

While Foxton is alive to its history and has a working Flax Stripper Museum to prove it, much of the rest of the flax-processing industry has totally disappeared. One other exception is at Marshlands, a few kilometres from Spring Creek, Marlborough. Here the mill built by John Chaytor in 1888 is still owned and preserved by his descendants and leased to the New Zealand Historic Places Trust. The last survivor in the area, it worked on until the 1960s, powered first by steam and then, when electricity became available in the Blenheim area in 1927, by electric motor. In 1924 a sawmill was added in order to provide work when wet winter weather prevented flax cutting in the swamps. Much of the mill remains in workable condition but at the time of writing faces an uncertain future.

Elsewhere across the scattered swamplands of New Zealand *Phormium tenax* regenerates abundantly, seemingly just waiting to be cropped, stripped, scutched and baled, but it is likely to just remain the happy haunt of the bellbird.

FLOUR MILLS

'Our time will be a good deal occupied
this summer erecting a water mill.'
GEORGE CLARKE, TE WAIMATE, 1833

The early missionaries were practical men. They came carrying farm implements as well as Bibles. Samuel Marsden's exploratory party of 1814 brought with them a hand-operated metal flour mill that delighted a local chief, Ruatara, who immediately ground some flour, made a cake and baked it in a frying pan.

From such modest beginnings sprang the rapid industrialisation of the milling industry, because bread was a necessity for transplanted Englishmen and Maori also quickly acquired a taste for it. Mills were built nationwide during the next 100 years. From small beginnings they culminated in monolithic piles that totally dominated the skyline of towns such as Timaru and Gore. Although early evidence on the ground is often scanty, thereafter sufficient of the fabric of our early flour mills has been preserved to allow this particular journey of industrialisation to be readily traced.

159

Early mills

The Church Missionary Society's farm at Waimate North employed a Mr McMullum in August 1833 to build a mill for five shillings per day plus rations. A stream was dammed, timber hand-sawn and ironwork manufactured in a primitive forge. Well over a year later work was complete. Even though the mechanics of milling initially proved difficult to master, by 1837 Waimate was producing over 20,000 kg of flour a year. The missionary farm soon wound down and, after a change of ownership, the mill seems to have been abandoned in the 1850s and nothing was left of this early experiment other than the earthworks of the dam.

Many towns boasted a flour mill from an early date, many of them wind-powered — a skyline adornment now sadly lost. Examples included Molesworth's Mill in the Hutt Valley, Wood's first mill in Christchurch and Auckland's 24-m-high Partington's Windmill, erected in Symonds Street in 1851 and only demolished nearly a century later when it was considered a structural risk.

New Plymouth has been luckier. The Egmont Flour Mill on Powderham Street — powered by steam, not wind — has been sympathetically restored, albeit for entertainment rather than industrial purposes. Established in 1868, it was a fine testament to the strength of small-town capitalism and a belief in progress that flourished despite the political vicissitudes of early Taranaki. It generally operated for about eight months a year, producing four tons of flour per day.

Maori mills

In a spirit of enlightened self-interest Governor George Grey gave financial aid to Maori agriculture, including investment in many rural flour mills. Maori provided much of the sustenance of the early European settlements and Grey thought they would be less inclined to warlike activities if they had a stake in local enterprise. The first such mill was built on Raglan Harbour in 1846. The most famous and enduring, Kawana Mill at Matahiwi on the Whanganui River, was erected in 1854. Using mill-stones from Australia and machinery from Britain, all brought up the Whanganui by canoe, the three-storey mill was powered by a waterwheel fed by a timber and earth headrace. The restored mill is now freely open to all that venture up the romantic Whanganui River road.

Clark's Mill, Maheno

The best preserved of the countryside mills of the 1860s and 1870s is Clark's Mill, tucked away just off State Highway 1 at Maheno, North Otago, and built from local limestone by the owners of the nearby Totara Estate. Originally a millrace from a river some distance away fed an overshot waterwheel that powered traditional horizontal millstones. Later a turbine was installed, together with metal rollers. The mill, now owned by the New Zealand Historic Places Trust, still displays this machinery in good working order.

Growth of automation

From the 1880s onwards milling became automated, urbanised and large scale. Roller technology replaced millstones, railways revolutionised transport and then electricity was widely adopted, first for lighting, later for power. Monolithic mills dominated city centres. The first fully automated mill in Auckland was J.C. Firth's Eight Hours Roller Mill on Quay Street. Opened with impeccably bad timing in

Clark's Mill, Maheno, North Otago.

Built from brick with Oamaru stone facings to the windows, the Crown Roller Mill, Dunedin, has been a distinctive city landmark since 1867. The mill was extended from three to five storeys in 1890 and converted to the use of steel rollers.

recession-bound 1888, it closed almost immediately when Firth's business empire, particularly his Waikato estates that were to supply grain to the mill, were foreclosed by the banks. But at least Firth left a legacy of good labour relations. The Eight Hours Mill was so called to reflect the unionist issue of the day, which Firth strongly supported, of three eight-hour shifts. Elsewhere, with a few honourable exceptions such as Woods of Christchurch, 12-hour days were commonplace. Soon the Northern Roller Mills emerged from the figurative embers of Firth's and another local mill. Located on Fort Street, it did not eventually close until mid-2000, though the structure has been much changed since the early days.

Woods Mill, Christchurch

For nearly half a century from 1856 the indomitable spirit of William Wood of Christchurch ground its way through all forms of milling technology and motive power. His original eight-storey windmill on Windmill Road, now Antigua Street, was followed by a water-powered mill at Riccarton. Then in 1890 he decided to fully embrace roller technology by erecting the four-storey, triple-brick Woods Mill, complete with chimney stack. Though it has long ceased its original function, Woods Mill still commands the skyline of Addington as surely as the owner's Imperial flour brand once dominated the local market.

Timaru mills

Timaru provides an industrial mill-scape unique in New Zealand. The earliest of the huge brick-built structures that crowd the railway line is the Belford Mill, which dates from 1878 and was built into a hillside to allow grain to enter on the third storey. Originally housing three pairs of millstones, Belford soon converted to rollers and produced the Golden Gem brand until after the Second World War. The building has subsequently been put to a variety of other industrial and entertainment uses. Nearby, the Silver Dust brand was produced by the Royal Flouring Mills built by James Bruce in 1882. Bruce's earlier mill had burned down but, ever the optimist, he took some local wheat to the United States, proved it was well suited to the latest roller technology and had his new state-of the-art, six-storey brick mill up and grinding after little more than a year. One of the largest buildings in New Zealand at the time, the mill housed 17 roller mills on its second floor, each gradually reducing the grain to an ever finer powder.

Bad luck continued to dog James Bruce, however. He soon fell out with the other directors and erected another mill nearby. Five storeys high and built of wood with a brick chimney, Bruce's new mill was to become the stuff of local legend. Initially the drying kiln twice caught fire. Then the market collapsed and after only six months the mill was forced to close. Within months a severe nor'-wester threatened to blow it over. The *Timaru Herald* of 5 October 1888 reported a drama-packed night:

> Quite early in the morning the news was flying all over town, 'Bruce's Mill is blown over' ... The wall framing of the building was not sufficiently braced. The second storey was the weakest ... the storeys above were carried forward four feet.

As the gale raged, 'making the building creak and groan in a very sinister manner', stout manila rope was wound around the huge butt of the brick chimney and

William Evans' Atlas Mill, Timaru (1888), and to the right the even earlier Landing Service building (1871). Originally on Timaru's harbourless waterfront, it has three portals from which to launch landing boats.

attached to timbers within the second floor of the mill. Then 'with strong sticks they twitched the ropes tight and then by wetting them tightened them still further' until the mill had been drawn upright by an estimated seven inches. Later chains were employed and the rescue completed successfully. However, the mill remained unused, except for storage, until it burned down in 1904. Then locals laconically commented that smoke rose from its chimney for the first time since 1888. A few years later the chimney finally found a useful role when incorporated into the local electric power plant.

A third famous name on Timaru flour bags, Atlas, was the brainchild of William Evans who built the five-storey Atlas Mill in 1888. A product of the well-trodden path of Kiwi entrepreneurs — Australian diggings, followed by Gabriel's Gully and then Hokitika — Evans was managing director of the mill for over 40 years and was finally persuaded to retire aged 92.

It's Christmas 2000 but Sergeant Dan, mascot of Creamoata rolled oats, has a tear in his eye because Fleming's Mill, Gore, has just closed after well over a century in operation.

Fleming's Mill, Gore

There's little about Fleming's Mill, Gore, to tickle the architectural fancy despite the presence of Sergeant Dan, the Creamoata man. Dan's image dominates the town as it did New Zealand breakfast tables for decades, but the main body of the mill itself is five storeys of 1919 reinforced concrete — best labelled functional. Next door the four-storey block dates from 1892. Yet the mill is certainly a heritage icon; the workaday reality behind high-quality marketing that sold Southland oats to hungry mouths for many generations. As well as Dan — 'I am the man says Sergeant Dan/ I care not one iota/ For who can be, as strong as me/ While I have my Creamoata' — there was the 'Eat Creamoata with a silver spoon' campaign. This included the first Invercargill to Auckland flight, in 1921, sponsored by Flemings. The aircraft flew low over various towns on its way north, with CREAMOATA emblazoned under each wing and passenger Herbert Fleming dropped silver spoons on tiny parachutes to the lucky consumers below. The pilot, who was unfamiliar with Auckland, knew he was in the right place when he saw Rangitoto. He then circled the city and landed on the lower slopes of One Tree Hill.

WOOLLEN MILLS

'... Why not use our own wool ... instead of sending it to England merely to be operated upon and returned to us enhanced in price.'

<small>LETTER TO *TIMARU HERALD*, 19 MARCH 1870</small>

It was a dilemma of almost Gilbertian absurdity. On the one hand, a land dotted with millions of sheep. On the other, a growing population of miners and farmers demanding tough, honest workgear and the occasional item of Sunday best. Yet, everything from miners' moleskin to finest worsted was imported, mainly from the furthest point of the globe.

Arthur Burns and Mosgiel Woollens

Even as the writer penned the letter quoted above, however, a singular Scotsman, Arthur Burns, was returning 'Home' aboard the *May Queen* intent on purchasing textile machinery and persuading skilled workers to try their luck in New Zealand.

Burns was both a novice in the finer points of spinning and weaving and to many of his fellows a seemingly improbable commercial proposition. Son of the Rev. Dr Thomas Burns, and grand-nephew of the poet Robbie Burns, Arthur served on a sailing ship to Hong Kong after leaving school. That had been heady stuff for an adventurous teenager and Burns used to recall being attacked by pirates and assisting with an assault by marines on Canton. Arthur and his father then emigrated to Otago on one the first two ships, the *Philip Laing*. Subsequently he farmed on the Otago Peninsula and then at Mosgiel on the Taieri. He also enlivened provincial politics with a rumbustious enthusiasm that stirred the local press to high-fevered criticism when reporting election meetings that tended towards the over-vigorous.

Rough at the edges he may have been but Arthur Burns undoubtedly possessed both a raw, restless energy and the foresight to recognise an opportunity. He was, writes Peter Stewart in *Patterns on the Plain* (1975), the history of Mosgiel Woollens, a 'strange mixture of progressive foresight and intemperate enthusiasm'. Domestic purchasing power had advanced on the back of the gold rushes and was to reach new heights during the Vogel-inspired boom of the 1870s. Possibly even more to the point for a canny Scot, a prize of £1500 was being offered by the Otago Provincial Council for the first 5000 yards (about 4570 m) of woollen cloth woven in the province.

165

Arthur Burns had a hard time persuading the capitalists of his native heath to back his scheme. Advertising in Edinburgh for a partner with capital, he received not a single reply. Undeterred, he mortgaged the farm and eventually returned with a load of textile machinery (mainly from Platt Brothers of Oldham), two dozen skilled hands and a partner to manage the mill, John Smail.

Soon the Mosgiel factory took shape next to Burns' old flour mill, part of which was used as a wool store. Mainly constructed from wood, the original textile mill also incorporated a boilerhouse and chimney stack built from bricks fired by the nearby Shiel Brick and Tile works, which had just installed a steam engine and a horizontal pug-mill. Messrs Kincaid and McQueen from the local foundry erected boilers, engines and shafting. Coal to fire the 7-m-long tubular boilers arrived by dray from Green Island. Carding machines and mules with 650 spindles, four blanket and tweed looms and finishing, washing and milling machinery were installed. By late September 1871 wool was being teased and carded and within a month Arthur Burns was proudly sporting the first pair of Mosgiel-made tweed trousers.

At Mosgiel, Arthur Burns started a trend of small-town mills utilising New Zealand's most abundant resource, wool. They also provided one of the few nineteenth-century employment opportunities for women — usually unmarried and always supervised by a male foreman. The mill closed only recently.

Burns' optimism was swiftly vindicated and he was to receive the dual benefit of the government bonus and a respectful press. Indeed, demand was such that profits were soon rolling in, additional plant was ordered and the business converted into a public company. New brick buildings were erected to the design of local architect H.F. Hardy, saving a small fortune in fire insurance premiums.

The textile boom

The instant success of Mosgiel precipitated a flurry of entrepreneurial activity around the South Island. A projected flax mill at Kaiapoi was swiftly switched to wool manufacture in response to a bonus offered by the Canterbury Provincial Council. A mill was built in the Kaikorai Valley, Dunedin, but could not keep up with the booming market in flannel and was quickly followed by another at nearby Roslyn in 1879.

One aspect of the textile boom was that visitors flocked to the Mosgiel mill on the newly built railway. This was all very complimentary but the company suspected industrial spying and had to restrict access. One inquiry seeking information was received in a letter from Oamaru but received short shrift by return.

Oamaru and Timaru

The Oamaru Mill was eventually floated on what seemed like a tide of local enthusiasm in 1881. In a fine example of small-town capitalism, shares were hawked around Oamaru and neighbouring areas. Sadly, local enthusiasm proved less overwhelming than anticipated and the venture was to be undercapitalised and precarious — in more senses than one — for some years.

The shortfall in Oamaru's initial funding was taken up by bank loans and a habit of persuading suppliers to take payment in shares rather than cash. The contract for the original building was won by a local builder willing to take part payment in this way. The power supply to the mill was provided by a second-hand boiler from Meek's flour mill paid for with £500 worth of shares.

After difficult early years the Oamaru Mill eventually reached a decent plateau of profitability and then, like many others, benefited hugely from the demand for uniforms during the First World War. It soon became apparent, however, that the original mill's physical foundations were even more vulnerable than its early finances. Situated on the north side of town and elegantly built from the famed local limestone, it was literally on the wrong side of the rail tracks that ran parallel to a rapidly eroding coastline. Shortly after the mill opened the cliff line was 32 m away. By 1896 the distance had shrunk dramatically to 22 m. By 1917, with the sea only 8 m away, a new building was erected inland from the railway line on the theory that any further erosion would be the responsibility of the government. For a short time Oamaru had two mills running simultaneously but the old building was eventually abandoned to the ravages of nature in 1921.

Oamaru Mill was to eventually merge with Timaru and Milton to become Alliance Textiles. (For a full history see *Spinning Yarns* [1981] by Gavin McLean.) In all three cases the early years saw small-town enthusiasm exceed small-town financial capacity. Timaru's Bank Street Mill (1885) in particular was to experience several bankruptcies and changes of ownership. Yet it eventually proved exceedingly durable and is still working at the time of writing.

Milton

In the small town of Milton, 55 km south-west of Dunedin, the woollen mill had a long gestation period, being first mooted in 1868 but not built until 1897. Then came a difficult birth when the delivery of machinery was delayed by industrial action in the United Kingdom and the drive shafts had to be powered for a time by two traction engines. Then the infant factory, in sickly financial health anyway, burned to the ground aged just over three years. Though rebuilt on the insurance money, profitability proved elusive for a time and the Bruce Woollen Manufacturing Company's annual meetings became the stuff of legend. With local money as well as local jobs on the line, vigorous debate was the order of the day.

In time prosperity settled on Milton and the textile company purchased the venerable McGill's flour mill nearby for use as a wool store. It was a fitting marriage, allowing the town to fully live up to its original name, for Milton was originally Mill Town before the local fathers took a poetical turn. In the early twenty-first century McGill's old mill is a haunting relic beside the main road, but the Alliance Textile factory works on vigorously to the rear.

8
FROZEN MEAT

'A cargo of frozen mutton … arrived in splendid condition.'
CABLEGRAM, DATELINE LONDON, 27 MAY 1882

The *Edwin Fox* had a most varied and exciting working life, with a curriculum vitae unparalleled among merchant ships in terms of adventure and longevity: Built Calcutta, 1853. Troop carrier, Crimean War. Transported general cargo for the colonies. Convict ship to Western Australia. Immigrant ship to New Zealand. As the ninth-oldest extant ship in the world, the *Edwin Fox* is one of the treasures of maritime history.

Now this venerable hulk rests proudly in a dry dock close to the passenger terminal at Picton, a major attraction for visitors disembarking in the South Island. In addition to having a romantic seafaring history, however, the *Edwin Fox* is also one of the two oldest links with the start of a major New Zealand industry — the export of frozen meat.

After the *Edwin Fox* made her final voyage in 1885, she was immediately pressed into service in New Zealand's newest and most dynamic industry. Moored at Port Chalmers, the masts were removed and salvaged boilers installed to power refrigeration equipment. Sheep were slaughtered on shore and then frozen and stored on the *Edwin Fox* at a rate of 400 per day. Where a few hundred immigrants had once travelled, now up to 14,000 sheep carcasses could be packed in until transferred to fast, modern ships bound for England.

The *Edwin Fox* was merely a stopgap measure, of course. The frozen meat industry was growing at such a pace at this time that dedicated meat works were soon built on shore. Within a few years the *Edwin Fox* was moved on to fulfil a similar function in Lyttelton, followed by Gisborne and Bluff. Then this incredible hulk was towed on a four-day voyage to Picton to do service for the Wairau Freezing

Edwin Fox moored at Picton during her time as a freezer storage ship.

(Edwin Fox Society)

Company. There she served for three seasons, freezing and storing meat killed at Spring Creek and then railed to the Picton wharf. The *Edwin Fox*'s 15 years in the meat industry finally ended when a shore facility was built at Picton in 1900. By then there cannot have been many British mouths that had not tasted sheep meat frozen on board the *Edwin Fox*.

Indignity followed retirement when the ship was used as a coal hulk until the 1950s. West Coast coal was stored on board and then transported to Picton's meat works down a slipway built from a vast hole cut in her side. The *Edwin Fox* then became derelict until purchased from the freezing company by the Edwin Fox Society in 1965 for one shilling (10 cents).

Today the *Edwin Fox*, one of the more unexpected industrial monuments of New Zealand, is lovingly cared for and receives thousands of visitors. But in the history of the meat trade at any rate, she has to give pride of place to the Totara Estate — the birthplace of the industry.

TOTARA ESTATE: SHIPPING FROZEN MEAT

Totara, just off State Highway 1 some 8 km south of Oamaru, has been one of New Zealand's premier sheep stations since the earliest days of European colonisation. Built of Oamaru stone — which guarantees longevity and grandeur — most estate

FROZEN MEAT

1. **Gisborne.** Kaiti freezing works: The Esplanade on the harbour front. Taruheru freezing works: by the Taruheru River, in Nelson Road.
2. **Patea.** The freezing works are by the Patea River on Portland Quay, on the left when entering town from Wanganui.
3. **Tokomaru Steam Engine Museum** is at 144 Highway 57, Tokomaru, Manawatu, 20 km south-west of Palmerston North. Phone 06 329 8867.
4. **Waipaoa** is 20 km north-west of Gisborne on SH 2.

5. **Christchurch.** Islington Meat Works: Waterloo Road, Islington on the west edge of the city.
6. **Dunedin.** Burnside Freezing Works: Eclipse Road, off Kaikorai Valley Road, near SH 1.
7. **Oamaru.** The old freezing works are between Humber Street and the shore, alongside the railway line.
8. **Picton.** Edwin Fox Maritime Centre is on Dunbar Wharf close by the Ferry Terminal. Phone 03 573 6868.
9. **Totara Estate** is just off SH 1, 8 km south of Oamaru. Phone 03 434 7169.

buildings date from around 1868. Operated as a museum these days by the New Zealand Historic Places Trust, the group of buildings — stables, men's quarters, granary and carcass shed — provide a fine insight into the organisation of a nineteenth-century sheep station.

Sadly, the slaughterhouse — the starting point in a lengthy logistical chain that was to revolutionise New Zealand farming — has long been demolished. Here, in a wooden shed, at 4 am on 6 December 1881, six butchers set to work killing sheep for the British market. The dream of William Soltau Davidson, the dynamic 35-year-old general manager of the Scottish-based New Zealand and Australian Land Company — not to mention those of thousands of Kiwi farmers — was about to come true.

Shipping frozen meat was not new. Successful voyages had been made from the United States to the United Kingdom and from Argentina to France in the previous few years. But the scale of possibilities really dawned on Davidson and the Land Company in 1880 when the steamer *Strathleven* successfully carried frozen beef and mutton from Australia to London.

The economics were compelling. Demand obviously existed from the rapidly

Totara Estate, icon of New Zealand's frozen meat industry.

expanding urban population of the Old Country. Supply from New Zealand was practically inexhaustible. Sheep were being reared almost solely for wool. New Zealand's small population could not possibly eat the vast amount of meat left over and other means of processing it were not particularly productive. Boiling down for tallow yielded a poor return. Canning, as practised by Thomson and Finlayson at Kakanui, for instance, was only an interim measure.

Oversupply was such that Davidson was to recall:

> … having to erect yards at the edge of cliffs into which some thousands of these old sheep were driven so that they might be knocked on the head and thrown over the precipice as waste product.

Davidson had all the self-confidence and drive typical of a Victorian entrepreneur. He had worked his way up the management ladder from shepherd on the Levels Estate near Timaru to the general manager's chair and was well placed to oversee the future growth of the meat trade with an experienced yet adventurous eye. Davidson did his homework thoroughly over a two-year period. A Bell-Coleman cold-air machine was purchased and installed on the Albion Shipping Company's sailing ship *Dunedin*, a decision that reveals Davidson as both pragmatic and far-sighted. A small shore-based station would prove a loser either way. If the voyage ended in failure, it would be useless; if successful, it would be too small. The Bell-Coleman cold-air system had been patented only in 1877 and the first ship fitted out in 1879, but it was to prove ideal for ocean-going vessels. It was non-toxic, an important consideration should a pipe burst in a confined space while at sea, and was obviously available worldwide at a time when other gases, such as ammonia and carbon dioxide, were not. Eventually, ammonia compression with brine circulation was to be the dominant freezing medium at land-based plants and highly efficient carbon dioxide plants prevailed at sea, but the technological changeover was to take several decades.

The Land Company's superintendent in New Zealand, the autocratic yet efficient Thomas Brydone, was instructed to oversee the preparation of facilities at Totara. Brydone, who never married and used a gentlemen's club in Dunedin as his home base, could near traumatise his staff merely by announcing his intention of descending on an estate in his charge. *Totara Estate*, by Martine Cuff (1982) quotes the children of long-time estate manager, John Macpherson, recalling their father 'getting into a state of agitation', and ordering wisps of wool to be whisked from the wire fences, at the prospect of a visit by 'TB'. The children, told not to whisper a word at the breakfast table, used to closely observe Brydone's table manners. A true Scotsman, educated at Perth Academy and a former land steward for the Earl of Buchan and then the Duke of Hamilton, Brydone had a methodical way with a bowl of porridge. Salt was sprinkled, a special bone spoon filled, dipped in a glass of milk and then consumed.

It is scarcely surprising that all initially went well with Brydone's meticulously laid plans. Up to 240 carefully selected sheep from the estate and the surrounding areas were killed each day in the wooden slaughterhouse at Totara and the carcasses left to hang overnight in the adjacent, specially ventilated carcass shed. (Blood and offal, incidentally, were fed through a gutter, which can still be seen, into a large pig-rearing yard. The story is told of young boys challenging each other to sprint across the yard dodging these lively carnivores.) Early next morning the carcasses were taken by dray to the nearby railway and transported in ice-chilled wagons to Port Chalmers. Davidson and Brydone jointly had the honour of carrying aboard the *Dunedin* the first carcass ever to be frozen in New Zealand.

All was fine for a few days — and then the crankshaft broke on the Bell-Coleman refrigeration equipment. It took a month to mend and the citizens of Dunedin happily feasted on cheap sheep meat. Eventually, the *Dunedin* was successfully fully laden and sailed on 15 February 1882.

An industry's maiden voyage

The voyage of the *Dunedin* proved dramatic. The funnel of the cooling equipment constantly threatened to set fire to the sails. The ship's hybrid appearance — surely what seemed like a steam ship in full sail must be in some kind of distress? — led to several offers of assistance from other vessels. When she was becalmed, the flow of air for the freezing equipment threatened to be insufficient. Captain John Whitson bravely crawled along the main air duct to cut additional holes — and nearly froze to death in the process. He had to be hauled out by a rope tied to his ankles and painfully defrosted. Finally, when the *Dunedin* neared England after the 98-day voyage, Whitson forgot the prearranged signal that all was well with the cargo. Davidson, who had gone ahead and had heard no news over this period, was temporarily distressed.

Yet only one carcass had deteriorated and the cargo sold for roughly twice what it would have fetched in New Zealand. The Land Company made a profit of over £4000 as well as receiving £500 reward from the New Zealand Government.

The whole operation, though meticulously planned, had nevertheless had a stroke of fine fortune with London meat prices high at the time of arrival. The next shipment from New Zealand, on the *Mataura*, proved less lucky and hit the Smithfield market at a time of glut and its cargo had to be hastily stored in conditions that were far from ideal. Yet another valuable lesson had been learned: a great deal of additional work had to be put into storage and distribution facilities in Britain.

The essential point had been made, however. One of the great springboards for the growth of New Zealand agriculture was now in place, for the *Dunedin* had carried a small quantity of butter as well as 4909 mutton and lamb carcasses. A vast market was now available to farmers in fat lambing or dairying. Add in the development of dedicated port facilities and the mushrooming number of freezing works and the face of New Zealand was changed for ever.

All was not universal sweetness and light in the nascent industry, of course. One problem was that everyone — Australia, Argentina and America — was into the frozen meat business. Another was that it was impossible for New Zealand farmers to step up the rearing of meat-producing breeds sufficiently quickly to fully utilise the burgeoning capacity of both the freezing works and the shipping lines. By the early 1890s around 40 vessels were engaged in the trade and cargoes of up to 70,000 carcasses were possible.

Farming does not move at such a pace and ships often left New Zealand loaded to less than capacity. This discouraged the shipping companies from lowering freight rates. The result, combined with the sometimes unpredictable nature of the London market, was that the smaller New Zealand farmer often thought that the changes in the meat industry had benefited only the middleman and the large producers who were more able to shoulder risk.

Despite the problems, the statistics of the first decade of frozen meat exports are compelling, however. From nothing, frozen meat had grown to 12 per cent of New Zealand's exports by 1893. This was still far behind wool but the gap was closing fast. The New Zealand economy was now growing rapidly off the sheep's buttocks as well as the sheep's back.

FREEZING WORKS ABOUND

The advent of freezing works materially affected many communities across the length and breadth of New Zealand. The major city, the small town blessed with a port and a pastoral hinterland, or the isolated, depressed region, all played a distinctive part in the story of the freezing industry.

Dunedin and Oamaru

Cities and their ports were swiftly up with the play. Indeed, Dunedin was planning its incursion into the trade as early as February 1881, just after news of the second successful shipment from Australia, on the SS *Protos,* hit the headlines. The *Otago Daily Times* urged immediate action in case Christchurch should 'show the way'. The New Zealand Refrigerating Company, under the chairmanship of industrialist and politician extraordinaire W.J.M. Larnach, was not incorporated until August that year, however, and further dithering followed, with no one sure exactly how to proceed. Larnach and others crossed the Tasman on fact-finding missions but reported that the Australians were also relying on little more than trial and error. Eventually a site was purchased in the Kaikorai Valley and work finally commenced

Freezing works at Oamaru, built on the foreshore in 1886 but abandoned within a generation when new works were built at nearby Pukeuri.

on the Burnside works in January 1882. A dry-air refrigeration system was purchased from Haslam of Derby who had bought the patent rights to the Bell-Coleman process, and the first meat — 150 sheep from Mr Shand's Taieri farm — were processed at New Zealand's pioneer freezing works on 8 August 1882.

Burnside had to be extended almost immediately and, despite problems with water supply and waste disposal, proved to be New Zealand's longest-lived freezing works. Almost inevitably the early buildings have been swallowed up by the massive extensions of later years. The original buildings of the company's offshoot have fared better, however. Burnside had been open only a short time when a branch slaughterhouse was built near Oamaru to kill stock to be frozen on John R. Reid's steamship *Elderslie* that carried 23,000 carcasses to Britain in 1884. Two years later the company built a more substantial freezing works from local limestone near Oamaru town centre, between the railway line and the foreshore. Such a constrained site denied future expansion and in 1914 an entirely new works was opened amid much fanfare at Pukeuri, a few kilometres to the north of town. Since then the old meat works at Oamaru have remained empty and forlorn, a neglected morsel in a land of plenty.

Christchurch

Dunedin folk were well advised to keep a wary eye on Christchurch competition, for the Belfast freezing works opened as early as February 1883. Once again a Haslam machine was used, though the company seems to have hedged its bets on new technology by also retaining facilities for canning. Six years later the Garden City boasted another freezing works, at Islington. The directors here were keen to avoid pitfalls encountered elsewhere and diversified as much as possible. Pelt curing, tallow rendering, bacon curing and sausage-skin manufacture were all additional items on the menu. The company boasted that every part of the animal was utilised except the squeal of the pigs — and they had recently heard that Professor Edison had patented a process for preserving that too. Indeed, a practical phonograph was demonstrated in Christchurch in 1891 and the company did later record the sound of (temporarily) contented hogs as proof that 'it kept ahead of its competitors'.

Islington was to be the hub of a national company for many years and developed into an industrial community. Although the majority of men were billeted in an

177

accommodation block, almost from the beginning more than 40 building sections were created in two streets for houses for married workers — though at £25 each the sections initially proved difficult to sell. Later an adjoining 45 acres were also sub-divided and London names used for the streets. A community centre was provided with a library, billiard room, dance hall and cafeteria. A general store operated as a private venture but later became a co-operative where employees could obtain a rebate on purchases.

Wellington and Wairarapa

Elsewhere around the country a degree of confusion and uncertainty about how exactly to proceed continued to accompany the euphoria generated by the successful voyage of the *Dunedin*. The port of Wellington and its hinterland, the Wairarapa, provide an excellent example.

The news was reported in the press on Monday, 29 May 1882. Two cablegrams were in fact received. The first, datelined 26 May, merely said the *Dunedin* had arrived safely, which raised almost as many questions as it answered. The second, datelined 27 May, added:

> … the cargo of frozen mutton … arrived in splendid condition. It was placed on the market today and realised an average price of 6 pence per pound.

Within days a public meeting was called in Carterton, in the Wairarapa, to discuss future developments. Within six weeks the prospectus of the Wellington Meat Export Company had been issued. Almost simultaneously the Gear Meat Preserving & Freezing Company also sold shares to the public. But enthusiasm was far outpacing capacity. Although the two companies had jumped wholeheartedly onto the bandwagon, neither was, in fact, ready to freeze its own meat. As a stopgap measure the Shaw Savill Line agreed to install freezing machinery on the venerable *Lady Jocelyn* which left for the United Kingdom in February 1883.

Thereafter the two Wellington freezing companies solved their immediate problems in differing fashions. The Wellington Meat Export Company opened a freezing works on the Waterloo Quay reclamation in September 1883. The Gear Company, however, already had an established abattoir at Petone and any meat frozen there would have faced an awkward little journey to the wharves in Wellington. The problem was resolved by fitting out the hull of the *Jubilee* with a Haslam freezing plant and operating her on the lines later so effectively adopted by the peripatetic *Edwin Fox.* Meat was slaughtered at the works in Petone and frozen onboard the *Jubilee* berthed nearby. When full the hulk was towed across the harbour to the waiting ocean-going steamships. It was said that the *Jubilee*, stripped of most of her rigging and covered in dust from her coal-fired boilers, was not a thing of beauty.

Auckland

Inevitably, Auckland outdid the general euphoria. The *Herald* reported that:

> … meat freezing is assuming the character of a mania … no doubt there will be fingers burnt — or frozen — in this business.

The prophecy came true remarkably quickly.

A hugely ambitious company, the New Zealand Frozen Meat and Storage Company was formed in July 1883 with a large capital base for the times of £200,000. Many of the directors were part of Auckland's financial inner circle. They included Dr John Logan Campbell, who was heavily involved in farming, timber and brewing, Thomas Russell, lawyer and businessman, J.C. Firth, owner of the Matamata estate and the roller milling company, and D.L. Murdoch, general manager of the Bank of New Zealand. Shareholders included the major finance houses and insurance companies. Dozens of small farmer-shareholders went along for the ride on what must have seemed a sure-fire success.

The company did things in style buying a five-acre harbourfront property for its cold store and head office. The latter was fitted out to impress with wrought-iron entrance gates, tiled floor and a 2-m-wide main staircase. The abattoir was out in the backblocks by the railway line at Westfield. Nearby the company built a substantial chemical fertiliser works.

Little went right for the company. Shipments to London proved more expensive than planned and met resistance from vested interests. Fertiliser sales were poor. Above all, the company was caught in the most disastrous trade slump of the century. It went into liquidation in 1889. Many directors faced ruin from this and other over-ambitious enterprises. The shareholders, big and small, lost every penny of their investment.

FREEZING WORKS IN SMALLER TOWNS

For the major cities freezing works were to be just another adjunct to economic growth, albeit an important one. For many small communities, eking out a precarious existence in the backblocks, the establishment of a freezing works was often seen as the only road to a golden age of economic prosperity. For some of them, however, the path proved to be pitted with potholes and wrong turnings. Nowhere provides a finer example of the full, turbulent life cycle of a freezing works town than the small South Taranaki settlement of Patea.

Patea

Patea was swiftly off the starting grid following the *Dunedin*'s successful voyage. The opportunities must have seemed immense, for until then the town's exports of farm products were limited to hides, skins, wool and tallow, together with modest shipments of butcher's meat to the gold diggings of the West Coast of the South Island. Additionally, in common with other small communities, a boiling-down plant pickled meat for the local market, though much was turned into fertiliser.

As early as 1883 plans were afoot to start the West Coast Meat & Produce Export Company on the site that was to ultimately house the modern freezing works. Initially meat was just slaughtered, cooked and canned by the company, but great things were clearly planned because Haslam refrigeration equipment had been purchased, although it was not operational when, in May 1885, fire destroyed both the building and a few dreams of economic fortune.

A second attempt, in 1888, was on a very small scale but this tiny factory was also eventually ravaged by fire. Not until 1904 was freezing undertaken on a substantial scale, possibly because, although the railway came to Patea as early as 1883, insulated wagons were not available. The new works proved to be a success and even boasted their own post office, 'Canville'. By the following year the works had been substantially expanded and were handling 50,000 sheep.

Yet more problems lay ahead. In 1907 a major industrial dispute involved both pay and the miserable working conditions — at that time each man completely dressed each individual carcass but without the benefit of changing or washing facilities. By 1910 trade was at a low ebb and the works became a producer co-operative.

Despite all these vicissitudes, the freezing works continued to expand. By 1920 nearly 90,000 sheep were killed but almost immediately substantial losses were incurred when a year's production was lost due to shipping problems. In the Depression of the 1930s the farmer co-operative became insolvent and the Vestey organisation bought and upgraded the plant. Solo butchering was replaced by a chain system. By the time of the Second World War, 320,000 sheep as well as calves, cattle and pigs were being handled each year. More disruption followed during the 1951 waterside industrial dispute. Even so, by 1955/56 the numbers had increased to a sheep-kill of 450,000. In the peak killing season up to 550 men were employed.

Patea Freezing Works, once the lifeblood of the town.

Further substantial investment was undertaken in the 1960s but Patea never enjoyed a reputation for good industrial relations or high productivity. When the overcapacity in the industry became apparent in the 1980s, Patea was one of the first works to close, in August 1982. The impact was traumatic. Patea was in part a rural service centre but primarily it was a freezing works town. Seven hundred of its 1000 jobs were at the works. Two-thirds of Patea's households gained an income there. The trade of the town's 60 businesses were crucially dependent on this cash flow.

Two decades later the population of Patea has halved, businesses have closed and property is as cheap as any in the North Island. On the far river bank, below the hill, lies the concrete behemoth of the old freezing works — a slumbering industrial giant that will never be reawakened.

All is not forgotten regarding Patea's industrial past, however. At the time of writing plans are afoot to display refrigeration machinery from the old freezing works at a small museum in vacated bank premises on the main street. The two prized exhibits will be a Linde horizontal ammonia machine imported to New Zealand by Nivens of Napier at the turn of the century, and a much newer, but intriguing, two-cylinder vertical machine manufactured by Gordons of Victoria in 1940. Niven particularly deserves an honourable mention in the annals of New Zealand's industrial history. Founded in 1886 by Messrs Niven and Galway, blacksmiths from Scotland, the company became a subsidiary of Nelson's freezing works empire about the turn of the century and was to give an enduring service to the industry, manufacturing, modifying and converting freezing machines.

Built in 1916 for the Imlay Freezing Works, Wanganui, this Filer & Stowell tandem compound engine could generate 335 hp, driving an ammonia compressor with a capacity of 200 tons of ice per day. It is now housed in the Tokomaru Steam Engine Museum, Manawatu.

(Tokomaru Steam Engine Museum)

Fittingly Patea will thus be at the forefront of the preservation of our long-neglected refrigeration heritage. Lack of public interest, coupled with the sheer bulk and weight of the machines, has generally minimised the conservation effort. Yet an entire raft of New Zealand industry has been entirely dependent on refrigeration, not only meat but also dairy products, fruit and seafood. It is too significant a heritage to let go by default.

Fortunately Patea is not entirely alone. A few leviathans of the meat trade are still receiving their share of care around the country. The privately funded Tokomaru Steam Engine Museum, near Palmerston North, has been particularly active. Its star exhibit is a 1916 Filer & Stowell tandem compound engine. Other refrigeration equipment is plentiful at Tokomaru, including a 225-hp Belliss & Morcom engine installed in the Waingawa Freezing Works, Masterton, also in 1916. The most venerable machine of all is lodged at McLeans Island, Christchurch. Here a Haslam air-blast machine, originally installed at the opening of Islington, but subsequently converted to ammonia, still awaits funding for a suitable building.

Poverty Bay

Across the North Island in Poverty Bay the introduction of freezing works must also have seemed like the missing link to economic prosperity. From the 1870s onwards the backblocks were cleared by bush-burning and initially offered fertile pasture. There were high hopes of rail links to the outside world, especially with Auckland and Wellington. Combined with the promise of direct exports of farm produce, the future looked promising indeed.

Sadly, Gisborne's economic jigsaw was never to be satisfactorily pieced together. Much of the rapidly cleared land proved highly vulnerable to the ravages of nature. The promised railway link to Wellington took what seemed like an eternity and was not finished until 1942. That with Auckland never even crossed the barrier of the Raukumaras. The establishment of freezing works, initially tentative, later precipitated savage competition within the industry. Two works proved short lived, but a third showed admirable staying power. When other freezing works were opened around the East Cape, at Tokomaru Bay and Hicks Bay, they too were only intermittently successful.

Initially Gisborne dipped its toes into the export trade when sheep were sent to

183

Taruheru, Gisborne's first freezing works, shortly after opening in 1889.

(W.F. Crawford Collection, Gisborne Museum & Arts Centre, A475)

Wellington to be frozen and shipped to the London market. Then came a brief flirtation up the blind alley of meat embalming, a process promoted by a company intent on supplying the Auckland market. Not until 1889 did the Nelson Brothers establish the works at Taruheru, by a small river on the edge of the city.

Mutton was slaughtered at Taruheru and ferried downstream by the steam launch *Tuna* to the freezing hulk *Prince of Wales* in Gisborne Harbour. The *Prince of Wales*, said to have been built in 1850 for the Hudson Bay trade, seems to have been perfect for the job, for with a metre-thick hull built from oak and sheathed with zinc, she was just as adept at keeping ice in as keeping it out. Fitted with a Haslam refrigerator, she easily coped with the modest daily output of 200 or so carcasses processed by the handful of butchers at Taruheru. Within a month the first load of 4100 carcasses was transhipped for the London market.

So successful was this operation that a freezing chamber was added to Taruheru in 1890 and killings soon reached 750 per day. The *Prince of Wales* was then shipped off to serve in Picton, Port Chalmers and Wellington before eventually being laid to rest in Queen Charlotte Sound.

The success of Taruheru precipitated competition. In 1896 the Gisborne Freezing Company opened its Kaiti works in the obvious place, the Gisborne harbourfront. So intense was competition between the two companies that the price paid for sheep was driven up to twice the previous level. This was too good to last from the farmers' perspective and in 1901 the Gisborne Freezing Company ceased trading. Prices then collapsed and a new company, The Gisborne Sheepfarmers' Frozen Meat Company, took over the works. The Kaiti works then rode out the economic rollercoaster that is the meat trade throughout most of the rest of the century. The original wood and galvanised-iron buildings were replaced by a red brick façade that became something of a feature on the harbourfront. Sadly, the old fellmongery became increasingly unsafe and, despite a 'C' heritage listing, was demolished in 1993, though other modern facilities at Kaiti worked on.

At Taruheru nature's revenge was insidious as the tiny Taruheru River silted up following land erosion. Transport proved impossible and the works closed as early as 1923. Now little is left of the pioneer works, other than a few fragments in the under-growth of the river bank, though the works are clearly not forgotten by the local community. In 1989 a plaque was unveiled on the site to commemorate the works' centenary.

During the First World War, an insubstantial shooting star of a company, the Poverty Bay Farmers Meat Company, flitted across the firmament. Under the guiding light of local lawyer, politician and farmer Douglas Lysnar, and supported by over 500 local farmers and businessmen, its Waipaoa freezing works hoped to cash in on the food shortages created by the war in Europe. The three-storey, ferro-concrete plant at Kaitaratahi, 20 km inland from Gisborne, was built to last by Jack Colley in 1915. He was eminently successful, for the gaunt rectangular skeleton dominates the landscape like the remnant of a mysterious blitzkrieg. In many ways the venture was well planned. The works were well sited for fresh water and ease of transport and employed up-to-date techniques, but other management decisions proved woeful. In particular, in an attempt to cut out the middleman the company overreached itself with the purchase of the badly designed freezing ship, the *Admiral Codrington*. By 1923 the company was insolvent and was later the subject of an inquiry by Royal Commission. The works were briefly resuscitated under Nelson Brothers management but then did not survive the ravages of the 1930s recession.

The Waipaoa plant is old enough to have used traditional killing methods, but sufficiently modern to be recorded as oral history. In the 1970s an early employee, Ted Stone, recalled his working life there for the *Gisborne Herald*. His memories included:

> … each man killing solo — killing, gutting, washing, everything, at two shillings and ninepence per head of stock; … two men being employed to dig a large hole each day to bury the offal; … another man working full time to scoop out fat before it reached the pipes.

He also remembered a community of about 27 company houses and whares with sleeping compartments for 200 men. As well as a store there was a company-run library available to residents for a subscription of one shilling per week.

9
DAIRY INDUSTRY

'… you led the way into what has become the mainstay of the district.'
ILLUMINATED ADDRESS TO CHEW CHONG, NEW PLYMOUTH, 1910

For an industry that was to become synonymous with co-operative organisation, the early days of dairy factories provide some of the most singular entrepreneurial tales of nineteenth-century New Zealand — none more so than the story of Chew Chong, a man with the keenest of eyes for a business opportunity.

Chew Chong left Canton (now Guangzhou) in China as a teenager to work in the European outpost of Singapore. Then, like so many successful businessmen, he tried his luck in the Victorian goldfields and for 11 years was a storekeeper in Castlemaine. Chew Chong then followed the flow of diggers to Central Otago where for a short time he exported scrap metal to China. By 1870, however, he was approaching middle age and had risen no higher than itinerant pedlar of household items and children's toys around the farms of Taranaki. It was a steady business, for the homesteads of the area were cut off from most other forms of retail activity and the tiny Chinese gentleman, replete in pigtail and coolie hat, was a very popular visitor. But for most people it would certainly not have been the foundations of fame and fortune.

On his travels Chew Chong was reminded of home by a fungus growing on tree stumps, many of which littered Taranaki following the era of bush-burning thought necessary to open up the country.

The fungus, colloquially 'Jew's ear' or 'Taranaki wool', or more formally *Auricularia polytricha*, was edible. Chew Chong did a little test marketing with the folk back in Canton. They thought it a prized foodstuff and a useful medicine. It was also said to engender a feeling of general well-being. Soon Chew Chong was exporting all he could lay his hands on. The farmers of Taranaki, many struggling just above subsistence level, were happy to oblige. Selling Taranaki wool was a double blessing.

DAIRY INDUSTRY

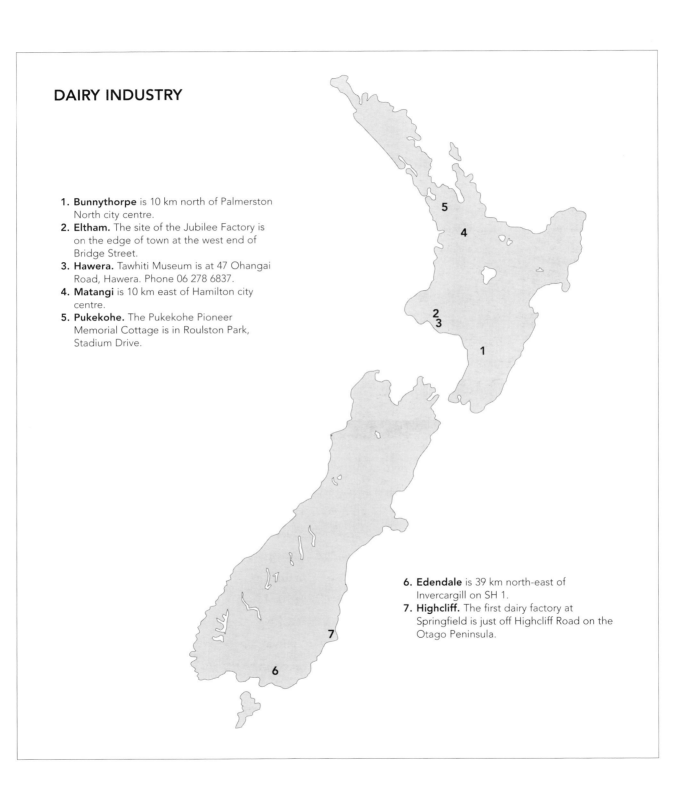

1. **Bunnythorpe** is 10 km north of Palmerston North city centre.
2. **Eltham.** The site of the Jubilee Factory is on the edge of town at the west end of Bridge Street.
3. **Hawera.** Tawhiti Museum is at 47 Ohangai Road, Hawera. Phone 06 278 6837.
4. **Matangi** is 10 km east of Hamilton city centre.
5. **Pukekohe.** The Pukekohe Pioneer Memorial Cottage is in Roulston Park, Stadium Drive.

6. **Edendale** is 39 km north-east of Invercargill on SH 1.
7. **Highcliff.** The first dairy factory at Springfield is just off Highcliff Road on the Otago Peninsula.

Chew Chong's Jubilee Dairy Factory at Eltham, 1887.

It was a rare cash crop, saleable at almost the same price per pound (in its dried form) as butter. It could also be gathered by the farmer's wife and children. In the second half of the 1870s and the early 1880s Taranaki wool was the major export of the region and the trade continued to flourish until around 1910. Even as late as 1950 isolated pockets of production existed in various New Zealand districts.

Although competition inevitably arose, Chew Chong remained pre-eminent in Taranaki's edible fungus trade for many years. By the mid-1870s he had opened a fungus store in Inglewood to augment his original shop in New Plymouth.

Later, taking advantage of the development of the railway, an improved Inglewood store was opened with all the jollity of a public dance, and premises were also established in the new settlement of Eltham where he conducted a variety of trades including those of butcher, baker, grocer and seedsman. Taranaki wool had started Chew Chong firmly on the road to a small fortune.

Other than fungus, the major farm product of the time was butter. Each farm had just a few cows and skimmed the milk manually in large flat dishes. The skim milk was usually fed to pigs while the cream was churned into butter in the farm kitchen. This was then sold to the nearest shopkeeper — if a market existed at all, which sometimes was not the case. Butter for local consumption was then wrapped in calico, or possibly dock or cabbage leaves, and often tied with flax cord. The rest was blended together in the hope of finding a wholesale outlet elsewhere in New Zealand or possibly overseas.

A major drawback for the struggling farming community was that butter often could not be sold for cash, only bartered. Chew Chong started accepting butter as well as fungus in exchange for his goods — and he paid cash for the balance, which rapidly increased his popularity. Butter from many farms was then mixed on Chew Chong's premises by a hand-operated machine not unlike a large egg whisk and transported to wherever markets could be found. Shipments to the Thames goldfield were profitable for a time. Later Chong exported butter to Australia and England. But problems inevitably arose. Using so many suppliers resulted in poor quality control and in pre-refrigeration days the packaging of butter in salt-lined kegs only heightened the problem. One consignment was described as 'cart-grease'.

With the advent of refrigerated transport, Chew Chong was one of the first off the mark, erecting a number of butter factories and skimming stations in and around Eltham. His Jubilee Factory, which separated whole milk, opened in the year of Queen Victoria's Golden Jubilee, 1887. Powered by an 8-hp undershot waterwheel at the end of a 100-m tunnel from the nearby river, it was regarded as an early model for the New Zealand dairy industry. Chew Chong was no butter expert but he was always open to new ideas and he had the sense to employ Sydney Morris, who was. New techniques pioneered at the Jubilee Factory included a rotary butter machine that churned, salted and worked the cream, and a refrigerated cool room. This effectively allowed an extension of working hours, especially on hot summer days. Chew Chong was also the first to organise a sharemilking system in Taranaki, although it had been used a few years earlier in Otago.

Soon after it opened, the Jubilee Factory received high praise for efficiency and cleanliness from the Dairy Inspectorate. At the Dunedin Exhibition in 1889/90 Chew Chong won first prize for export-quality butter. He had come a long way from his 'cart-grease' days.

Chew Chong's legacy

It is easy to overstate Chew Chong's achievements. His was not the first dairy factory in Taranaki, for instance. This honour probably goes to Peter Peterson. In the early 1880s Peterson was milking 120 cows on his property near Hawera and also purchasing milk from his neighbours. He introduced one of the first separators into the district and traded butter to Wellington and cheese to Tasmania.

Nor did Chew Chong's place in the limelight of Taranaki dairying last long. For just a short period his empire and the Crown Dairy Company dominated the local industry but from 1892 onwards many of his suppliers organised themselves into co-operatives and Chong had to close some factories, including the Jubilee Factory in 1901.

Yet Chong's achievements should satisfy the most demanding of critics of the age of Victorian entrepreneurs. He did much to develop a cash economy in the desolate economic landscape of early Taranaki; he introduced new technology; he demanded the high standards necessary to turn dairying into a true export industry. All this was a remarkable lifetime's work for a once-penniless Chinese peasant. Yet in addition he also managed to endear himself to his adopted country-folk, not least by his offer to travel the countryside during influenza epidemics with free Chinese remedies.

Chew Chong lived on until 1920. His memory can still be traced around Taranaki. Walk westwards along Bridge Street, Eltham (which has another claim to historical fame, becoming the first tar-sealed road in New Zealand, in 1906) across the railway line and just before the river a historical noticeboard marks the site of the Jubilee Factory. More substantially, Chew Chong's Eltham butchery — a late 1880s building ideally suited to its task, with high ceilings, side and ceiling ventilation and originally an open front — has been relocated to the Tawhiti Museum where it houses a detailed exhibition of his life and times.

SOUTHERN VENTURES

Highcliff, Otago Peninsula

About the time Chew Chong was first tramping his lonely path between the pioneer farms of Taranaki, a successful co-operative dairying venture was being established in a stone-built farmstead that still stands just off Highcliff Road on the Otago

Peninsula. In the winter of 1871 Scots-born John Mathieson and a few of his neighbours agreed to form a co-operative cheese-making company. Those attending the meeting applied for shares in the company and guaranteed a supply of milk. Operating from the barn and the farm kitchen, the company produced a remarkable 4500 kg of cheese in its first season. New members were attracted and although the company soon relocated, it continued in business for many years supplying the Dunedin market, or if prices there were low, the cities of Australia, especially Adelaide. Nobody grew rich from the Highcliff experiment but the co-operative principle worked well in terms of both efficiency and fair dealing and many regard it as a model for the organisation of twentieth-century dairying.

Yet the immediate future undoubtedly lay with corporate entrepreneurs. Highcliff excepted, many early attempts at co-operative dairies were unsuccessful due to both business and technical shortcomings. Co-operatives were to grab the limelight later but for the time being it often took hard-nosed entrepreneurs like

The first co-operative dairy factory, at Highcliff, Otago Peninsula.

William Davidson and Thomas Brydone of the New Zealand and Australian Land Company to harness the rapid technological change of this period — milk separators, milking machines and particularly refrigeration — to stringent management techniques.

Edendale

Even as the *Dunedin* sailed out of Port Chalmers in February 1882, Davidson and Brydone were hedging their heavy bet on the future of frozen meat with a side stake on the refrigerated transport of butter and cheese. The previous year the New Zealand Government had offered a substantial £500 reward for the first export cargo of 50 tons of cheese or 25 tons of butter. The Land Company intended to collect; a small amount of butter on board the *Dunedin* had come from its estate at Edendale, to the north-east of Invercargill.

Brydone set about organising Edendale along lines noted by Davidson when he had visited a model factory at Ingersoll, Canada. There was room for improvement. The Edendale Estate was among the poorest in the Land Company's extensive portfolio. Davidson was to marvel why his predecessors had bought it at all and bemoaned the fact that 'sacks of gold were spent on … sour land in Southland'. But eventually the estate was much improved by liberal applications of lime.

A two-storey wooden factory was erected near the Land Company's private railway siding. The concrete floor extended for about 300 mm up the walls to exclude 'unauthorised visitors in the shape of rats'. The rest of the walls were insulated. Four milking sheds, also concrete-floored and well supplied with water, were also constructed. Here the Land Company's own herd of 300 cows was milked by the women and boys from the Edendale township for payment of one penny per cow and a free bucket of milk to take home. For difficult cows the rate was doubled.

Altogether, constructing the factory was an expensive venture for the times, at a cost of £1200. However, the government reward, which was claimed in its second season, reduced the outlay substantially.

For details of the early methods of cheese-making at the factory we are indebted to a reporter from the *Southland Times* who visited Edendale in March 1882 and whose findings are summarised in *Historic Account of the Southland Dairy Co-operative*.

Milk was received from surrounding farms as well as the company's own herd. Next, it was:

weighed and tested using a lactometer in the receiving room … and then put in a tin vat big enough for the milk of up to 200 cows. It was heated in a steam-filled jacket and a Danish rennet extract added. Once curdling was completed a many-bladed knife diced the curd and a wire stirrer was used to gently agitate the mass until the required acidity was reached …. The vat could be tilted to drain off the whey, which was siphoned off to a tank to later be fed to pigs.

[After mixing with salt] the curd is placed in the cheese-vats … of novel construction. They are made of iron and are telescopic; that is, they are made of cylindrical parts, fitting into each other, and shortening as the cheese contracts under pressure.

Twenty-five cheeses at a time were then pressed longitudinally by a ratchet lever. Finally, the curing process was also automated, with cheeses being rotated in sets of 12 by use of a spindle turning a stout frame.

Edendale produced its first cheese on 18 January 1882. Although the factory was equipped from the earliest days to also produce butter, this option was initially ignored for reasons of profitability. Later, up-to-date technology was also used for butter-making.

Edendale Dairy Factory, 1895.

(MAKING NEW ZEALAND COLLECTION, ALEXANDER TURNBULL LIBRARY, NATIONAL LIBRARY OF NEW ZEALAND/TE PUNA MĀTAURANGA O AOTEAROA, 000607¼ MNZ)

For 20 years Edendale continued to develop as a model factory, always at the forefront of change. In 1892 it helped pioneer the use of Babcock testers, a vast improvement on the old lactometers. Soon the company was paying suppliers by butterfat content rather than by the gallon. The first milking machines used in New Zealand were also tried out on Edendale farms. Education was also high on the agenda. In 1895 Edendale, along with Stratford, was used as New Zealand's first dairy school. Over 100 students attended courses that lasted about a month during the 'dry' season. Many future factory managers started out at Edendale.

Davidson and Brydone seem to have intended to turn Edendale into a co-operative venture from an early date — with the Land Company benefiting from the sale of the vast estate. Brydone suggested as much to the settlers as early as 1884 but the idea fell through due to poor transport infrastructure. A decade later, however, the company no longer ran its own herds, receiving all its milk from independent suppliers. In 1903 the government bought what was left of the estate and then sold it on to individual settlers. The factory was collectively purchased in 1904 and the number of suppliers immediately doubled.

Today the Southland Dairy Co-operative operates an ultra-modern dairy complex on the site of the old Edendale factory. Little is left of its distinguished past, although there is a plaque to the memory of Thomas Brydone inscribed: 'of him it can be truly said he filled every unforgiving minute with sixty seconds worth of distance run'.

NORTHERN VENTURES

Pukekohe

A street name on the outskirts of town is all that remains of the early dairy industry in Pukekohe. The name — Factory Road — fails to specify the nature of the industry and you would certainly be hard pressed to find any physical evidence of it among the prosperous market gardens of the twenty-first century. But in many late nineteenth-century townships in the North Island the industry would have been self-evident. Dairy factories were springing up across South Auckland, Waikato, Taranaki, Manawatu, and the Tararuas. The Pukekohe factory was to have a special place in our story, however. Under the guidance of Wesley Spragg, the New Zealand

Dairy Association became a major player in the industry and then grew into the giant New Zealand Co-operative Dairy Company.

After spending time on the goldfields — in his case Thames — Spragg entered the dairy industry in Auckland around 1883/84 and organised the dairy department of the New Zealand Frozen Meat & Storage Company. The company bought and blended farm-made butter from around the Auckland region. This was then shipped in 112-pound (about 50-kg) kegs to Australia and to the many logging camps scattered around the top half of the North Island. Smaller consignments were sold locally. It was a sizeable business for the time, shipping about 300 tons of butter each year, but in common with other butter blenders, product quality was inconsistent. As we have seen there were also problems elsewhere in the company and it was soon wound up.

One supplier to the New Zealand Frozen Meat & Storage Company was Pukekohe storekeeper James Roulston, who bartered goods for butter with local farmers. Roulston's ledgers recording his transactions in the early 1880s still survive in Pukekohe's Pioneer Memorial Cottage in Roulston Park. They make an interesting study of an often cash-less society — or, more precisely, one in which pounds, shillings and pence were the acknowledged units of valuation but only rarely actually changed hands.

Roulston supplied his customers with the basics of life such as tea, textiles, spices and hardware. All were conventionally priced in currency. Payment was made in the form of supplies of butter to Roulston's store. The butter was valued according to condition and seasonal factors. For example, during October 1884 James Preston made one delivery of 14 pounds of butter valued at 10 pence per pound and four other deliveries aggregating 154 pounds of butter valued at eight pence per pound. Total value: £5-14-4. But it had been a bad budgeting month for Mr and Mrs Preston. They had purchased goods of greater value from Roulston and their total indebtedness to him increased to over £35. This process continued throughout the year, with no cash actually changing hands.

Similar monthly accounts litter the ledger. Almost all Roulston's customers were paying for their purchases solely in butter, or, occasionally in other farm produce. In 1880 John Reynolds settled his account in butter, eggs and fowls. In 1883 a Mr McCracken, who may have been down on his luck, paid in butter, 12 days labour valued at five shillings per day, roots, hay and, oddly, one payment in cash.

In terms of both quality control and industrial development the butter-barter system was a dead end. But the potential of the Pukekohe area was obvious and Spragg turned his eyes south from Auckland, determined to establish a creamery industry on the lines developing successfully elsewhere. An existing, rather ramshackle, cheese and bacon factory was purchased and converted to a milk-receiving station. The separated cream was transported to Auckland for butter manufacture.

This half measure was soon improved upon and Spragg's newly formed New Zealand Dairy Association rapidly developed the Factory Road site into a fully fledged butter factory. By 1892 the *New Zealand Farmer* was able to report that the factory was processing cream from between 250 and 300 farmers. A suitably impressed journalist wrote:

> The premises consist of a boiler room and engine room…a separating room running six large Laval separators; a cream cooling room; a refrigerating insulated compartment; a butter making room containing five churns, four round Danish and a large box churn, a butter worker, draining vats etc.

The Waikato

Over the next few decades Wesley Spragg — exemplary employer, prominent Congregational Church layman and firm temperance advocate — was to bring together many of the loose strands of the local dairy industry. In 1896 his New Zealand Dairy Association amalgamated with its arch rival, the Waikato interests of Henry Reynolds.

Henry Reynolds, a man of prodigious organisational skills and considerable vision, first made his mark as manager of the vast Piako Swamp estate. By the early 1880s Reynolds had established the Woodlands estate, praised as a model of rural self-sufficiency. The estate grazed 2300 cattle. A three-storeyed building housed a sawmill, thresher and chaff cutter, all powered by waterwheels. Woodlands was the centrepiece of social activity and Premiers and Governor-Generals were honoured guests.

In 1886 Reynolds addressed his skills to the dairy industry and built a factory at Pukekura, west of Cambridge. Initially the butter was canned, packed in boxes and transported to Auckland. Soon Reynolds was shipping butter to Australia, China,

Hong Kong and then England. In London Reynolds supervised the erection of a large cool store at Hay's Wharf on the south bank of the Thames and, being nobody's fool, organised an efficient distribution system to prevent his cheap butter being repackaged as Danish and sold at a premium price. By the early 1890s Reynolds had factories at Ngaruawahia and Newstead and a string of skimming stations as far south as northern Taranaki.

By 1896, however, Reynolds was in financial difficulties and his butter interests were taken over by Spragg's company. It might have seemed incongruous to the entrepreneurs of the time but the most significant item in the acquisition was probably just a name. 'Anchor' — variously reported to have originated from a tattoo on Reynolds's arm or one he saw on the arm of an ex-mariner — was to grow into one of New Zealand's premier international brand names.

By the turn of the century the combined organisation was producing 1200 tons of butter per annum, two-thirds of which was destined for the British market. The following year, with Spragg's encouragement, the company became a co-operative. By 1916 — by which time the Waikato interests of Ambury, English & Company had also been absorbed and Spragg had just retired as Chairman — the Pukekohe factory alone had over 1000 suppliers, a network of 31 skimming stations and produced 1309 tons of butter. The Ngaruawahia factory was of a similar size and there were also creameries at Waiuku and Frankton Junction. The dairy industry of Franklin County and the northern Waikato had come a long way since the days of farm kitchen manufacture and a barter system based on butter.

In 1923 the historic creamery in Factory Lane went the way of so many of New Zealand's industrial monuments, being burned to the ground. Its replacement, on the other side of town at Paerata, was to be part of the local scene and a major factor in one of New Zealand's premier industries for the next three generations.

Powdered milk at Bunnythorpe
Of all the goods displayed in Debenham's department store in London's Oxford Street in the early twentieth century, few would seem less likely to make the shopper's pulse race than the sight of a can of milk powder. Yet to Maurice Nathan it looked like a fortune ready for the taking.

Maurice Nathan was a London director of a Wellington import/export business started by his father, Joseph. Nathan senior, the sixth son of a poor Jewish tailor in the East End, had been exceptionally successful since leaving London as a teenager in 1853. After a brief and unprofitable spell in Melbourne, he settled in Wellington. Initially mainly an importer in partnership with Jacob Joseph, he eventually expanded into the purchase of land in Wellington's hinterland. After the full farming potential of the Manawatu was opened up by the construction of the Wellington & Manawatu Railway, Joseph Nathan became a major player in the export of butter and cheese. Nathan companies owned 17 creameries and also held shares in other dairy factories.

In common with most of the industry, the Nathan-owned dairy factories suffered from the perennial problem of disposing of surplus milk after cream had been skimmed for butter-making. If the surplus milk could be dried and exported in cans an entire new side to the dairy business would be opened up.

There had been earlier attempts at a milk-drying process but they had not been commercially successful. In early 1904 Joseph Nathan & Company purchased the Australasian rights to the new, efficient milk-drying machines developed in the United States. A small company-owned dairy factory in Makino, just north of Feilding, was converted into a milk-drying factory. Four drying machines and two boilers were bought and John Merrett, an English engineer, was employed. That year

Bunnythorpe dried milk factory, closed 1974.

Nathan's exhibited their milk powder at the Manawatu A&P Show. Then they put on a special train to take 200 farmers to inspect the drying operation at Makino in order to convince their suppliers of its viability. By the closed dairy season of the winter of 1904 they were so obviously onto a winner that the entire operation was transferred to a new, purpose-built factory at Bunnythorpe.

Powdered milk was to be manufactured on the Bunnythorpe site for the next 70 years, though the initial years were far from trouble free with two buildings being destroyed by fire in rapid succession. At around 2.30 on the morning of 4 January 1906 the two-storeyed corrugated-iron building was gutted. Months later, in the early hours of a Sunday morning, two loud explosions wrecked its replacement. Industrial sabotage was suspected but not proven in court. The current building at Bunnythorpe, which is no longer used for its original purpose, was erected in 1944.

Although Nathan's milk powder was an immediate success under the original brand name Defiance, something more consumer-friendly was thought necessary. The first idea was Lacto but, apparently, this did not appeal to the Registrar of Trademarks. By what proved to be a happy combination of Lacto and galactin, Greek for milk, the name Glaxo was born. Registered as a trademark in 1906, within a few years it was a household name for the 'Food that Builds Bonnie Babies'.

Soon Glaxo's empire expanded northwards. A factory was opened near Te Aroha, followed by others at Matamata and Matangi, just outside Hamilton, as joint ventures with the New Zealand Dairy Association. When Prime Minister Bill Massey officially opened it in November 1919 the *New Zealand Herald* reported that the Matangi factory '… is to handle the largest quantity of milk under one roof in the world. The building with employees' cottages etc cost £40,000 and the machinery £45,000.' The Matangi factory, once a world-beater and still more pleasing on the eye than most industrial buildings, survives to this day, though like so many of its kin around the country, it now enjoys an alternative use.

By the end of January 1922 the Glaxo group was producing 4318 tons of dried milk but soon the company's growth was to lie well beyond the realms of milk powder. After a number of mergers it was to become one of the most successful pharmaceutical companies in the world.

10
PUBLIC UTILITIES

ELECTRICITY

'Strange but dazzling brilliancy …'
INANGAHUA TIMES, 3 AUGUST 1888

At seven o'clock on the evening of 1 August 1888 the citizens of Reefton lined the banks of the Inangahua River to witness the future in the form of bottled sunshine.

They had initially been sold the idea of a town electricity supply by Walter Prince, electrical engineer and salesman extraordinaire. Prince, a rather shadowy figure, arrived in New Zealand in the early 1880s and was associated with ex-Premier Julius Vogel, who was hawking electrical equipment around Australasia at this time. Prince, like Vogel, was not a man to shy away from grandiose plans or grandiloquent language — hence the 'bottled sunshine', or as a variation, 'bottled lightning'. Electricity, said Prince, was 'the greatest natural force the world has ever seen, brought under man's control and made his willing vassal'. He was right — but it probably helped if other people installed it.

Prince outlined his plans at a meeting in Dawson's Hotel (since demolished) on Reefton's Broadway in December 1886. The persuasive salesman met a receptive audience, for Reefton folk were of both an entrepreneurial disposition and also in funds at this time. The Reefton Electrical Transmission of Power and Lighting Company was formed with 65 shareholders. All except Prince seem to have been local residents or business people, including hairdressers, clerks, tailors and tinsmiths. A water intake was built at Black's Point and a 1.8-km water race (including 91 m through a solid rock tunnel) was connected to the powerhouse just outside town. There a Rafel vertical turbine drove a Crompton bipolar dynamo capable of lighting 500 lamps of 20 candlepower each. The cost was £7000.

201

PUBLIC UTILITIES

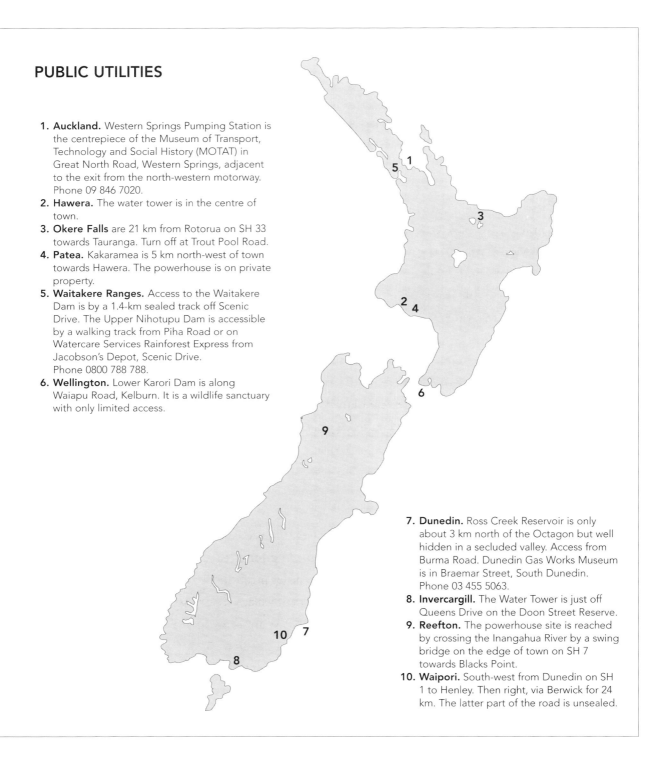

1. **Auckland.** Western Springs Pumping Station is the centrepiece of the Museum of Transport, Technology and Social History (MOTAT) in Great North Road, Western Springs, adjacent to the exit from the north-western motorway. Phone 09 846 7020.
2. **Hawera.** The water tower is in the centre of town.
3. **Okere Falls** are 21 km from Rotorua on SH 33 towards Tauranga. Turn off at Trout Pool Road.
4. **Patea.** Kakaramea is 5 km north-west of town towards Hawera. The powerhouse is on private property.
5. **Waitakere Ranges.** Access to the Waitakere Dam is by a 1.4-km sealed track off Scenic Drive. The Upper Nihotupu Dam is accessible by a walking track from Piha Road or on Watercare Services Rainforest Express from Jacobson's Depot, Scenic Drive. Phone 0800 788 788.
6. **Wellington.** Lower Karori Dam is along Waiapu Road, Kelburn. It is a wildlife sanctuary with only limited access.

7. **Dunedin.** Ross Creek Reservoir is only about 3 km north of the Octagon but well hidden in a secluded valley. Access from Burma Road. Dunedin Gas Works Museum is in Braemar Street, South Dunedin. Phone 03 455 5063.
8. **Invercargill.** The Water Tower is just off Queens Drive on the Doon Street Reserve.
9. **Reefton.** The powerhouse site is reached by crossing the Inangahua River by a swing bridge on the edge of town on SH 7 towards Blacks Point.
10. **Waipori.** South-west from Dunedin on SH 1 to Henley. Then right, via Berwick for 24 km. The latter part of the road is unsealed.

Reefton's was to be the first public power supply in New Zealand. Although electricity had certainly been used in the country previously, it was sometimes little more than a curiosity. The window of a jeweller's shop on Lambton Quay, Wellington, had been illuminated as early as 1879. A few travelling circuses used it as an added attraction. More seriously, industry had been experimenting for some time. Walter Prince had been involved in at least two such commercial developments, the lighting of Lyttelton Wharf in 1883, which had suffered from interminable insulation problems, and the hydroelectric power plant at the remote Phoenix Mine in Bullendale a few years later. Elsewhere, textile mills were also keen on the new technology. The mill at Roslyn in Dunedin had electric light by 1882, Kaiapoi by the following year and Mosgiel in 1885.

At Reefton, however, a commercial company was to illuminate most of the town. Thus Reefton was to predate some of the fashionable parts of the northern hemisphere and all the major New Zealand cities, some of which, delayed by the vested interest of gas-lighting companies, did not have an effective system until the twentieth century.

As water gushed into the turbine that evening in 1888 Reefton folk were suitably amazed. Ever the salesman, Prince had erected an arc lamp on a pole outside the powerhouse. The local newspaper reported:

> … around the station it was as bright as day … Onlookers were so unused to electric light they became confused by shadows cast from fences and vegetation mistaking shadows for objects and trying to step over them.

A few days later another demonstration was laid on at the Oddfellows Hall. Soon many of the homes and businesses of central Reefton signed up for a glimpse of the future. For £1 the local tinsmith installed the wiring, sometimes including doorbells. Then, for a fee of £3 per annum per light installed, power was available from dusk to dawn. The town's street lighting was embellished by distinctive mushroom-shaped globes.

All did not go entirely to plan, however. Prince was rather better at selling electric lighting systems than installing them and, to be fair, there were always going to be problems with untested technology in the most distant outpost of the Empire. There were many outages, especially in the part of town where cables had been laid underground to avoid the overhead telegraph wires. The subterranean wires had been placed in wooden boxes using green timber with disastrous consequences after rain. There was sufficient dissatisfaction for Prince's contract to be terminated and his shares in the company forfeited. He departed to try his powers of persuasion on the townsfolk of Auckland and Thames. Later it was found that wires of varying gauge had been used and were imperfectly insulated.

The epoch-making 1888 Reefton powerhouse has gone, but the foundations of its 1908 replacement, including the Boving turbine, remain partly intact.

Reefton's epoch-making public power supply survived these early vicissitudes and was steadily improved and gave long and productive service to the people of the town. The original turbine and dynamo were used until 1908 before being sold and shipped to Melbourne. Thereafter the system functioned effectively until after the Second World War.

Today the line of the water race can still be tracked through the undergrowth by the Inangahua River, and the concrete water intake remains visible across the river from Black's Point. The power-station site has been highlighted by the proud folk of Reefton with a Powerhouse Walk. Opened to celebrate the centenary of electricity supply in the town — when there was also a Grand Electrical Ball with the ballroom lit by magic lantern slides of the town's glory days — the walk is an excellent way to enjoy one of New Zealand's most distinguished industrial towns. Sadly, the 1888 powerhouse site has been largely obliterated but the 1908 Boving turbine is still just about intact, as are its intake and outlet tunnels.

It takes only a little imagination for visitors exploring the age of 'bottled sunshine' to visualise the wonder of the onlookers that August evening back in 1888. Then, according to the *Inangahua Times*:

> … the bright luminous rays of the arc light burst forth lighting up the whole scene with strange but dazzling brilliancy … The spectacle was weirdly beautiful.

Cities see the light

Almost immediately after Reefton's pioneering venture, Wellington empowered the Gulcher Company to illuminate parts of the city. Power from stations in Panama

Street and Manners Street first flowed in 1889 but was so unreliable that an Auckland journalist commented it was about as effective as a 'fat and healthy glow worm'. This was thought a bit rich coming from a city where municipal power generation was extraordinarily slow to take off.

Auckland had several temporary flirtations with electricity from the early 1880s onwards but they always seemed to expire under the combined weight of economic recession and the vested interest of the gas company. The city remained lit by the pale, shadowy glow of incandescent gas burners. Not until an agreement was reached in 1903 to use power generated for the tramways was Queen Street effectively lit. Other streets, such as Karangahape Road and Symonds Street, had to wait until 1910 or later. In Christchurch a protracted rear-guard action by vested interests also delayed the generation of electricity — this time from the city's rubbish dump — until 1903.

Dunedin and the Waipori powerhouse

Dunedin was also late in jumping onto the electricity bandwagon but it eventually did so in style with the municipally owned Waipori hydroelectric project which, continually developed throughout the twentieth century, was to make Dunedin largely self-sufficient in electricity for much of that time.

Yet Waipori suffered extreme birth pangs, nearly losing out to competing schemes involving cheaper, more accessible but less far-sighted powerhouse developments on the Lee Stream or the Taieri River. Indeed 500 m of a planned 2.3-km tunnel had already been dug from the Lee Stream when the City Corporation, enmeshed in engineering problems and acrimonious parliamentary legislation, switched horse-power mid-stream and bought out the private company that had been developing Waipori since 1902.

The Waipori River, which rises in the Lammerlaw Hills, drops by over 200 m over a distance of 4 km at one stage, an ideal location for a hydro station. A weir had already been built, together with a small tunnel and over 1.5 km of wooden fluming. The rest of the fluming, a penstock, 200 m of hand-riveted steel pipe, the powerhouse and 40 km of transmission line to a sub-station at Halfway Bush outside Dunedin, still awaited attention. But finishing the job at this remote site was no easy matter. For instance, it took a team of 24 horses to cart the first 10-ton generator over

Foundations of the original Waipori powerhouse.

the tortuous 38-km track from the railhead at Lawrence. When cement was hauled from Outram the ruts were so deep that the dray axles were polished to a high sheen by the clay soil.

The Waipori scheme was formally opened in April 1907, operating on two 1000-kW units. A small village sprang into existence, with barracks for the workers and cottages for more senior staff. In a whimsical moment the supervising electrical engineer, a capable and demanding American, Edgar Stark, named these Faraday House, Volta Villa and Ampere Cottage. Life on this remote wooded hillside was not without its pleasures, with a bowling green, tennis court, community hall and a heated swimming pool.

Demand for electricity was such that massive expansion was almost immediately necessary at Waipori. A tunnel replaced the fluming, a series of dams were built and the generating capacity was doubled. Within a few years two more generators were added, bringing total capacity to 6000 kW. Further developments continued throughout the century and now a series of tunnels, surge chambers and four power stations are able to produce 81 MW of electricity. Behind the modern station on the original powerhouse site a substantial concrete base is all that remains of the first building, which continued in use until the mid-1970s and was demolished soon afterwards.

Rotorua district

Elsewhere in the country, necessity could be the mother of electricity supply. When the railway reached Rotorua in 1894 there was a pleasing boom in tourist numbers — and a less exhilarating increase in sewage. At that time the town was under the control of the Lands and Survey Department and in order to pump the waste and light the city, the government made its first major foray into electricity generation and supply. Premier Richard Seddon promised the development would 'put Rotorua in a thoroughly sanitary position …' and 'make this marvellous region one of the most attractive health resorts of the world.'

In 1899 tenders were called for the construction of a powerhouse beneath the Okere Falls at the outlet from Lake Rotoiti. It was a modest affair, for a survey of local opinion had generated only lukewarm response, but construction took longer than anticipated for its foundations were almost in the river at the base of the falls. Eventually, water from a 60-m wooden flume drove two Waverley turbines linked to two 50-kW Mordey generators. On the night of Monday 20 May 1901 several of

Power station at Okere Falls.

(ROTORUA MUSEUM OF ART AND HISTORY/TE WHARE TAONGA O TE ARAWA, CP2054)

Rotorua's public buildings were lit for the first time, including the post office, the railway station and the baths and sanatorium grounds. Happily, everything had been completed for Rotorua to suitably impress its royal visitors, the future King George V and Queen Mary, a few weeks later.

Almost inevitably, this successful demonstration sparked a surge in demand and within a few years capacity at Okere Falls had to be doubled. Hotels, the lakefront parade and the meeting house at Ohinemutu were all lit. The carnival grounds and dance platform were temporarily illuminated in February 1908 and a bowling tournament was played under lights on three evenings. Later that year the elegant new bathhouse was officially opened and mains electricity became an important tool in the science of balneology — the treatment of diseases by baths or medicinal springs. Battery-powered apparatus had been used in the older Blue Baths since 1887 but now the balneologist, Arthur S. Wohlmann, could comment that Rotorua had a 'very complete installation of apparatus'.

The Okere Falls power station served Rotorua until the mid-1930s. The falls, a pleasant boat trip from the city, had always been an attraction in their own right but now the power station provided an exciting additional feature. It was finally dismantled in 1941. Today the Okere Falls still attract visitors, many rafting or canoeing a river in which the remains of the powerhouse machinery and part of the fluming are clearly visible. One of the original turbines has been salvaged and is displayed nearby.

Progress in Taranaki — Patea

It took the small South Taranaki town of Patea to lead the way in one significant aspect of electricity generation and usage. The Patea Electric Lighting Scheme was the first municipally owned and operated system in the country. It was also one of the most unusual.

About 5 km north-west of the town, at Kakaramea, a stream tumbles over the cliff face into the South Taranaki Bight. In 1899 Patea Borough Council approached R.T. Turnbull of Wellington for his expert opinion on the feasibility and cost of installing a turbine to utilise the fall of 70 feet (21 m) at a flow rate of 528 cubic feet per minute. An enthusiastic Turnbull was retained to supervise the work. After a few delays a 40-kW hydro system was commissioned, amid much fanfare, on Easter Saturday 1902.

On an unusually inclement night there were a few teething troubles and the lights flickered occasionally, causing one doubting local to reportedly comment: 'How do the fools expect lamps to stay alight in a wind like this.'

Word of Patea's success spread across the land. The Town Clerk had the satisfaction of fielding enquiries about installing similar systems from communities scattered from Mosgiel to Whangarei. No doubt the most pleasure was gained from the report published a few months later in ill-lit Auckland's *Weekly News*, under the headline PROGRESS IN TARANAKI:

> When the project of supplying Patea with electric light was first mooted it was denounced as quixotic and impracticable. But the experiment has turned out an unqualified success. There has not been a hitch, a failure, or an accident in the work from the commencement...It was commenced last March and now the light is installed in all the business premises with the exception of four. All the churches in town are fitted with it. All the hotels have adopted it and the streets are so well lighted that practically there is no night in the town.

The only snag was the proximity of the turbines to salt water and there was subsequently an explosion at the powerhouse. The present remains of the powerhouse, which are on private property, date from about 1920.

Gas works were once a feature of most major towns and cities, initially mainly for street lighting. The Dunedin Gaslight and Coke Company's works were the first in New Zealand, opening in 1863 under the management of Stephen Stamp Hutchison. Closure did not come until the late 1980s. The works are now an industrial museum. None of the original buildings, then on the original waterfront, survives, but the chimney, purifier house and parts of the main building are about a century old.

WATER

'... a riotously popular commodity.'
G.W.A. Bush, *Decently and In Order*

Watering Auckland — a perennial problem

In 1872 Auckland suffered one of its recurring water-supply problems. As usual, a period of drought was the immediate culprit. The underlying cause, of course, was that the city was rapidly outgrowing its infrastructure.

At that time the city's 13,000 inhabitants mainly received their water supply through a small-bore pipe from a spring on the Domain that is now a duck pond.

After a protracted drought this proved totally inadequate. Hawkers were selling water on the streets. The Fort Britomart cannon were fired at the clouds that gathered frustratingly over the harbour each evening, to try to encourage rainfall. As an emergency measure the City Council had to supplement its supply by purchasing water from the well at Seccombe's brewery in Khyber Pass.

Dire necessity and the availability of loan finance from Julius Vogel's expansionist budgets became happy bedfellows. After seemingly endless debate and investigation, but with the drought lingering on, land and water rights were purchased at Low and Motion's Mill at Western Springs. William Errington was employed as architect and engineer of a pumping station to lift the waters of Western Springs to newly built reservoirs in Ponsonby, Khyber Pass and eventually on top of Mount Eden. From the reservoirs water was gravity fed to the city. Errington proved to be just the man for the job. Trained as an engineer in the United Kingdom, he moved to Australia as a young man and worked on the construction of the *Lady Barkly* in Ballarat. He was then instrumental in solving the water problems of Thames' gold mines by installing and managing the town's Big Pump. Later he was also responsible for the construction of the Calliope dry dock at Devonport.

Western Springs Pumping Station, built to Errington's plan by T & S Morrin, was functioning by March 1877. Inside, one of the wonders of the Industrial Revolution, a double compound condensing steam engine, was to be Auckland's saviour for a generation and more. Manufactured by John Key & Sons of Kirkcaldy, Scotland and powered by four huge Lancashire boilers, the great beam engine was the stuff of Victorian engineering dreams: a huge, rhythmic triumph of science over nature. To many folk — usually male — there was an intense visual pleasure in the working of beam engines that was passed down to later generations tinkering with all manner of machinery in garden sheds. For such aficionados a beam engine in full throttle was something whose beauty far outweighed its utility but, for the statistically minded, in a 12-hour working day that started around four in the morning the great engine at Western Springs raised about one million gallons of water.

Almost inevitably, when Western Springs water first came on stream, rain poured on Auckland. Only a few folk paid the connection fee in the first months. Soon, however, the city's thirst was to prove almost insatiable. Output soared over tenfold in the next decade. Western Springs struggled to cope with demand and at times

Waitakere Dam under construction, 1909.

supply had to be cut off at night and the streets cleaned with salt water from the Waitemata Harbour. Consulting engineer, R.L. Mestayer, hugely experienced in Britain's water-supply industry, thought the position 'critical in the extreme … in fact on the verge of a water famine'. There was no shortage of ideas for future supply, including utilising Lake Pupuke on the North Shore by slinging a pipeline across a proposed harbour bridge. Another report recommended utilising the Waikato River — an idea that would eventually come to fruition over a century later.

Ideas and investigations were one thing, action entirely another and Aucklanders soon grew cynical about the likelihood of a satisfactory solution. Questions were also being asked about the purity of the existing water supply, with the collecting ponds being disturbingly close to refuse dumps and a night-soil disposal area. After much heart searching, and interminable reports, Auckland City decided to tap the potential of the Waitakere Ranges. Temporary wooden dams, built from heart totara, were rapidly constructed on the Nihotupu Stream and Quinn's Creek and a pipeline was slung somewhat precariously around the contours of the hillsides down to the city.

Modelled on the driving dams long in use in the kauri logging industry — without trapdoors of course — the wooden dams were up and flowing by February 1902. They were finished in the nick of time, for in the previous month Auckland had to suffer 12-hour cuts in water supply.

Work on the first of a series of permanent dams commenced in 1907. The Waitakere Plum Concrete Dam (so called because to save money 'plums' of solid rock were placed in the concrete as it was poured) was built from sand from the Kaipara Harbour, Wilson's cement, rock from a nearby quarry and the plentiful local supply of kauri for boxing timber. A 25-km pipeline fed Ponsonby reservoir near the city. Progress was painfully slow, however, due to floods and difficulty with access to the site, and the dam was not completed until December 1910. Its height was later raised by five metres to 25 m. The upper part of the narrow-gauge tramway built to service the dam site from New Zealand Railway's Swanson Station is now a scenic narrow-gauge railway.

Auckland's next excursion into dam construction was mooted almost as soon as Waitakere was complete, but the Upper Nihotupu Dam was not destined to be finished until 1923, partly due to shortages of materials and personnel during the First World War. Massively over budget, Auckland City Council eventually took over the contract from the original builder and completed the job using day labour.

At twice the height of the Waitakere Dam, the Upper Nihotupu Dam is an imposing structure readily accessible either on foot or along the tramway built for its construction. This is now used partly for recreation and partly to service the dam's pipeline, much of which is original and seemingly indestructible. En route along the tramline the regrowth bush of Quinn's Creek allows little more than speculation as to the siting of the original wooden dams that met Auckland's hour of need back in 1902. Way below, towards the Manukau Harbour, the Lower Nihotupu Dam, built in 1948, now hides another tramline once used to haul construction materials from the wharf at Big Muddy Creek to a steam winch that scaled the steep hillside to the Upper Nihotupu line. Happily, one remnant of this tramline, a tiny, five-ton Orenstein & Koppel locomotive, originally built in Berlin in 1906, is still exhibited nearby. Below the dam a large picnic area is all that is left of Seaver Camp, a work camp that became the near permanent home of many labourers as the contract dragged out. It is fittingly named after a 'camp mother' who became an institution as she laboured to feed the hungry masses and also support a family and an invalid husband down in Auckland.

As for Western Springs, regular use of the old pumping station ceased in the late 1920s and in 1936 a decision was made to dispose of the machinery. The four boilers were scrapped the following year. Only the timely intervention of enthusiasts prevented the beam engine suffering the same fate. Last to go was the pumphouse chimney — brick by brick. With building materials in short supply after the Second World War, an enterprising local resident paid £50 for the chimney. He shifted 32,000 bricks in two weeks and built his house in Massey Road, Mangere.

In 1964 the Western Springs pumphouse became the centrepiece of the Museum of Transport, Technology and Social History.

Water in other towns and cities

Many other towns and cities tackled their water-supply problems with more panache and urgency than Auckland. Usually the incentive to spend money, municipal or private, came from an explosion of population.

The laurels for the oldest water-supply dam go to the Phoenix Dam near Lawrence, built in 1863 primarily to supply desperately needed water to the nearby gold diggings but soon used for town water supply also. A few years later Wellington was booming as a consequence of becoming both the seat of government and the first port of call for many immigrants. By 1874 the Lower Karori Dam had been built, but only after compensation had been paid to several gold mines in the valley. Luckily, prospecting here had proved singularly unsuccessful so the cost was not great.

The oldest dam in the land actually constructed as a town water-supply venture is Dunedin's Ross Creek Dam, completed in 1867. In the previous decade the population of the city had exploded as a result of the gold rushes. The existing water supply was 'only fit for sewage' according to one disgruntled resident. Fire risk was also ever-present. An impoverished city council contracted out the work, though it did provide loan

Valve-tower, Ross Creek Reservoir, Dunedin.

guarantees, and it is to Ralph Donkin, engineer, and D. Proudfoot, builder, that we owe one of the country's most enduring industrial monuments. Twenty-three metres high, the dam has a puddled clay core for water retention, a form of construction that was to continue to be much used in New Zealand. At its rear a smaller dam was built to collect sediment. For a time this was removed in traditional Otago fashion by the use of a hydraulic elevator. Massive stone flood channels flank the valley sides and the original valve tower is lasting proof of Ralph Donkin's eye for elegance as well as his grasp of civil engineering. Tucked away in the hills just 3 km from the centre of Dunedin, Ross Creek still supplies water for the city as well as providing an idyllic setting for walking and jogging.

Certainly, not all towns were created equal in terms of water supply. While New Zealand's topography is such that most major centres could rely on water pumped either from natural springs or from dams in nearby ranges, for many plains-dwellers towers had to be constructed to provide an artificial head of water.

Frequently it was the threat of fire that finally pitchforked local authorities into action. Often the fires were deliberately lit. 'Bush-burn' was the accepted method of creating workable agricultural land from native forest but often raged out of control. In the drought-ridden summer of 1885/86, for instance, much of rural New Zealand seemed to be ablaze. Many farmers lost all they possessed and were thankful to escape with their lives. Townsfolk were also at grave risk. On the night of 6/7 January 1886 Stratford was a total inferno as bush fires swept irresistibly down the slopes of Mt Egmont/Taranaki.

Nearby Hawera — which translates from Maori as 'the burnt place' — seemed doomed to a succession of fires in the late nineteenth century. Yet here, as elsewhere, the town was merely hastily rebuilt after each conflagration, with little heed to the need for a water supply adequate to protect its wooden buildings. It took a further fire, in 1912, and the resultant table thumping of the insurance companies, to pressurise the council into action. The cheapest effective option was the construction of a water tower. Work started almost immediately on an impressive structure 54 m high near the town centre. By early 1914, however, there was a problem. The tower had developed a lean of three-quarters of a metre to the south and townsfolk were more than a little apprehensive. Urgent underpinning went on day and night and the tower was declared safe by examining experts. Time has proved them correct.

Invercargill solved its water-supply problem a good deal earlier than most towns and much more elegantly. Even so, its water tower was only completed in 1889 after long and tedious debate following the 1875 fire that destroyed the Albion Hotel and many other buildings. There was firm opposition to anything as utilitarian as a water tower on the city's green belt. This probably accounted for the trouble taken to make it as attractive as possible and the acceptance of an ornate design by William Sharp. It was probably his first ever commission in private practice, for Sharp had just lost his job after about a decade as an engineer with the Invercargill Public Works Department, a victim of the long recession of the 1880s. At over 42 m tall and with a water-tank capacity of 300,000 litres, the water tower fulfilled its operational requirements admirably and proved to be such an adornment to the city that it won an accolade as an 'architectural treasure' in the late twentieth century. Between times the tower had its rotting cupola removed in the 1930s but was happily recrowned in time for its centennial in 1889.

Invercargill Water Tower, elegant and functional.

11
BUILDING MATERIALS

CEMENT

> 'The Portland Cement industry … was started by men
> with small capital, large hearts and hopes, no experience,
> and little dreaming of the trials and tribulations in store …'
> T.H. WILSON

Nathaniel Wilson was a pragmatic and adaptable man but he would be amazed to see his old cement works 100 years on. In recent years the ruins by the Mahurangi River near Warkworth have at times hosted pop concerts and the occasional wedding. The towering walls of un-reinforced concrete, some now juxtaposed at improbable angles, form a distinctive backdrop for either event. In what might seem like flights of literary fancy, the cement works have even been described as New Zealand's nearest equivalent to a ruined medieval monastery or a war-ravaged castle. Yet in some ways both analogies are fitting for there is no doubt that Nathaniel fought many a battle, and doubtless said quite a few prayers, during his long struggle to establish one of New Zealand's premier industrial companies.

The main body of the cement works dates from 1903 but the industrial history of the site goes back much further. Nathaniel Wilson, born in 1836, emigrated as a child on the *Jane Gifford* in 1842. Initially his father worked in Auckland as a blacksmith with the army. Later the family moved to the copper mine on Kawau Island, which, despite the tough life of an industrial settlement, must have been an enchanting home for an adventurous boy from Glasgow. The Kawau mine proved short-lived and the family returned to Auckland where Nathaniel served his time as an apprentice shoemaker. He then took the aspiring entrepreneur's almost obligatory short-lived turn on the goldfields of Victoria.

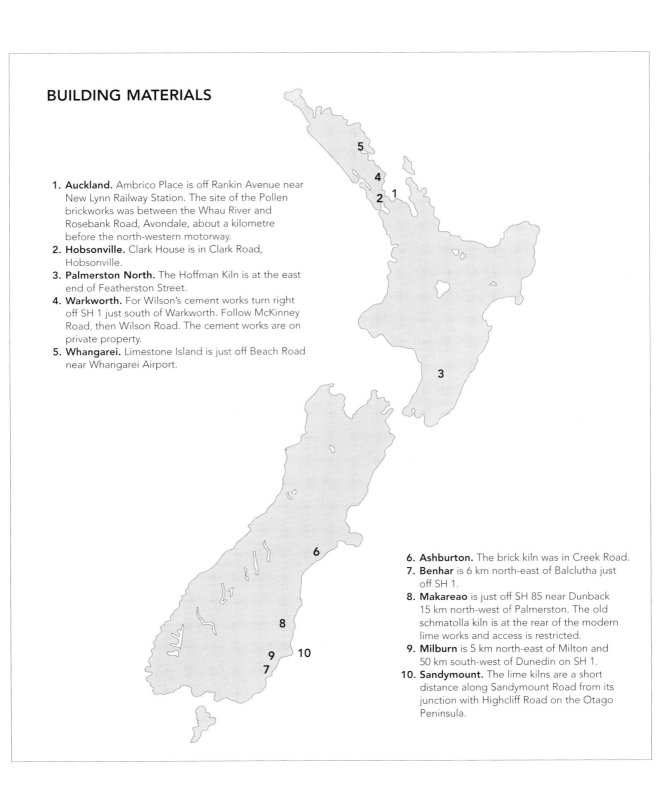

BUILDING MATERIALS

1. **Auckland.** Ambrico Place is off Rankin Avenue near New Lynn Railway Station. The site of the Pollen brickworks was between the Whau River and Rosebank Road, Avondale, about a kilometre before the north-western motorway.
2. **Hobsonville.** Clark House is in Clark Road, Hobsonville.
3. **Palmerston North.** The Hoffman Kiln is at the east end of Featherston Street.
4. **Warkworth.** For Wilson's cement works turn right off SH 1 just south of Warkworth. Follow McKinney Road, then Wilson Road. The cement works are on private property.
5. **Whangarei.** Limestone Island is just off Beach Road near Whangarei Airport.

6. **Ashburton.** The brick kiln was in Creek Road.
7. **Benhar** is 6 km north-east of Balclutha just off SH 1.
8. **Makareao** is just off SH 85 near Dunback 15 km north-west of Palmerston. The old schmatolla kiln is at the rear of the modern lime works and access is restricted.
9. **Milburn** is 5 km north-east of Milton and 50 km south-west of Dunedin on SH 1.
10. **Sandymount.** The lime kilns are a short distance along Sandymount Road from its junction with Highcliff Road on the Otago Peninsula.

By the late 1850s the family was farming just south of Warkworth next to the Mahurangi River, though father and son also kept up their respective trades. By 1866 they were also exploiting deposits of limestone in a small way for the manufacture of hydraulic lime. They probably took a lead from John Southgate who had been running a similar operation nearby since the 1850s.

Initially trade proved sporadic but the boom years of the 1870s led to several large contracts, including the Parnell railway tunnel and part of the Auckland docks. Then an unfortunate flirtation with the construction of concrete houses in Auckland in the early 1880s almost proved terminal. The problem cannot have been product quality, for at least two of the houses, in Richmond Road, Grey Lynn, are still inhabited in the early twenty-first century. Indeed the manufacture of hydraulic lime bounded ahead. By 1883 Wilson's (Nathaniel had been joined by his brothers James and John a few years previously) had 18 small kilns in constant operation, fired by coke from the Auckland Gas Company. A boiler and a single-cylinder engine, both manufactured by Fraser and Tinne of Auckland, were operating and a crushing mill had been bought from Edgar Allan & Company of England.

But technology was advancing apace and Nathaniel was not one to be left behind.

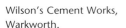

Wilson's Cement Works,
Warkworth.

(YVONNE COLES COLLECTION)

Portland cement, now popular in England, was being imported to New Zealand. Via his friend J.A. Pond, the Government Analyst, Nathaniel Wilson obtained a copy of a handbook on its manufacture and according to his son T.H. Wilson, author of the company's history, 'from the pencil marks … there is no doubt he studied it deeply'. There followed a period of intense and often disappointing experimentation, with the pestle and mortar pressed into heavy service. Perseverance was eventually rewarded and T. H. Wilson records that 'the first Portland cement made in New Zealand, in fact the first Portland cement produced in the Southern Hemisphere' was manufactured in 1884 and offered in saleable quantities in 1885.

Problems perfecting cement manufacture continued for many years, however, and the company survived on the profits that continued to flow from hydraulic lime. The necessary degree of grinding and crushing and the duration and intensity of burning varied significantly from English conditions. A good deal of time was wasted up the blind alley of adding caustic soda, which for many years was a closely guarded secret. A process of continually refilling the kilns over a number of days exuded clouds of carbonic acid gas with most unpleasant effects. T.H. Wilson recalled:

> If the men stayed in the gas too long they would get an uncommonly bad headache; in fact you would think the top of your head was being lifted off … At times they would get such a dose that they would become insensible and have to be carried out into the paddock and put in the shade where they would come around after a short time …

Thankfully, this process was later abandoned and the kilns allowed to burn out from the initial filling.

The quality of the limestone from the quarry varied alarmingly, prejudicing the reputation of the finished product. For a time Nathaniel tried to solve the problem alone, afraid of giving away trade secrets if he consulted outside experts. Eventually J.A. Pond once again came to the rescue, analysing the lime content of the local rock and providing a method of measuring it. Any shortfall in carbonate was then made up by the addition of pipi shells harvested about 5 km downriver from the cement works. Later, shells were shipped by scow from Clevedon, south of Auckland. There was also a problem with the quality of coke after the Auckland Gas Company replaced Westport coal with Newcastle coal. Briefly Wilson's manufactured its own coke on site.

For many years the company also battled consumer prejudice towards home product against that imported from the United Kingdom — a problem encountered by a wide range of local industry at this time. To an extent this was justified by the initial variable product quality. By the 1890s, however, improved quality control and a resurgent building market allowed a substantial expansion by the company. Three large kilns were built, each producing over 50 tons of cement clinker in an eight to 10-day cycle.

By the turn of the century the company was experimenting with revolutionary American technology. Limestone was now dried in a revolving cylinder, ground in tube mills and fed automatically by a screw conveyor into 18-m-long, 2-m-diameter, rotary kilns that revolved slowly in a gently inclined plane. Substantial cost savings were made and, aided by a booming market, the company bounded ahead. Production advanced from 1500 tons in 1897 to 20,000 tons in 1903. John Wilson & Company obtained a Stock Market quotation and employed 180 men. Many of the existing structures at Warkworth date from this time. With solid concrete walls standing 12 m high, it would take a lot more than the occasional pop concert to dislodge them.

The Warkworth plant eventually closed in 1928 and production was concentrated near Whangarei Harbour which offered excellent limestone, coal from the mines at Kamo and Hikurangi and deep-water port facilities. Cement had been manufactured in these parts since the late nineteenth century when the works on Limestone Island, just below the modern airport, was established. Later the Dominion Portland Cement Company started manufacturing from a first-rate facility on the mainland at Portland. Eventually a batch of amalgamations saw all production concentrated at the Portland facility that is still working to this day.

Sandymount Lime Kilns and Milburn Cement
At the other end of the country, at Fairfield near Dunedin, another Scot, James McDonald, was also making an early entry into the cement market. Like Nathaniel Wilson he too encountered early production problems. Sadly he did not survive the grim days of the late 1880s, being swamped by a tidal wave of debt in 1888. His assets were then bought by the newly incorporated Milburn Lime and Cement Company.

McDonald had also been burning lime at Sandymount, on the Otago Peninsula, for many years prior to his disastrous dabble into cement manufacture. His lime kilns there date from 1865 and are still in an excellent state of preservation. The largest kiln, a round, tapering stone tower, is set into a limestone cliff face and originally had a wooden loading platform that extended from the outcrop to the top of the kiln. The base of the tower has brick-lined fireplaces and a large opening for the removal of burnt lime. Nearby there are two smaller kilns.

Unlike the Sandymount Lime Kilns, the cement works bought by Milburn from McDonald did not last long, for the company soon moved to a more convenient site at Pelichet Bay, between Logan's Point and Ravensbourne. Initially, Pelichet Bay was a modest two-kiln operation producing about 50 tons of cement clinker per week from a plant comprising a hand-fired boiler, a steam engine and a central driving shaft that powered the various mills. Raw materials included burnt lime, harbour mud, and coke from the Dunedin gas works. For the next 40 years Milburn's Clydesdale horse-drays were an everyday sight, hauling 56-kg bags of cement through the streets of the city. In 1901 a new rotary kiln was purchased and capacity increased to between 150 and 200 tons a week. Pelichet Bay worked on until 1929 when a new plant was opened at Burnside.

Sandymount Lime Kilns, Otago Peninsula, built 1865.

Initially most of the company's burnt lime was obtained from the hills just beyond Milburn, near Milton, south-west of Dunedin, where the quarrying of lime and phosphate has continued to be a flourishing industry to this day. In 1909, however, a new source was acquired when the company bought the government's quarry and kilns at Makareao, near Dunback, about 80 km north of the city. A 22-m-high, coal gas-fired kiln was built using technology imported from Germany. This elliptical Schmatolla Kiln produced about 30 tons of burnt lime per day for about 20 years. One of New Zealand's finest industrial monuments, it still stands behind the modern limeworks.

221

BRICKS AND CERAMICS

'Thomas Henderson begs to acquaint the public of Auckland
that he can supply them with bricks of a superior quality …'
ADVERTISEMENT, *AUCKLAND HERALD*, 1 MARCH 1843

So many kilns, so few survivors. Jack Diamond, doyen of industrial historians, estimated there were over 100 brickyards in Auckland alone in the 90 years following the establishment of the city in 1840. Most, like Thomas Henderson's, were small-scale and short-lived affairs. In the early days isolated outcrops of fine-quality clay were worked with little more than a shovel, barrow, moulds and a field kiln, which was usually just an oblong stack of bricks with the spaces packed with coal or wood. The whole lot was set alight with variable results. Bricks towards the centre might be adequately fired but the quality on the extremities was not so hot. When a pocket of clay was worked out, the brickmaker left for pastures new. No wonder that when Diamond and his wife canoed their way along the inlets of the Upper Waitemata Harbour in the 1960s to conduct their pioneering survey of the archaeology of the industry, all that remained of many sites was wasteland strewn with broken bricks.

With the passage of time there is now even less to remind us of the once flourishing brick and ceramic industry, even of the larger companies. For example, George Boyd's Newton Pottery, situated in the gully by the side of Great North Road, produced an amazing variety of tiles, pipes, chimney pots, garden ornaments and domestic tableware for a quarter century from about 1860 onwards but has long since disappeared.

Dr Pollen's brickworks

Even earlier, Dr Daniel Pollen purchased land and built a brickworks out on the wastelands of the Whau Peninsula, probably in the mid-1850s. By that time Pollen had experienced the amazing variety of life on offer in colonial times. He was present at the signing of the Treaty of Waitangi, invested successfully in Auckland's early land sales, and had been the city's coroner and the medical officer to the copper-mining company on Kawau Island. Later he entered politics, holding a number of posts including Premier of New Zealand for a brief time.

Dr Pollen's brick-making foray was substantial, wide ranging (the site also included the kiln of James Wright, the potter) and long lasting (25 years or so). The good news is the site has been subject to a detailed DOC archaeological investigation so this part of New Zealand's industrial history has not been entirely lost. The bad news, however, is that much of Pollen's brickworks, in common with others, now lies under the concrete and asphalt of a heavily commercialised area. The nearby Pollen homestead, where he died in 1896, has also been demolished. Almost inevitably for one of our more forgotten forebears, even Pollen's grave is marked only by a modest headstone in Avondale's tiny, unfashionable Orchard Street cemetery.

Clark Pottery

If the area around the Whau Peninsula was to become the home of brick-making, Hobsonville at the head of the harbour became synonymous with ceramics, especially under the remarkable dynasty founded by Rice Owen Clark.

Like many an early entrepreneur, Clark experienced his full share of tribulation before making his fortune. Early Wellington was a grave disappointment to many, not least the classically educated Clark, who arrived there in 1841 and soon found that his work experience with a wine merchant and at Lloyds was totally unmarketable. After labouring as a road builder and pit-sawer, Clark then worked as a land surveyor, schoolteacher and market gardener before moving to Auckland. By 1854 Clark and his family were living on the wide open spaces of Hobsonville on the Upper Waitemata Harbour in a house roughly built from ponga logs, plastered with a mixture of cow manure and clay and lined with newspaper. Clark struggled to cultivate the heavy clay soil of his farm, for which drainage was obviously essential. He experimented making field drains by wrapping strips of pressed clay around the trunks of small trees to dry in the sun and then firing both clay and tree trunk in a white-hot open fire. The results were primitive but effective and soon Clark's well-drained market garden was showing a good return from selling produce to the hungry masses of Auckland. Clark then imported a pipe-making machine from England. An enterprise that eventually covered two acres at Limeburners' Bay, and was to be one of the premier ceramic manufacturers in the Antipodes, was under way.

Little is now left of the early industry that once cluttered the Hobsonville shoreline. The old Clark pottery has been reduced to a scattering of shards on the

Clark House, Hobsonville, distinctively built from ceramic blocks.

seashore. Further along among the mangroves and pongas there is slightly more evidence of the once-flourishing works of Joshua Carder but it adds up to only mangled metal and scattered bricks. Nearby, however, there are other reminders of a dynasty that produced, among others, Rice Owen Clark I, II and III and Thomas Edwin Clark.

Directly behind the site of the old pottery, the church largely financed by R.O. Clark I in 1875 still commemorates a man who became a cornerstone of local Protestantism. Unsurprisingly, there are brick-built tombs in the graveyard. Around the corner is the remarkable two-storey family home built in 1902 from ceramic building blocks.

Ceramic blocks, about the size of modern concrete blocks, were a technological innovation that never really got off the ground. Clark adapted one of three pipe-making machines to the manufacture of fully glazed hollow blocks with horizontal dividers to prevent dampness. Besides Clark House, a few other local buildings and Warkworth Town Hall were built using them. One modest drawback is reported to be an occasional ghostly creaking at night as the blocks cool after the heat of the day. On the other hand a benefit, at least theoretically, was that they seem to have been thought of as conduits for centrally heated air. Indeed, in the basement of Clark House there are what appear to be large ceramic central heating pipes leading into the body of the building. A tunnel then heads in the direction of the old pottery with the seeming intention of transmitting hot air to the house. Yet the tunnel soon veers away at an unpromising angle and exits after about 15 m on the face of the small hill on which Clark House is built. To add to the mystery, old folk well remember the house being dreadfully cold in winter. It is all slightly odd but looks like an experiment that failed.

In other regards Clark House is an architectural gem, for the Clark family had come a long way since its ponga-hut days. There is extensive use of cast-iron ornamentation on the verandahs, a bedroom ceiling that is a masterpiece in native timber, floors tiled in stunning geometric patterns and stained-glass doors and windows.

New Lynn brickmakers

Although the Clarks made conventional bricks as well as pipes and the ill-fated ceramic blocks, the centre of Auckland brick-making was to be increasingly concentrated around New Lynn. William Hunt, who had previously made a fortune in iron in England, took early advantage of the coming of the railways to start a yard in St George's Road in 1882. This he soon sold to fellow Methodist, flourmiller John Bycroft. Later, some of the household names of Auckland brick-making — J & J Craig, the Gardner Brothers and the redoubtable Albert Crum — dominated the local landscape. Yet bricks always appeared to be the poor relation of the Auckland building trade and slowly but surely a process of amalgamation and then closure eliminated the local industry. Now just about all that remains of the once-proud industry is an old kiln preserved slightly incongruously on Ambrico Reserve in the midst of a spanking new townhouse development. Nearby, in New Lynn town centre, there is a monument to the proud history of the local industry built from local bricks of various vintages, each stamped proudly with the maker's name — Archibald, Glenburn, the New Zealand Brick Company, Carder Brothers, J & J Craig, Crum, Hunt and many others. It adds up to an impressive list totalling 44 major sites.

Hoffman kilns

It took Friedrick Hoffman of Germany to bring a degree of permanence to the structures of the brick-making industry. Until around 1858, when Hoffman invented the kiln that bears his name, brick-making was a haphazard activity in small-scale, single-chamber kilns that were fired, cooled and emptied — and then the whole process started again. Hoffman kilns allowed simultaneous firing and cooling. Kilns now multiplied in size and lasted for generations.

Hoffman kilns, or a variant, became common in many New Zealand towns. For example, Ashburton gloried in a fine circular Hoffman for many years. With each chamber firing around 5000 bricks, the kiln produced over a million bricks per year and supplied the fabric of many of the schools, churches and homes of the town. In reality the kiln's 12 chambers were entrances to a common circular tunnel. Fuelled from above, 11 chambers could be fired while the twelfth was being emptied and refilled. Such continuous firing demanded three shifts of stokers. It is said that the kiln fire once burned continuously for 13 years.

Built around 1880, the kiln was worked by Albert Crum for a decade from 1895 until he departed northwards to fire up the Auckland brick trade. The kiln then passed into the hands of his brothers and remained a family business until closure through want of suitable clay, in 1978. Like many industrial monuments, it then lingered awhile, with the forces of nostalgia and economics pulling vigorously in opposing directions. It was eventually demolished in 1988 and the site is now zoned residential.

The Hoffman kiln at Palmerston North is one of the unsung glories of New Zealand's industrial heritage. With 14 chambers in oblong rather than circular formation, it was probably built in 1904 by Robert Price Edwards. It is a substantial facility with a theoretical total capacity of about 140,000 bricks per fortnight. In reality output was usually less than this. In any case it was always the quality of production rather than quantity that was important in brick-making, as Albert Crum was often at pains to point out to his competitors.

All went well with the kiln on Featherston Street until the quality of the clay from

Crum's Hoffman kiln, Ashburton, served the town for a century but was demolished in 1988.

(ASHBURTON MUSEUM)

the back section started to deteriorate in the 1940s. Then clay had to be shipped in, eventually from as far away as Plimmerton. Later the demand for red bricks fell away in the face of competition from Huntly. The last firing was in 1960. Since then Palmerston North's Hoffman kiln has survived only precariously.

Benhar

The pottery at Benhar straddled a curve in the South Island Main Trunk line for most of the twentieth century — pipe works and Hoffman kiln on one side, ceramic factory on the other. As the southern express slowed to take the bend, passengers were reminded of their intimate familiarity with the works of Peter McSkimming and his family, manufacturers of a popular line in sanitary ware.

Peter McSkimming's move from Glasgow to Otago in 1878 has the familiar ring of a wannabe gold miner turned entrepreneur. Almost inevitably his years in Lawrence and Waitahuna were unfruitful and he was soon working in John Nelson's brick and pipe-making works and coal mine at Benhar, a few kilometres from Balclutha. By 1894 the family had bought the works. Just after the turn of the century they made the timely and profitable decision to diversify into sanitary ware and the

Hoffman kiln, Benhar, survivor of the disastrous 1990 fire at the famous ceramic works.

227

company township of Benhar was developed on the hillside under the stern, paternalistic, god-fearing eye of Peter McSkimming. Even today his memory lingers on in local folklore with stories of compulsory church attendance and workers fined if caught smoking but, conversely, £5 notes being left in newborn babies' cribs.

As the company grew, three elegant coal-fired bottle kilns dominated the ceramic works for many years, only to be later replaced by a modern LPG tunnel kiln. The works continued to trade profitably until the fateful night in February 1990 when it was substantially gutted by fire, leaving only the company office, part of a warehouse and the Hoffman kiln unscathed. Indeed, the Hoffman remains in excellent condition, partly through lack of use over the years. Long-time employees recall it being utilised only as a store and boiler room throughout their careers. The strongly held belief locally is that the necessity to run a Hoffman on a continuing basis conflicted with McSkimming's strict Sabbatarian beliefs — and for once profit lost out to principle.

The one-time company village of Benhar now happily denies the norms of ghost-town New Zealand. Far from plunging into terminal decline with the closure of the pottery, the village thrives as a pleasant, inexpensive dormitory to nearby Balclutha. On top of the hill Lesmahagow, built by the McSkimmings, also flourishes as a family home and luxurious B & B. Brick-built with extensive ornamentation and gardens sheltered by brick pergolas, it is a fine memorial to a remarkable family.

12
SOME OTHER INDUSTRIES
— ENGINEERING, MINING, GUM DIGGING

ENGINEERING

'Their place was not amongst the ledgers.'
C.W. VENNELL, *MEN OF METAL*

From the earliest days New Zealand's industrial expansion crucially depended on the import of capital goods and technical know-how from 'Home'. Increasingly, however, a diverse and effective domestic support mechanism emerged, ranging from the humble blacksmith to substantial engineering companies.

In Auckland Fraser and Tinne, who would have a go at most things, had extensive engineering works on Stanley Street. Down in Christchurch Andersons started small but eventually concentrated on large contracts such as railway viaducts, gold dredges and coastal steamers. Henry Ely Shacklock, ironfounder of Dunedin, became a household name when he specialised in a kitchen range, the Orion, specially adapted to New Zealand conditions. His original factory has gone but a stone-built store on Princes Street is still standing. Charles Judd established his Thames foundry very soon after the town was founded and his company went on to make equipment for the gold and timber industries for several generations. Based in Napier, Nivens made their name erecting freezing works and installing refrigeration equipment. On the West Coast, Davidson's Hokitika foundry became famous for its log-haulers while the Dispatch Foundry in Greymouth — which still stands, though substantially modified — had a go at making or servicing most items for the gold and timber industries, including bush locomotives.

OTHER INDUSTRIES

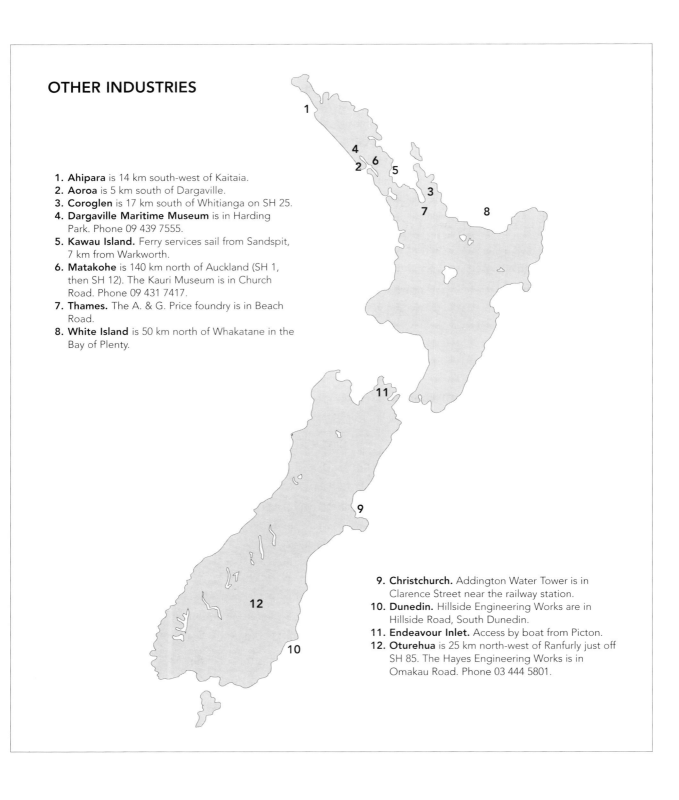

1. **Ahipara** is 14 km south-west of Kaitaia.
2. **Aoroa** is 5 km south of Dargaville.
3. **Coroglen** is 17 km south of Whitianga on SH 25.
4. **Dargaville Maritime Museum** is in Harding Park. Phone 09 439 7555.
5. **Kawau Island.** Ferry services sail from Sandspit, 7 km from Warkworth.
6. **Matakohe** is 140 km north of Auckland (SH 1, then SH 12). The Kauri Museum is in Church Road. Phone 09 431 7417.
7. **Thames.** The A. & G. Price foundry is in Beach Road.
8. **White Island** is 50 km north of Whakatane in the Bay of Plenty.

9. **Christchurch.** Addington Water Tower is in Clarence Street near the railway station.
10. **Dunedin.** Hillside Engineering Works are in Hillside Road, South Dunedin.
11. **Endeavour Inlet.** Access by boat from Picton.
12. **Oturehua** is 25 km north-west of Ranfurly just off SH 85. The Hayes Engineering Works is in Omakau Road. Phone 03 444 5801.

With the rapid growth of the rail network in the 1870s railway workshops were established in many centres, including Auckland, Wanganui and Petone. In Addington, Christchurch, the site of the former workshops is marked by a ferro-concrete water tower erected in 1883. It was built by prison labour on soft ground, and its designer, Peter Ellis, had the harrowing task of allowing for settlement — which duly took place as planned. The most famous workshops of all are Hillside, Dunedin. Originally just a repair works, locomotive manufacture began in 1897. Over the next 70 years 190 were built.

This is only part of a mighty list that bears witness to Kiwi ingenuity and commitment at its finest. But to get the full flavour of the 'can-do' nature of the industry, we cannot do better than look in detail at two prime examples, A & G Price and the Hayes Engineering Works.

The 22-m water tower at the site of the Addington railway workshops, Christchurch.

A. & G. Price

If a tapestry were to be woven to illustrate the saga of New Zealand industry over the past century and a half, images of the products of A. & G. Price would be dotted all over it. The manufactures of this most adaptable and enduring of engineering companies found their way to the furthest corners of the country — in flax mills, in stamper batteries, on railway tracks, in the depth of the forests and on coastal steamers. The word ubiquitous might well have been coined with the firm of A. & G. Price in mind.

Alfred and George Price had all the attributes of successful nineteenth-century industrialists. Inventive and hard-working, they also had keen eyes for new developments and the good fortune, or good judgement, to be in the right place at the right time. Onehunga and Thames in the late nineteenth century presented a succession of heaven-sent opportunities for such industrious, adaptable engineers.

Emigrants from England's West Country, the Price brothers first struck pay-dirt in the usually stony ground of the flax industry. Money was to be made by the first manufacturers of a successful flax-stripping machine — especially if their invention coincided with one of the brief boom times of the industry. Working from a shed and a stable in Onehunga in the late 1860s, Alfred and George did exactly that.

231

Simultaneously, gold was discovered in Thames and A. & G. Price built a foundry on the waterfront close by some of the country's richest mines. Soon the Prices had a booming business in the sale of stamper batteries and ancillary equipment. Although subsequently expanded and modernised, their premises at the north end of town are still on the same site today.

Meanwhile, back in Onehunga, yet another door opened when the railway line was extended from Auckland into the Waikato in the 1870s. A. & G. Price stepped once more into unknown engineering territory and manufactured the required rolling stock. The successful delivery of 10 carriages and 12 wagons marked the beginning of an association with rail transport that was to be the backbone of the company. A. & G. Price were to build and overhaul hundreds of locomotives for New Zealand Railways and private enterprises over the years.

From the mid-1870s work concentrated at Thames, though all was not plain sailing. Good business was to be had as new mines opened, or as existing ones were deepened and required huge boilers and other equipment for pumping operations. However, sudden closures could leave behind mountains of bad debts. Yet, just occasionally, a mine closure could be turned to advantage. In 1883 the Prince Imperial Mine was wound up and A. & G. Price bid £250 for the company at public auction, mainly in order to secure its machinery. Almost incidentally they had also acquired its mining rights and were persuaded to reopen the mine as the New Prince Imperial. The new company struck rich quartz almost immediately. After 12 months under new ownership the mine had yielded nearly 40 per cent of the Thames field's output for that year. The prescient — or lucky — proprietors enjoyed a huge dividend.

Such a bonanza might well have distracted lesser men but the Price brothers lived and breathed the challenge of practical engineering. 'Their place was not amongst the ledgers', wrote the company's historian, C.W. Vennell. These they left in the capable hands of John Watson, who had emigrated with Alfred Price aboard the *Green Jacket* in 1863. So, as the century wore on the brothers continued to get their hands dirty, solving a multitude of mechanical problems on the Thames and the Ohinemuri goldfields: the huge water pumps that dominated the Thames field; the massive, but fruitless, mine and battery at Waiorongomai near Te Aroha; the eminently successful Waihi Gold Mining Company; and the succession of battery sites that string along the Karangahake Gorge — the Crown, the Woodstock and the Talisman.

Then there was timber. Again it may have been good fortune, or possibly foresight, that led to the brothers relocating their business to the midst of a major kauri-milling region, but they once more grasped the opportunity with skill and enthusiasm. A. & G. Price probably produced their first timber jack in the early 1870s, refining a centuries-old English design to give maximum power with minimum weight. Over the next century over 25,000 Price timber jacks found their way to every nook and cranny of New Zealand forest. Inexpensive, at £6-10-0 to £9-10-0 each, they were the minimum requirement for shifting logs over short distances. Further work was forthcoming from the timber trade in the manufacture of waterwheels and pelton wheels, a Price speciality.

As the nineteenth century progressed machinery built by the Price brothers was also installed by many other industries. A survey of the company's accounts reveals a vast variety of clients. Work was undertaken on castings for the Chelsea Sugar Refinery; winding gear for the Huntly coal mines; additional engine, boiler and pumping gear for the Western Springs Pumping Station; the engine and rag boiler for the paper mill at Riverhead, and many more companies.

It follows that the contribution of A. & G. Price to the industrial heritage of New Zealand cannot be found in the busy factory on the outskirts of Thames. It is scattered across the land. Out in the bush rusting boilers are likely to display the nameplate of A. & G. Price. Price railway engines and bush lokeys can be found in many of our heritage rail centres. The timber museums at Matakohe and Putaruru have fine examples of the ubiquitous timber jack and other products. It adds up to an almost endless and proud heritage.

Hayes Engineering Works

It is a long way from A. & G. Price of Thames to the Hayes Engineering Works of Oturehua, Central Otago, both in space and time. Little has outwardly changed at the Hayes Works. Firmly embedded in early twentieth-century rural New Zealand, they seem shrouded in an enchanted time warp.

Ernest Hayes was a brilliant, intuitive engineer whose name, like A. & G. Price, lives on to the present day. Unlike A. & G. Price, however, the Hayes business relocated to a major city, Christchurch, half a century ago, leaving behind an engineering complex that had changed little since Ernest's day — and he retired in 1926. By then

233

The Hayes Engineering Works, near Oturehua, Otago.

he had followed a path of empirical engineering outstanding in its originality, even by Kiwi standards. In a land where most things were fixed by the enterprising use of a piece of number 8 fencing wire, Hayes was a champion.

Ernest Hayes emigrated from Warwickshire in 1882 and for many years ran a flour mill and a farm at Oturehua, then known as Rough Ridge. Around 1895 he invented a small apparatus for slicing strips of pollard, a bran-based rabbit poison. Initially he made these devices by hand but when demand took off he mechanised the operation by way of a hand-operated lathe made from a gatepost and a chaff-cutter wheel. His wife Hannah provided the sales force as she cycled energetically around the farms of Central Otago and South Canterbury. Over the next three decades the engineering genius of Ernest Hayes manifested itself in an amazing variety of other products. These included cart jacks, wire coilers, windmills with Hayes patent revolving towers for farm water supply, pulley blocks, cattle stops, gate fasteners, portable rabbit smokers and the most famous of all, a parallel wire strainer for farm fences, a device that gained lasting renown throughout New Zealand and overseas.

The arrival of the railway at the turn of the century led to the closure of the flour mill in Oturehua, with grain being transported to Dunedin for processing. Hayes then concentrated on his engineering business. A stone workshop was erected in 1902 and was extended using sun-dried bricks a few years later. An office and stables quickly followed. These buildings all survive to this day, as does the earlier Hayes homestead.

Perhaps most intriguing of all is the original power-supply system. In 1910 Hayes built a 12-m-high windmill that totally dominated both the works and the valley. It provided power throughout the works via a series of overhead pulleys and belts that would have been familiar to Hayes from his flour-milling days. The transmission system is still in working order, powering machine tools that also bear the stamp of Hayes' original turn of mind. The conducted tour of the works these days gives a glimpse of a treasure trove of engineering ingenuity sufficient to keep the average enthusiast intrigued and contented for hours.

The wind of Central Otago is a variable commodity, however, and the mill was replaced in 1927 by a pelton wheel, driven by a race from a dam on the hill. Only the base of the old windmill now exists but the pelton wheel can still be operated. The first of the company's farm water-pump windmills has been returned and stands proudly in the middle of a works that make a fitting memorial to both Ernest Hayes and thousands of other, unheralded, intuitive Kiwi engineers.

OTHER MINING

'In a cavern, in a canyon, excavating for a mine …'
PERCY MONTROSE

Copper on Kawau

New Zealand's mining heritage often comes wonderfully packaged. Nature has been generous in compensating the most hazardous of industries with spectacular locations. Waiuta on a clear spring day sparkles in a bowl of the Southern Alps. The view from Denniston — when available — goes on for ever. The rugged mining townships of Central Otago, such as Macetown or Bullendale, knew nature at its most awesome and challenging.

235

Nowhere is as lovely as Kawau Island. To sail from Sandspit down the Matakana estuary can be a dreamtime experience. Disembark at Mansion House, the former home of Sir George Grey, at times both Governor and Premier of New Zealand, and the fairytale aura of Kawau is confirmed. The house is elegant and the garden rejoices in Phoenix palm, Moreton Bay fig, and bunya bunya pine. A peacock even struts its stuff for visitors.

Europeans first came to Kawau in the early 1840s, intent on serious mining, not leisure. Mansion House was originally a mine manager's house, pleasant enough for its time with a total of 10 rooms. With the aid of the foremost architect of the day, Frederick Thatcher, Grey, who bought the island in 1862, transformed it into a small palace by the addition of another 20 rooms and acres of kauri panelling.

Pumphouse, Kawau Island.

The mine itself lies a half-hour walk through the pines and redwoods at the rear of the house. The first shaft was sunk in to extract manganese for export but almost immediately a rich seam of copper was unearthed. This was mined from shafts on the hillside above Dispute Cove. These were then linked by horizontal tunnels at various levels. The ore was carted in manually operated trucks and then hauled to the surface by horse-operated windlasses. It became a sizeable operation — the biggest-ever copper mine in New Zealand.

With much of the mine workings below sea level, a pumphouse was erected around 1847. Then, with the ore proving impractical to transport in an untreated state, a smelter was erected in a nearby bay. Soon several hundred Cornish miners and Welsh smelters had settled into a small community.

Flooding was always a problem, however, and seems to have been compounded by the operations of a rival mining company run by Auckland entrepreneurs Frederick Whitaker and Theophilus Heale. The Kawau Company had the rights to mine the island but the interlopers secured rights to the adjacent seabed. The story has grown a little murky over the years but it seems that the new workings allowed the sea into the existing mine. It is also evident that much of the most productive lode had already been extracted and subsequent attempts to reopen the mine proved fruitless.

These days there is still plenty to remind day-trippers of Kawau's early mining history. Copper ore litters the beach around the Kawau mine. The old adits in the cliff face are stained a dramatic turquoise. An abandoned boiler lies on the shore beneath the old scene-stealing pumphouse. The soft Mahurangi sandstone used in this building has eroded extensively over the years, though the bricks of the chimney have fared slightly better. Ongoing care is a necessity to stabilise one of our more picturesque industrial monuments.

Sulphur on White Island

If Kawau has a hint of fairyland, White Island must be halfway to Hades. Indeed, it has been described as desolate and god-forsaken, but also awe-inspiring.

White Island is an active volcano in the middle of the Bay of Plenty, part of the same geological structure as the great mountains of the central North Island. It often emits plumes of threatening smoke and occasionally erupts. White Island's horse-shoe crater is over a kilometre long with fumaroles along the western edge that give temperature readings up to 900 degrees Celsius and are subject to bouts of elemental explosion. Some have been given names such as 'Noisy Nellie', 'Big Donald' and 'Schubert's Fairy'. One visitor described them as the equivalent of 40,000 boilers blowing off steam simultaneously. Tantalisingly, White Island also has remarkable concentrations of workable sulphur.

Although Cook named it, the intrepid missionaries Henry and William Williams were the first Europeans to set foot on the island in 1826. From the 1840s onwards there are vague stories of piecemeal sulphur mining. The first systematic exploitation was not until the years after 1885, however, when 5000 tons were mined and a small sulphuric-acid plant set up in Tauranga. This operation soon folded and not until 1913 were there further serious mining forays. It was then suggested that 40,000 tons of pure sulphur were there for the taking plus large deposits of fertiliser. Buildings were erected and refining equipment operated successfully for a short time.

Then on the night of Thursday, 10 September 1914, an eruption precipitated a mud and sulphur flow that swept all before it from the crater to the sea. It took some time for the news of the disaster to reach the outside world. Not until Monday, 14 September, did the *Auckland Star* report:

The place is devastated. The whole side of the hill has fallen into the crater, fresh holes are numerous, and the area on the island known as 'the flat', on which [the] men resided, is now buried under 20 feet of debris. It is feared that all the residents of the island have been buried alive. Sergeant Ferguson of Opotiki visited the island yesterday. He stated that the living quarters are buried, that the surf boats have been smashed, and that there is no hope that anyone has escaped.

Eleven men died.

Despite the lessons of this tragedy, further sulphur mining was attempted in the late 1920s and early 1930s. The company went into liquidation in 1934. In total around 10,000 tons of sulphur are estimated to have been mined over the years.

Antimony at Endeavour Inlet

Mining at Endeavour Inlet in Queen Charlotte Sound encapsulated much that was characteristic of extractive industries in nineteenth-century New Zealand. Various ventures spluttered briefly into life and then expired just as swiftly. Distance from the primary market, Britain, proved to be a continuing hindrance. Revenues were always at the mercy of wildly fluctuating world prices. Quality of ore proved distressingly variable. Technologically, a great deal of Kiwi ingenuity was expended on new smelting techniques that were ultimately found wanting. A small, tight-knit community was established and, indeed, thrived for a time in a remote yet beautiful corner of the country but soon completely disappeared.

After all this endeavour — the place was well named — none of the various venturers ever made a decent return on their investment. The workforce scraped a hand-to-mouth existence in conditions often hazardous to health. And one man wasted so much of himself financially and emotionally at Endeavour Inlet that he met the most tragic of ends.

The story of mining here is told by the historian of Marlborough mining, Mike Johnston, in *Gold in a Tin Dish* (1993). Stibnite, the sulphide of antimony, was first discovered in these parts in the early 1870s. The soft grey-blue metal had been useful as a cosmetic as far back as Biblical times but by the nineteenth century it was mainly used in the manufacture of pewter, printing type and gunmetal. The world market for the metal was small and prices often waxed and waned alarmingly. But prospects at Endeavour Inlet looked good. The initial outcrop of ore, in a landslide only a few kilometres from the sea, appeared to be of a gratifyingly high grade. If mining coincided with a price boom, an excellent return would surely result.

An initial attempt at exploiting the ore body was established in 1874 but failed because of problems at the smelting stage. In the mid-1880s, however, prices went through the roof and a new mining syndicate was formed that soon floated off the Endeavour Inlet Antimony Company with Jaketh Wearne as mine manager.

Wearne left his native Cornwall in 1859 as a young man bound for the Victoria goldfields. He then continued down the well-worn path to Central Otago, the West Coast and Reefton. Then he ran two small mines in Wellington and Nelson. The job at Endeavour Inlet must have seemed like a godsend, for Wearne's employers were well capitalised and had ambitious plans. Skilled workmen were recruited from Britain. A three-storey dressing shed was constructed to sift, sort and pulverise the ore. Nearby, a 25-m-long smelting works had three furnaces that concentrated the antimony content of the ore from around 50 per cent to as much as 99 per cent. A decent-sized community, housed in modest but respectable company housing, grew up on the flat near the inlet. A school was started and a post office established.

Sadly, during the time-lag between first committing the capital expenditure and reaping the hoped-for reward, the price of antimony collapsed. Some high-grade product was exported but in 1887 the company had to be refinanced by London investors. Luckily Jaketh Wearne kept his job.

More money was poured into the mining and smelting complex, increasing capacity to 900 tons per annum and the workforce to 75. But the new company had the recurring problem of liquid antimony attacking the fabric of the furnaces and with the variable quality of the ore, and in 1892 it went into liquidation. The Star Antimony Company was formed in its stead: manager, Jaketh Wearne. Antimony prices remained low, however, and two further attempts at constructing a durable furnace failed. By the turn of the century Endeavour Inlet was deserted.

Inevitably, prices rose again a few years later and equally inevitably Jaketh Wearne returned to Endeavour Inlet, backed by Wellington money. Prices then crashed once more and this small-scale venture collapsed. On 16 July 1907 Jaketh Wearne killed himself by taking hydrochloric acid.

KAURI GUM

*'… hopeless … the deuced stuff is not worth half
or even a quarter freight home.'*
JOHN LOGAN CAMPBELL, 1846

One of history's curiosities is that when Lieutenant James Cook circumnavigated New Zealand in 1769 in the company of two fine naturalists scant attention seems to have been paid to the giant kauri trees that covered large parts of the top half of the North Island. However, while in Mercury Bay he did note the existence of small lumps of kauri gum, first on the beach and then sticking to the mangroves 'and by that means found from whence it came'.

Just what to do with the extruded, hardened resin of the kauri tree continued to puzzle the early settlers. Some used it to light fires. Enterprising John Logan Campbell was at first convinced it must be good for something and chanced his arm with a consignment to the London market along with a cargo of spars from the Kaipara Harbour. His partner, William Brown, accompanied the cargo and hawked it hopefully around manufacturers of sealing wax, candles and marine glue. But in London and elsewhere there was little enthusiasm for kauri gum in the 1840s and generally Brown & Campbell had difficulty recouping the £5 per ton paid to Maori collectors, never mind the freight costs.

From mid-century onwards, however, kauri gum was in increasing demand for the manufacture of varnish and developed into a major industry. Gum was to hold first or second place among Auckland's exports in most years up to the First World War. Total annual quantities exported commonly averaged about 9000 tons. The larger merchant houses — Nathans, Mitchelson, Dargaville and Brown & Campbell — grew rich from a trade that surpassed gold in importance for the local economy. Thereafter trade inevitably declined as the resource was depleted and synthetics entered the market, but modest quantities were still being exported a generation later.

Initially it was easy pickings — surface gum being harvested by Maori and sold to European merchants. As demand increased subterranean deposits from long departed kauri forests were exploited by means of long spears and spades. Gumfields became a distinct feature of the landscape. Initially they were located relatively close to the Auckland market, around Papakura and Riverhead, for instance. Soon the Northern Wairoa was heavily involved the trade, as were areas of the Coromandel Peninsula, the Hokianga and the Far North.

The larger nuggets of gum were relatively easily located by individual diggers but eventually a degree of organisation and co-operation entered the industry. Gum was dug from long trenches by teams of horny-handed spade-men, particularly new emigrant Dalmatians. Dubbed 'Austrians', they were generally tough, hard working and law abiding but were nevertheless often treated with a degree of disdain by the locals, not wholly dissimilar to the attitude towards the Chinese on the goldfields.

By the end of the nineteenth century there were perhaps 8000 men in the industry. Many were full-time gum diggers living in primitive bush camps, often alone but occasionally persuading their wives to share their rough homes. In treeless areas sack and sod shanties were commonplace, while in wooded areas ponga logs and nikau fronds were put to good use. Others drifted in and out of the business as mood or economic necessity dictated. In the Northern Wairoa the cash for farm improvements often came from occasional forays into gum digging. There was even an urban trade for a time. Gum diggers once travelled daily on the ferries from Auckland to the North Shore to harvest the gum of the kauri forests that had covered much of Northcote, Birkenhead and East Coast Bays.

Little remains of the once extensive kauri-gum industry except an excellent photographic record, such as this one taken by the Northwood Brothers at Sweetwater in the Far North.

(NORTHWOOD COLLECTION, ALEXANDER TURNBULL LIBRARY, NATIONAL LIBRARY OF NEW ZEALAND/TE PUNA MĀTAURANGA O AOTEAROA, 051975^1/2)

241

Altogether kauri gum added up to a substantial industry but it is one that has left nary a trace of its being to the naked eye. This partly reflects the fact that much kauri gum land lay on rich alluvial plains. The diggers performed a useful service draining swamps and removing tree stumps from what is now some of our best farmland. Moreover, relatively little machinery was used in the early days. Later, small nuggets previously thought uneconomic came into play after demand increased for the manufacture of linoleum. Then machines were developed to wash and grade tiny morsels of gum. Initially these were simple hand-operated machines not unlike a butter churn. Later large oil-driven machines with a series of filters and screens and operated by several men were in common use. A few have survived, including one powered by a 1914 Blackstone oil engine that has recently been housed in the Dargaville Maritime Museum. In a few outlying areas the sites of gum-digger's camps can occasionally be recognised from traces of human habitation. Many were listed in a survey of the industry conducted by John Coster and Gabrielle Johnston in 1980.

The camps were rarely far from a settlement of sorts that provided at least a trading post, hotel and store. Sadly, many of these are now little more than names on the map. For instance, Coroglen is now just a pub, a community hall and stockyards that have seen better days, at the junction of State Highway 25 and the old Tapu road on the Coromandel Peninsula. Prior to its name change in 1922, however, Gumtown was the service centre for numerous bush camps that rejoiced in names such as Rat Camp, Welcome Jack and, somewhat despairingly, No Gum and Starvation Camp. For a time Gumtown, also a major logging centre, was the largest population centre on the peninsula north of Thames and briefly boasted a truly impressive hotel and its own race meeting.

Communications were terrible, however, with everything being transported by packhorse or downriver to Mercury Bay by boat, particularly the coal-fired *Little George.* Today communications could not be better as holiday-makers speed frantically between the holiday resorts of Whitianga and Tairua. Northland is littered with former gum towns. Ahipara, south-west of Kaitaia, is said to have once had a local population of around 1000. Aoroa supported an estimated 300 diggers and Red Hill had shops, a school and a hall back in its glory days.

13
A MISCELLANY OF INDUSTRIAL SITES

LYTTELTON TIMEBALL STATION

Lyttelton's Timeball Station perches high on a hillside like a miniature castle on the Rhine. When today's luxury liners arrive in port it must look a little incongruous — a tower and battlements set immediately above one of New Zealand's busiest container terminals.

Yet the Timeball Station, built in 1876, was a strictly functional building, part of the ingenious solution to an age-old problem of the sea, the calculation of longitude. The fixing of latitude was relatively easily solved, first by use of a cross-staff and then by a sextant. But not until the dogged English clockmaker John Harrison dedicated his life to perfecting a reliable chronometer could a ship's captain accurately measure longitude and thus firmly fix the ship's position. From the time of Cook's second voyage to the Pacific navigation had been revolutionised by the ingenuity of John Harrison.

Yet a practical problem still remained. Chronometers developed errors on ocean voyages and had to be checked against exact Greenwich time. To this end a series of Timeball mechanisms were erected worldwide. The first was at Greenwich in 1833. Within a few decades there was one in each of New Zealand's major ports. Mainly they were placed on top of existing port or government buildings — but the proud folk of Canterbury did things in style and engaged Thomas Cane to design and William Brassington to build Lyttelton's enduring edifice. They did a fine job, only to be let down by the quality of the local scoria which was found to be far from damp-proof, a serious problem because the Timeball Station was a family home as well as an overgrown timepiece. So, within a few years the outside walls were encased in stucco, which makes the building's appearance less majestic close up than it is from down by the harbourside.

MISCELLANEOUS SITES

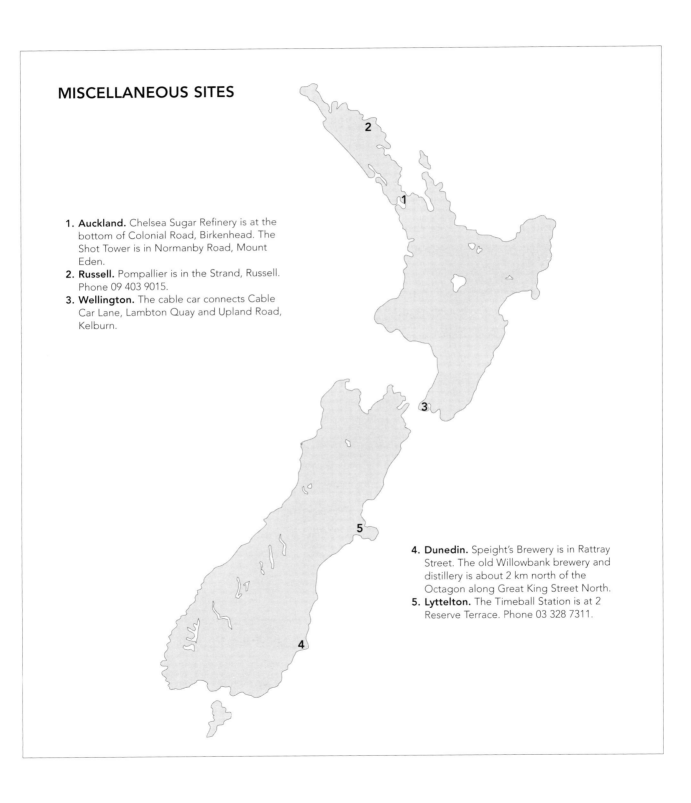

1. **Auckland.** Chelsea Sugar Refinery is at the bottom of Colonial Road, Birkenhead. The Shot Tower is in Normanby Road, Mount Eden.
2. **Russell.** Pompallier is in the Strand, Russell. Phone 09 403 9015.
3. **Wellington.** The cable car connects Cable Car Lane, Lambton Quay and Upland Road, Kelburn.

4. **Dunedin.** Speight's Brewery is in Rattray Street. The old Willowbank brewery and distillery is about 2 km north of the Octagon along Great King Street North.
5. **Lyttelton.** The Timeball Station is at 2 Reserve Terrace. Phone 03 328 7311.

Lyttelton's Timeball Station aided seafarers for 58 years until overtaken by wireless technology in 1934. At 1 pm each afternoon throughout those years a telegraphic time signal was received from the Colonial Observatory in Wellington. This activated the electromechanical mechanism that lowered the timeball 3 m down an Oregon pine mast in eight seconds amid a cacophony of mechanical grinding and screeching. Ships in the harbour knew the exact time from the second the ball started its descent and could check their chronometers. It took over 80 turns of the hand-wheel to return the zinc ball to the top of the mast.

At the turn of the Millennium Lyttelton's Timeball Station once again enjoyed a moment of glory. Having been restored by its original builders, Siemens, the ball was lowered to mark the historic moment for an audience of millions on television. Other Timeball Stations around the world then followed suit.

Lyttelton's Timeball Station may look decidedly romantic but it was, in fact, entirely functional, a vital aid to shipping for 58 years.

CHELSEA SUGAR REFINERY

Travel northwards over the Auckland Harbour Bridge and there are many distractions on or beside one of the world's most attractive harbours. One that probably arouses least comment is the Chelsea Sugar Refinery. Yet, painted a dashing shade of pink beside an azure harbour and set against the green backdrop of leafy Birkenhead suburbs, Chelsea is not easily ignored and has been an Auckland icon for well over a century.

In 1881 Edward Knox, the Chairman of the Colonial Sugar Refining Company, visited several sites around New Zealand with a view to starting a refinery. At that time the shoreline at Duck Creek was wild, bleak and seemingly uninviting. However, the clean water supply, deep anchorage and proximity to the sugar plantations of the Pacific Islands, Indonesia and Central America won the day. The availability of local partners willing to partly finance the venture also helped because the sugar works was a substantial enterprise. Auckland in the early 1880s was awash with spirited capitalists and most of the big names of the day — Thomas Russell, Frederick

Whitaker, J.C. Firth, David Nathan, A.G. Horton, W.S. and J.L. Wilson, David Murdoch and Allan Kerr Taylor — were in on the venture. During 1883 and 1884 about 150 building workers moved across the harbour from Auckland to a canvas construction site on the northern shore. Part of a hillside was removed and the spoil used to reclaim about one hectare of harbour. One and a half million bricks were fired from the clay deposits of the area in a specially erected kiln and used to construct the refinery and the water dams. Wisely, Duck Creek was rapidly dropped as a name in favour of the more marketable Chelsea.

Soon after the opening of the refinery the *Auckland Star* sent a reporter on a tour of inspection. He was suitably amazed at the transformation of a desolate spot into 'Sugaropolis', the most modern, automated manufacturing plant in New Zealand up to that time. Indeed the unnamed scribe waxed lyrical at the size and complexity of it all and took his readers on a tour of inspection. Firstly, the raw sugar 'a soft sticky mass, suggestive of perspiring toffy' (sic) was stacked 9 m high by hydraulic power. Then after melting in two huge, circular pans the liquid sugar passed into the 27-m by 18-m refinery to be filtered through large bags of best Orleans cotton:

Chelsea Sugar Refinery, a Birkenhead landmark since 1884.

Each bag is encased in a flaxen sheath, and when distended they bear a striking similitude to puddings of plethoric proportions. In order to facilitate the process of filtration they have to be surrounded by an atmosphere of steam to keep the liquor hot and hence the workmen … have to adopt a costume which may be described as Central African in its primitive simplicity.

Our intrepid correspondent then climbed the eight flights of steps — 'each successive flight narrower and steeper than its predecessor' — to the top of the char cylinder house where he observed the partly purified liquid being filtered again in 20 'immense cast-iron cylinders'. When full with liquid sugar and charcoal each weighed around 50 tons, so 'it may be understood how massive are the pillars required to sustain the exceptional weight of such a floor'.

Then the purified liquor was conveyed for crystallisation in two enormous vacuum pans where the highly skilled sugar boiler tested samples withdrawn from the pan '… for uniformity of the crystals … by holding them up between his eye and the light'. Finally, the refined sugar was lifted by hydraulics to the top of the Fine Sugar Store and 'emptied through a hatchway on to a perfectly clean floor underneath'. Packaged into bags, Chelsea Sugar headed for the consumer and our correspondent, exhausted but mightily impressed, attempted to head for home 'as the sun was setting'. But he had missed the last ferry, no small matter in those days. After 'idly fluttering our handkerchiefs for some time as signals of distress' the Auckland Timber Company's steamer *Terror* came to a timely rescue.

The new enterprise suffered not only the normal commissioning problems but also soon ran into a period of low sugar prices. By the late 1880s the economy nose-dived and the local company was forced to amalgamate into the Colonial Sugar Refining Company. When the recession ended the refinery expanded rapidly and by 1908 employed 250 men (but no women — Chelsea was a male bastion until the late 1930s). The original four-storey refinery buildings — still recognisable even in the twenty-first century — were substantially augmented. By the 1950s there were 450 workers at Chelsea.

Chelsea was developed as a company town, for in the early years Auckland's North Shore offered little other than fruit growing and gum digging. The company, conscious of the need to attract staff and have them quickly available in case of emergency, built a model village of 35 wooden cottages that hugged the hillside

247

behind the works. Each cottage had a large garden to encourage self-sufficiency. A schoolroom, reading room and church were provided. An independently managed store was built so there would be no suggestion of stooping to the infamous 'truck' system, whereby workers were effectively paid in goods rather than cash. Sadly, the cottages proved to be damp and many families moved out. By 1900 the village was largely occupied by single men and had acquired a reputation for rowdyism. The cottages, by then known as the Barracks, were condemned in 1905. Some were demolished but others were moved to various parts of Birkenhead. Later four still-extant brick duplexes were built on the site for essential workers. Elsewhere the company provided extensive housing loans for its workers. It is estimated that about 130 houses were financed between 1910 and 1926 — over a third of the total built in Birkenhead in that period.

Shot Tower, Mt Eden.

THE SHOT TOWER

The Shot Tower, icon of Mt Eden, has been known to puzzle passing visitors, and, indeed, quite a few Aucklanders. This is hardly surprising for there is nothing quite like it worldwide. It was once one of many towers used to manufacture lead shot for cartridges since the first was constructed in Bristol in 1782. Yet all the other surviving examples — in the USA, Australia and the UK — are constructed from masonry. Uniquely, Mt Eden's was built from riveted steel. Its lattice-work structure silhouettes starkly in the clear Auckland sky.

Originally the Shot Tower was part of a sizeable munitions factory that evolved at the foot of Mt Eden from 1885 onwards when the Colonial Ammunition Company, colloquially known as CAC, was formed by Major John Whitney and W.H. Hazard in response to the commonly held fear of a Russian invasion. The tower itself was added in 1914. The process of manufacture was straightforward. Bars of solid lead were hoisted in a lift to the small corrugated-iron shed at the top of the tower. There they were heated in a cauldron. The molten lead then passed through two large pans, the latter of which was perforated with hundreds of small holes. The lead pellets then dropped 30 m into a trough of water at ground level. The perfect spheres were next polished by graphite in a revolving barrel and then packed into cartridges. The tower had a capacity of between 700 and 1000 tons of shot per annum.

When the tower ceased production in the 1980s the last shot maker was reported as saying it was a shame to see it go but there would be some very happy rabbits around. The tower has faced an uncertain future for some time despite being registered Category One by the Historic Places Trust, which is campaigning to save this unique piece of our industrial heritage.

SPEIGHT'S BREWERY

When Captain Cook moored at Dusky Sound in 1773 after nearly four months at sea he put down a brew of molasses and rimu bark and leaves, its fermentation triggered by unfermented beer he had on board. Though unlikely to be a great tipple by modern standards, to some of the crew it tasted 'rather like champagne' and, more to the point, it kept the scurvy at bay. It was also the start of an irresistible trend.

In 1835 Joel Polack established a brewery at the whaling port of Kororareka, a market just waiting to be tapped. Then breweries sprang up in the major European settlements established in the early 1840s. Renwick and Hooper of Nelson were probably first, in late 1841 or early 1842, followed by Brown and Campbell in Auckland later that year. Richard Seccombe, who was later to become a major player in the Auckland market, commenced business in New Plymouth in 1843.

Thereafter a multitude of local breweries mushroomed across the land, but over the years almost all were to disappear under the forces of modernisation and amalgamation and only a few, such as the current home of the Coaltown Museum in Westport, survive to the present day.

Speight's Brewery on Rattray Street has been a Dunedin icon in one form or another since 1876 when James Speight, Charles Greenslade and William Dawson opened what might have been just a further short-lived addition to the gaggle of breweries in the city. But the three friends, respectively businessman, maltster and brewer, were to prove a potent combination. On the back of several prize-winning brews, Speight's soon outgrew all local competition and indeed all other breweries in New Zealand.

Speight's success was down in part to the complementary skills of the three partners but also to sheer hard work, of which there was plenty in the early days. While Greenslade and Dawson humped sacks and barrels around malt-house and brewhouse, the convivial Speight was daily on the road drumming up sales. Also, like many other successful entrepreneurs, they were in the right place at the right time. New Zealand in general, and Dunedin in particular, was booming in the 1870s and our ambitious trio had all previously worked for James Wilson at his Well Park Brewery on the Rattray Street site. When Wilson decided to move his operation a few kilometres out to Willowbank, Speight, Greenslade and Dawson snapped up the existing plant. As it happens, although there is nothing left of the original Speight's brewery, the stone structure on the Willowbank site has survived, first as a brewery and then for many years as a distillery.

By 1880 Speight's had won two first prizes and four seconds at the Melbourne Exhibition and sales boomed. Further market share was gained when its major rival, Marshall & Copeland, went out of business in 1887 — the year in which James Speight died of an occupational hazard, cirrhosis of the liver, and William Dawson was elected Mayor of Dunedin, aged just 35. Both Dawson and Greenslade went on to become extremely wealthy men. By the 1890s Speight's was the biggest New Zealand brewery and by 1923, when nine of the leading breweries in the land merged to form New Zealand Breweries Limited, it was almost the size of the rest put together.

Today Speight's street frontage includes Robert Forrest's elegant 1913 Shamrock Building, constructed as a fermentation house and now housing a bar and a restaurant. The New Brewery (1940) lies a little further up the hill. Between the two are the buildings that still remain from the rapid reconstruction of the 1880s and 1890s.

WELLINGTON CABLE CAR

In strict technological terms Wellington's cable car is really a funicular — but that is hardly a word to trip readily off the tongues of the weary workers of Lambton Quay as they wend their way homewards to Kelburn. Opened in 1902, with a steady gradient of 1 in 5, the original system was double-tracked, with only the descending car coupled to a driving cable operated from the steam-driven powerhouse at Kelburn.

An entirely separate cable wound around an independent drum joining the two cars so that one balanced the other.

With 425,000 customers in its first year, the system was such a success that increased capacity was created in the form of converted horse tramcars that were attached as trailers. Horse-drawn coaches met the cable car at the summit and entirely new commuter suburbs rapidly developed in the former wastelands high above Lambton Quay. By 1926 patronage had increased remarkably to two million people.

Electrification followed in 1933 and the original stylish powerhouse was almost entirely replaced by the existing structure. After safely transporting over 100 million passengers over the years, the cable car suffered an accident in 1973. Despite much local displeasure the system was condemned and soon replaced by a single-track Swiss-built automatic funicular system, with a passing bay in the middle. When plans were afoot to remove the powerhouse in the 1990s, however, protest was both vigorous and successful. Today it houses a small museum displaying an original gripcar built in 1901 by Mark Sinclair of Dunedin and a trailer that started life as a horse tram in the late 1880s or early 1890s. The basement contains winding gear from 1901 and electric motors from 1933. The museum is a fitting memorial to the sound practice and ingenuity of the original engineer, James Fulton, and the sweat and toil of the workmen, including prison labour from the old Terrace jail, who did the heavy spade work of digging tunnels and cuttings a century ago.

POMPALLIER

When Bishop Pompallier of the French Roman Catholic Mission arrived in Russell, then Kororareka, he found the well-established Anglican and Methodist missionaries of the Bay of Islands already printing religious tracts in Maori, sometimes with a vehemently anti-Catholic tone. A Marist compound was established on the waterfront in 1839 and within two years work had started on a printery and a Gaveaux press was imported from France. The missionaries were dirt-poor so they built in the peasant tradition of Lyon, rammed earth. Soil, beach sand, rock and burned lime from sea shells, which cost nothing but hard work, were used on the building's ground floor. Upstairs local timber framing was filled with earth.

Pompallier, Russell. Would that all factories looked like this.

Under the dynamic guidance of Jean Yvert, who had taken a three-week crash-course in printing and bookbinding in Caen before leaving home, the Marists were soon able to match the Protestant press. During the 1840s Maori language texts, pamphlets and books were printed and bound, including one that ran to 648 pages in an edition of 6000.

At the back of the building, almost as an afterthought, the Marists built a two-storey lean-to tannery complete with tan pits in the earth and a drying loft above. Necessity was evident here too, for by the end of 1842 the Brothers' shoes were in tatters.

The Pompallier printing works and tannery lasted until 1850 when the Bishop relocated to Auckland. The building was used as a commercial tannery for some years and then became a much-modified private home. Eventually it was left derelict. In the early 1990s the New Zealand Historic Places Trust restored the country's oldest surviving industrial building to its original form. It is now open as a working museum.

BIBLIOGRAPHY

Ashby, Ted. *Phantom Fleet.* A.H. & A.W. Reed Ltd, Wellington, 1975.

Beardsley, Eric. *Blackball '08.* Collins, Auckland, 1984.

Bird, Warren. *Viaducts Against the Sky.* Craig Publishing Co. Ltd, Invercargill, 1998.

Boese, Kay. *Tides of History.* Bay of Islands County Council, Whangarei, 1977.

Bromby, Robin. *An Eyewitness History of New Zealand.* Curry O'Neill Ross, South Yarra, 1985.

Bush, G.W.A. *Decently and In Order.* Collins, Auckland, 1971.

Caughey, Angela. *The Interpreter: The Biography of Richard 'Dickie' Barrett.* David Bateman, Auckland, 1998.

Coney, Sandra. *Piha — A History in Images.* The Keyhole Press, Auckland, 1997.

Crawshaw, Norman. *From Clouds to Sea.* Coal New Zealand, Westport, 1996.

Dalziel, Raewyn. *Julius Vogel. Business Politician.* Auckland University Press/Oxford University Press, Auckland, 1986.

Dangerfield, J.A. *The First Railway in Otago and the Lewis Coal Mine near Coal Point Molyneux.* 1991.

Department of Internal Affairs. *Dictionary of New Zealand Biography.* Volumes I, II, and III. Bridget Williams Books, Department of Internal Affairs, Auckland University Press, Wellington and Auckland; 1990, 1993 and 1996.

Diamond, J.T. and Hayward, B.W. *Kauri Timber Dams.* Auckland, 1975.

Diamond, John. *Once the Wilderness.* Lodestar, Auckland, 1977.

Eccles, Alfred and Reed, A.H. *John Jones of Otago.* A.H. & A.W. Reed, Wellington, 1949.

Ewing, Ross and Macpherson, Ross. *The History of New Zealand Aviation.* Heinemann, Auckland, 1986.

Field, Tom and Olssen, Erik. *Relics of the Goldfields.* John McIndoe, Dunedin, 1976.

Furkert, F.W. *Early New Zealand Engineers.* A.H. & A.W. Reed, Wellington, 1953.

Garner, John. *Guide to New Zealand Rail Heritage.* IPL Books, Wellington, 1996.

Grady, Don. *Perano Whalers of Cook Strait.* A.H. & A.W. Reed, Wellington, 1982.

Grady, Don. *Sealers & Whalers in New Zealand Waters.* Reed Methuen, Auckland, 1986.

Haddon, Kathy. *Birkenhead, the Way We Were.* David Ling Publishing, Auckland, 1993.

Halkett, John. *The Native Forests of New Zealand.* GP Publications Ltd, Wellington 1991.

Harris, Jan. *Tohora: The Story of Fyffe House, Kai Koura.* New Zealand Historic Places Trust, Wellington, 1994.

Hawken, Rachel and Walker, Lloyd (eds.). *Heads, Harbour and Hills: An Awhitu History.* Awhitu History Society Inc., Waiuku, 1999.

Hayward, B.W. and Diamond, J.T. *Historic Archaeological Sites of the Waitakere Ranges.* Auckland, 1978.

Johnson, David. *Wellington Harbour.* Wellington Maritime Museum Trust, Wellington, 1996.

Johnston, Mike. *Gold in a Tin Dish. Volume 2: The History of the Eastern Marlborough Goldfields.* Nikau Press, Nelson, 1993.

Johnston, Mike. *Nelson's First Railway.* Nikau Press, Nelson, 1996.

Kernohan, David. *Wellington's Old Buildings.* Victoria University Press, Wellington 1994.

Lambert, Gail and Lambert, Ron. *An Illustrated History of Taranaki.* The Dunmore Press, Palmerston North, 1983.

Lee, Jack. *The Bay of Islands.* Reed, Auckland, 1996.

Loach, Cyril. *A History of the New Zealand Refrigerating Company.* New Zealand Refrigerating Company, Christchurch, 1969.

Lowe, David. *The Piha Tramway.* The Lodestar Press, Auckland, 1974.

Mackay, Duncan. *Frontier New Zealand.* HarperCollins, Auckland, 1992.

Mahoney, J.D. *Down at the Station.* The Dunmore Press, Palmerston North, 1987.

Mahoney, Paul. *The Era of the Bush Trams in New Zealand.* IPL Books, Wellington, 1998.

Martin, John (ed.). *People, Politics and Power Stations.* Bridget Williams Books and Electricity Corporation of New Zealand, Wellington, 1991.

McClure, Margaret. *The Story of Birkenhead*. Birkenhead City Council, Auckland, 1987.

McDonald, K.C. *City of Dunedin. A Century of Civic Enterprise*. Dunedin City Corporation, Dunedin, 1965.

McGill, David and Sheehan, Grant. *Landmarks*. Godwit, Auckland, 1997.

McGill, David. *Ghost Towns of New Zealand*. Reed, Auckland, 1980.

McKinnon, Malcolm (ed). *New Zealand Historical Atlas*. David Bateman, Auckland, 1997.

McLauchlan, Gordon. *The Story of Beer*. Viking Penguin, Auckland, 1994.

McLean, G.J. *Spinning Yarns. A Centennial History of Alliance Textiles Limited and its Predecessors*. Alliance Textiles, Dunedin, 1981.

McLean, Gavin. *Wellington — The First Years of European Settlement, 1840–1850*. Penguin Books (NZ) Ltd, Auckland, 2000.

Millen, Julia. *From Joseph Nathan to Glaxo Welcome*. Glaxo Welcome New Zealand Limited, Palmerston North, 1991.

Miller, Athol. *The Clark Family History*. 1989.

Moore, Phil and Ritchie, Neville. *Coromandel Gold*. The Dunmore Press Ltd, Palmerston North, 1996.

Morris, Gerard (ed.). *Waiuta, the Gold Mine, the Town, the People*. Friends of Waiuta, Reefton, 1986.

Offer, R.E. *Walls for Water*. The Dunmore Press, Palmerston North, 1997.

Perriam, Terry. *Where It All Began. A History of the Waitaki-Pukeuri Freezing Works*. Waitaki International Limited,

Pickering, Mark. *Stepping Back: Exploring South Island History*. Shoal Bay Press, Christchurch, 1998.

Pierre, Bill A. *North Island Main Trunk*. Reed, Wellington, 1981.

Porter, Frances (ed.). *Historic Buildings of New Zealand. North Island; Historic Buildings of New Zealand. South Island*. Methuen New Zealand, Auckland, 1983.

Reese, Daniel. *Was It All Cricket?* George Allen & Unwin, London, 1948.

Rickard, L.S. *The Whaling Trade in Old New Zealand*. Minerva, 1965.

Riddle, Janet. *Saltspray & Sawdust*. Gumtown Publishers, Whitianga, 1996.

Ryburn, Wayne. *Tall Spars, Steamers & Gum. A History of the Kaipara from Early European Settlement 1854–1947*. Kaipara Publications, Auckland, 1999.

Salmon, J.H.M. *A History of Gold Mining in New Zealand.* Government Printer,
Wellington, 1963.

Scott, Dick. *Fire On The Clay: The Pakeha Comes to West Auckland.* Southern Cross
Books, Auckland, 1979.

Scott, Dick. *Stock in Trade. Hellaby's First Hundred Years 1873–1973.* Southern
Cross Books, Auckland, 1973.

Simpson, Thomas E. *Kauri to Radiata.* Hodder & Stoughton, Auckland, 1973.

Stewart, Graham. *Fares Please — Horse, Steam and Cable Trams of New Zealand.*
Grantham House, Wellington, 1997.

Stewart, Graham. *The End of the Penny Section.* Grantham House, Wellington,
1993.

Stewart, Peter. *Patterns on the Plain: A Centennial History of Mosgiel Woollens
Limited.* Mosgiel, 1975.

Stone, R.C.J. *Makers of Fortune. A Colonial Business Community and its Fall.*
Auckland University Press/Oxford University Press, Auckland, 1973.

Stone, R.C.J. *Young Logan Campbell.* Auckland University Press, Auckland, 1982.

Terry, Charles. *New Zealand: Its Advantages and Prospects as a British Colony.* 1842.

Thornton, Geoffrey. *Cast in Concrete.* Reed, Auckland, 1996.

Thornton, Geoffrey. *New Zealand's Industrial Heritage.* A.H. & A.W. Reed,
Wellington, 1982.

Trotter, Michael and McCulloch, Beverley. *Digging Up The Past.* Viking, Auckland,
1997.

Vennell, C.W. *Men of Metal. The Story of A & G Price Ltd. 1868–1968.* Wilson &
Horton Ltd, Auckland, 1968.

Warr, Eric. *From Bush-burn to Butter.* Butterworths, Wellington, 1988.

Wilson, John (ed.). *The Past Today: Historic Places in New Zealand.* Pacific
Publishers, Auckland, 1987.

Wilson, T.H. *The Birth and Growth of Wilson's Portland Cement in New Zealand.*
Type & Dup. Bureau, 1956.

Wood, Brian. *Disaster at Brunner.* Greymouth, 1996.

Wright, Matthew. *New Zealand Engineering Heritage.* Reed, Auckland, 1999.

Pamphlets, Booklets and Articles

Ayson, Bob. *Miranui — the Story of New Zealand's Largest Flax Mill.* Southern Press Industrial Archaeology Series, 1977.

Best, Simon. *The Whau Brickworks and Pottery.* Department of Conservation, Auckland, 1993.

Blackball History Group. *Historic Blackball.* Blackball, 1993.

Chapman, Chris. 'A Historic Mill at Gore.' *Historic Places*, July 1993.

Craddock, F.W. *Golden Canyon.* Pegasus, Christchurch, 1973.

Cuff, Martine E. *Totara Estate.* New Zealand Historic Places Trust, Wellington, 1982.

Department of Conservation. *Macetown.* Department of Conservation, Dunedin, 1997.

Department of Conservation. *St Bathans.* Department of Conservation, Dunedin.

Green, R. Brett. *Auckland to Onehunga Railway Centennial. 1873–1973.* The Railway Enthusiasts Society (Inc).

Hannah, Myra. *Operation Waterwheel.* Alexandra District Historical Association, Alexandra, 1972.

Hodge, Peter. 'Short but Sweet.' *Historic Places*, September 1993.

Information Section, State Coal Mines. *Coal & Coal Mining in New Zealand.* 1987.

Kellaway, Laura. 'Frankton: When Rail Ruled.' *Historic Places*, July 1996.

Luke, Peter. *Sugar Workers, Sugar Town.* New Zealand Sugar Company, Auckland, 1984.

Milburn Cement. *100 Years Helping Build a Nation.* Milburn New Zealand Ltd, 1988.

New Zealand Flour Millers Association. *Flour Milling and Baking in New Zealand: The First 150 Years.* New Zealand Association of Bakers, Wellington, 1983.

New Zealand Historic Places Trust. *Hayes Engineering Works.* New Zealand Historic Places Trust, 1986.

New Zealand Historic Places Trust. *Lyttelton Timeball Station.* New Zealand Historic Places Trust, 1987.

New Zealand Historic Places Trust. *Welcome to Pompallier.* New Zealand Historic Places Trust.

Orepuki: A Hundred Years of Memories. Craig Printing Company, 1971.

Reefton Electricity Centennial Committee. *Powerhouse Walk.* Reefton.

Reynolds, David. 'An Industrial Icon.' *Historic Places*, May 2001.

Robinson, Sheila. 'A Tale of Five Freezing Works.' *Historic Places*, December 1989.

Scanlan, A.B. *Taranaki's First Railway.*

Southland Dairy Co-operative Ltd. *Edendale: Heart of Dairying in the South.* 1998.

Stafford, Don. *Rotorua Electricity: A Brief History of Power for the Rotorua District.* Rotorua Area Electricity Authority, Rotorua, 1988.

Thornton, Geoffrey. 'The Makatote Viaduct.' *Historic Places*, March 1988.

Thornton, Geoffrey. 'The Makohine Viaduct.' *Historic Places*, September, 1987.

Verran, David. *Flour Mill Workers, 1889–1990.* NZ Labour History website, www.geocities.com/nzhistory

Wilson, Lorraine. *A Short History of the Beam Engine and Western Springs Waterworks, Auckland.* MOTAT, Auckland, 1994.

Newpapers and Periodicals

Auckland Star, Gisborne Herald, Hawke's Bay Courier, New Zealand Farmer, New Zealand Herald, New Zealand Wesleyan, Nelson Examiner, Opotiki News, Otago Witness, Sunday Star-Times, Patea Mail, Rotorua Daily Post, Timaru Herald, Wanganui Herald.

INDEX